Revolution to Devolution

Revolution to Devolution
Reflections on Welsh Democracy

Kenneth O. Morgan

University of Wales Press
Cardiff
2014

British Library Cataloguing-in-Publication Data.
A catalogue record for this book is available from the British Library.

ISBN   978-1-7831-6088-4 (hardback)
        978-1-7831-6087-7 (paperback)
e-ISBN 978-1-7831-6089-1

The University of Wales Press acknowledges the financial support of the Welsh Books Council.

Typeset in Wales by Eira Fenn Gaunt, Cardiff
Printed by CPI Antony Rowe, Chippenham

To Joseph and Clara, Thomas and Samuel:
Cymru Fydd, the Wales that is to be

CONTENTS

Contents

FOREWORD

Just over fifty years ago, I published my first book with the University of Wales Press. It was a short essay on Lloyd George's career from a mainly Welsh perspective, which appeared in February 1963. Four months later appeared a far more significant work, one which perhaps has helped to define my career ever since, entitled *Wales in British Politics 1868–1922*. I was far from home when it was published, touring in Lima, Peru, after completing a year's research on American history at Columbia University in New York. Its appearance was not personally auspicious. It came out on 18 June, Waterloo Day, and it was nearly my Waterloo as well. I decided to take my two travelling companions, an Englishman and an American girl, out to celebrate at a Chinese restaurant in downtown Lima, the meal washed down (not for long, alas!) by Peruvian champagne. The results were predictably terrible: we spent the next three days in bed with severe food poisoning. However, things could only get better, as they say, and I returned to Aberystwyth three months later to find that the book had received many pleasant reviews in the interim. Fifty-one years on, it is, remarkably, still in print. I received a short time ago a cheque for £7.50, reflecting the fact that it had sold all of three copies in 2012–13. To me, one was a miracle.

Ever since 1963, even though I have published many other books in the meantime on modern British and American history and politics with Oxford University Press and other publishers, including some large biographies, the University of Wales Press has remained close to my heart. I have published around half a dozen other books with the University of Wales Press over the years, to my great pleasure. In 1995, the Press produced *Modern Wales: Politics, Places and People*, a volume of essays to mark my retirement, and in 2004 a *festschrift* for my old friend, Professor

Ralph Griffiths, and myself to mark the end of my forty-two and our joint thirty-eight years of editorship of the *Welsh History Review*. I hope I have offered something in return. I was able to use the University's Central Services Committee (largely through the Welsh language) to keep the Press alive when I was Vice-Chancellor of the University of Wales in 1993–5, fighting off a threat led by some English scientists who wished to close it down. So it still endures and flourishes, as one of the precious legacies of the now regrettably diminished University of Wales, which was for over a hundred years one of our greatest and most prestigious national institutions. It is thus a particular joy for me to publish this new work with its Press, both to mark the half-century of my writing for them, and also to note my eightieth birthday.

The themes of this volume follow up those which have been important in my career ever since *Wales in British Politics* appeared. First, there has been consideration of the variations of democracy, especially political democracy. My book was often compared early on with other local or regional studies, notably Peter Clarke's splendid book *Lancashire and the New Liberalism* (1971). That work showed the vitality of the New Liberalism there, notably in Manchester under the influence of L. T. Hobhouse, whereas my book tended to show how relatively weak it was in nonconformist Wales. Paul Thompson's very different conclusions again, in his challenging work *Socialists, Liberals and Labour: the Struggle for London 1885–1914* (1967), were also adduced for further comparison. I broadened my research considerably in my *Rebirth of a Nation: Wales 1880–1980* (1981) to look at the Welsh political culture in the widest sense, including religion and the arts, with much more attention now paid to the origins of the Labour Party, including ancillary movements like the Unofficial Reform Committee and the Plebs League. I was also struck by the continuing failure of the Conservatives to make any impact in Wales in a long-running series of parliamentary disasters for them. At last, as some of us foresaw, the advent of devolution has given them proper opportunities to do so.

Second, my work has focused on the emergence and recognition of the Welsh national identity (and, increasingly on Scotland and English regional-ism as well as on European national minorities). I remain convinced that the years after 1868 were the seed-bed of modern Welsh nationality. To adapt General de Gaulle, it created 'a certain idea of Wales'. It gave its cultural and (to a degree) ethnic nationalism the framework of civic and communal identity as well. The whole notion of a distinct, definable Welsh nationality was a revelation at the time, which tended to see Wales, if at all, in terms of Darwinian stereotypes about the cultural and physical difference between the Saxon and the Celt, as did Mathew Arnold. Officially, however, in the notorious phrase, it was a case of 'For Wales, see England'. That late-Victorian period created new institutions such as the National Museum, the National Library, the national federal University, and the revived impact of the national *eisteddfod* as a forum for a kind of people's culture – not to mention a glorious rugby team. But political democracy was always the essential key, in establishing national priorities, in separate Welsh legislation from secondary education to Church disestablishment, in incremental administrative devolution, and in a glittering generation of younger political leaders, with Tom Ellis and David Lloyd George as the eloquent symbols of Cymru Fydd, Young Wales. Many decades later, after a long phase of unionism, the achieve-ment of devolution in 1999 has carried that movement on apace.

And finally, in a way I certainly did not anticipate in 1963 when the public mood was strongly Fabian/unionist, I think my work has made some contribution to the debate on Britishness, however that shadowy concept may be defined. I have always looked at Wales as a British historian working mostly in England, and therefore my book, proved to be somewhat prophetic. Almost unintentionally, it played its part in examining the pluralism of Britain, the distinctiveness and limitations of the Welsh sense of nationhood, and the differences between Wales, Scotland and Ireland in the mix of the United Kingdom. Despite the partial advance of Welsh political nationalism, hard to detect in 1963, I have always been struck by the contrasts between Wales and Ireland, where the campaign for self-government was so fundamental a theme of later-nineteenth and early-twentieth century Britain. As I put it in *Wales in British Politics*, 'the object of the one was equality, the aim of the other was exclusion', so far as the United Kingdom was concerned. Scotland, with its distinctive institutions, the law, education and church, surviving from the Union in 1707, was different again. These profound differences were reflected, perhaps excessively so, in the asymmetrical devolution accorded to Scotland, Wales and Northern Ireland by the Blair government in 1997. They have helped to ensure that the pluralism of the union-state of Britain has been emphasised. It led in March 2014 to the final Silk Commission Report in Wales to which the government has responded, and to the coming referendum in Scotland, with an increasingly federal tendency in governance resulting, whatever the result in Scotland. Certainly, since the coming of devolution, the United Kingdom will never look the same again. Its unity will increasingly come into question, like that of Spain, Belgium and other member states of the European Union.

This volume, by bringing together a series of closely-related essays, follows up these key themes. Its justification lies partly in the fact that both the public context and I myself have changed since then. The overall starting-point is very different from that of my volume *Modern Wales* in 1995, with the entire situation transformed by the coming into effect of devolution four years later. What it is worth, my own perspective has also changed. For forty years I studied these matters as an academic historian, working safely in the cloistered calm of the university library or the confined debates of the seminar. But since 2000 I have been in the House of Lords, as a legislator and so-called 'working peer' disguised as 'Morgan of Aberdyfi', my home village; I have thus been able to consider democracy, nationhood and other matters as a first-hand observer, and, to a degree, as a public participant. It has given me a very different perception.

The twelve essays in this volume are all the result of work since 1995. Most of them are the product of public lectures, some of which later appeared, in whole or in part, in print. All focus on these earlier themes. Chapter 1 considers how historians of Wales have viewed the turbulent course of Welsh democracy since the early nineteenth century, how far they have seen Wales as torn apart by conflict, political, social, religious and linguistic, and how as a place able to resolve its internal differences through consensus, perhaps now through national consensus. Chapter 2 considers the many varieties of Welsh democracy since the 1789 revolution in France, political and industrial, with Liberal, Labour, Nationalist and Conservative variants of the democratic ethos able to express themselves. I also consider how Wales at the present time, whose people remain subjects of the crown rather than citizens in the same way as the Americans or the French, still falls well short of fulfilling earlier democratic aspirations. Chapter 3 follows a wider overseas trajectory and examines how far ideas of democracy in Wales were influenced by events in the United States, particularly the victory of the North in its Civil War and the towering role of Abraham Lincoln, a long-term Welsh hero. Chapters 4, 5 and 6 discuss three notable individual practitioners of democratic politics – Henry Richard, who led the democratic upsurge against 'feudalism' in 1868 and also introduced an international dimension of his own in the peace movement; David Lloyd George, the most powerful Welsh tribune of his day who was also remarkably effective at close quarters as legislator and executive force in parliament itself, perhaps more so even than Churchill; and Herbert Lewis, a quiet man of politics with a strong commitment to local government and education, but also a courageous ally of Lloyd George in some of his most perilous passages. Herbert Lewis, like Dr Christopher Addison whose life I once jointly wrote, illustrates the insight to be gleaned from examining an honourable politician of middle-ranking stature.

The emphasis swings in chapter 7 to see the response of Welsh democracy and its national ideals to the crisis of the First World War, a period of enduring transformation in Wales in a way that it may be hoped the official commemoration of the First World War in 2014–18 will not neglect. The theme here is protest as much as patriotism. Chapter 9 follows this with a consideration of both world wars, and their comparative impact, mainly social, economic and cultural, on Wales and the other nations of the United Kingdom. The conventional wisdom on the comparative legacies of both world wars seems to need extensive modification. One of the consequences of the First World War for Wales was a new and heightened nationalism, as shown in the formation of Plaid Genedlaethol Cymru in 1925. Another is considered in chapter 8, a new sense of internationalism, as shown in the career of David Davies and the League of Nations Union, and Alfred Zimmern's brief tenure of the pioneer chair of International Politics at Aberystwyth. It also suggests a realist internationalism that contrasts with the utopianism and pacifism of Henry Richard. Chapter 10 looks at the Labour movement, and the nature of the democratic aspirations of the Labour Party in its supreme period of power in 1940–51. Wales, like Britain generally, still broadly subscribes to the 'legend of '45' with Nye Bevan and Jim Griffiths as its giants. Chapter 11, a lecture originally delivered in Cardiff in 1998, and deliberately left unchanged here, looks at the forces behind the advance of devolution and the expectations that it aroused then. And finally, chapter 12 takes the discussion on into a European context, considered primarily historically in the careers of four highly distinctive Welshmen, but also in terms of the challenges of today in a nation so long strongly European but now perhaps in some disarray as insular Euro-scepticism, whipped up by the English media, continues to grow across Offa's Dyke. Together, I hope, these reflections provide further analysis of key aspects inherent in the Welsh past, in the light of a new context and a new world.

A work produced in my eightieth year must inevitably reflect the enormous wisdom and warmth I have received from so many colleagues over the years, in Wales and in Oxford especially, but perhaps most of all from my closest and most loyal academic co-workers in Swansea, in my early lecturing career, and in Aberystwyth towards the end. I must reiterate my gratitude to the University of Wales yet again, particularly to Sarah Lewis whose efficiency has been exemplary and whose enthusiasm has been a huge encouragement; the same applies to the anonymous reviewer at the University of Wales Press to whom I am also very grateful. I am greatly indebted, too, to the editorial skills of Dafydd Jones. It is not only the world outside that has changed since my retirement volume appeared in 1995; so has my life, and to my enormous advantage. I have met and married Elizabeth of Bordeaux, a proud, beautiful Scottish-French Huguenot, the ideal academic comrade and the perfect wife. Introducing her to Welsh-speaking Wales, even including the Bala *eisteddfod* one fine day, has been a constant joy as has been her enthusiastic response to it. After driving with me along many of the by-ways of Wales, one Welsh word that Elizabeth certainly knows now is *araf* (slow)! My family life as for nearly forty years past has been sustained, in good times and in bad, and for all twelve months of the year, by the love, loyalty and courage of my quite wonderful son and daughter, David and Katherine. They have not only kept me alive; they have also brought their respective spouses, Liz and Tim, into my world. And they have given me four lovely grandchildren, Joseph and Clara Morgan-Yonge, Thomas and Samuel Spillane, the last two christened by the Reverend Alan Boddy who also married Elizabeth and me in St Mary's Undercroft chapel, Westminster. I dedicate this book to them, and for a reason. This is not just a series of reflections on the past, including his own past, by an elderly man now in retirement. In a deeper sense, it is about them. It is about the future, my beloved Wales's future and their own future. I hope and intend to continue chronicling that future in the miles to go before I sleep.

Kenneth O. Morgan
Long Hanborough, Waterloo Day 2014

Acknowledgements

Earlier versions of some of the material in this volume have previously appeared or were delivered at the following places:

1. David Howell and Kenneth O. Morgan (eds), *Crime, Protest and Police in Modern British Society* (Cardiff, 1999), pp. 16–41.

2. Lecture delivered to Llafur (the Welsh People's History Society) conference, National Assembly, Cardiff, 8 November 2009.

3. Lecture delivered at St Catherine's College, Oxford, 4 July 2009, and printed in Richard Cawardine and Jay Sexton (eds), *The Global Lincoln* (New York and Oxford, 2011), pp. 139–56.

4. Lecture delivered to the United Nations Association, Bangor, 13 May 2010, and printed in *Welsh History Review*, 25/3 (June 2011), 401–23.

5. Lecture delivered at Speaker's House, Westminster, 17 January 2011, and printed in Philip Norton (ed.), *Eminent Parliamentarians* (London, 2012), pp. 17–36.

6. *Flintshire Historical Society Journal*, 36 (2003), 114–35.

7. Lecture delivered to the Lloyd George Society, Llandrindod Wells, 15 February 2014.

8. Lecture delivered at Aberystwyth University, 14 May 2010, and printed in *Transactions of the Honourable Society of Cymmrodorion* (2010), 119–30.

9. Prothero Lecture delivered to the Royal Historical Society at University College London, 2 July 1996, and printed in *Transactions of the Royal Historical Society*, 6th ser., 7 (1997), 131–53.

10. Duncan Tanner, Chris Williams and Deian Hopkin (eds), *The Labour Party in Wales, 1900–2000* (Cardiff, 2000), pp. 166–88.

11. Lecture delivered to the British Academy, Cardiff, 18 September 1998, and printed in Bridget Taylor and Katarina Thomson (eds), *Wales and Scotland: Nations Again?* (Cardiff, 1999), pp. 199–220.

12. Lecture delivered to the British Academy, London, 31 May 2013.

ABBREVIATIONS

BL   The British Library

NLW   The National Library of Wales, Aberystwyth

Parl. Deb. Parliamentary Debates

PRO   The Public Record Office

TNA   The National Archive

I

Consensus and Conflict in Modern Welsh History

David J. V. Jones, in his brief but brilliant career, played a pivotal role in Welsh history's coming of age. When he graduated at Aberystwyth as a young man of twenty-one in 1962, there was scant awareness in the British historical world that Wales in the modern period had a history of its own. Most of the major literature, after all, focused either on early medieval Wales, prior to the English conquest in 1282, or else on the rule of the Tudors. Debates on the significance of the Act of Union loomed large. David Williams's pioneering studies of Welsh Chartism (1939) and the Rebecca Riots (1955) were isolated achievements which stood almost alone. A journal called the *Welsh History Review* had come into being at Swansea only two years earlier; the seminal, if greatly contrasting, work of Gwyn A. Williams and Ieuan Gwynedd Jones was just beginning to appear. The building blocks of Oxford University's history syllabus were three compulsory papers on English (certainly not British) history, heavily political and constitutional in emphasis. The ghosts of Stubbs and Tout stalked the land. Continental novelties like the French *Annales* school need never have been. At that time, British history like British government was centralist and metropolitan in emphasis. There was in 1962 no Welsh Office, no S4C, certainly no vision of devolution. Plaid Cymru was a small minority which lost nearly all its deposits with monotonous regularity. The impact of Saunders Lewis's BBC lecture *Tynged yr Iaith* (The Fate of the Language) that February had still to be measured. The Welsh appeared to be relatively marginalised in British public and political life. To adapt the title of a famous stage review of the day, these Celts seemed almost beyond the fringe. Their modern history was similarly disregarded.

By the late 1980s, when David Jones was in full flow as an author, an extraordinary transformation had taken place. In the previous twenty-five years, history had become one of Wales's major growth industries. In particular, Welsh history in the nineteenth and early twentieth centuries, since the era of industrialisation, had been done justice at last. David himself had been a dominant figure in this process. Between 1964 and 1989 he had written five major monographs, along with a score or more of learned articles, almost all of them concerned with Welsh popular protest in the early nineteenth century. But indeed the sixties, seventies and eighties were a time of extraordinary vitality for almost all aspects of the writing of the history of Wales, from the age of Hywel Dda to that of David Lloyd George and well beyond. It was one of the great success stories of British historiography in the post-war period. An array of imposing and acclaimed books and articles had poured forth in a mighty torrent. By 1987, four volumes of a six-volume *Oxford History of Wales* had been published. The *Welsh History Review* was striding confidently towards its fourth decade. It had been joined by innovative newer journals, notably *Llafur*, which aimed successfully, as a journal of labour history, to create links between the academic community and the world of work. It straddled the great divide between scholarly writing and a wider social memory. All the Welsh university colleges had schools of graduate students; the staid gatherings of the Board of Celtic Studies in Gregynog were humming with life. Journals and scholars in England, Ireland, North America and the Commonwealth were also showing a new awareness of the centrality of the experience of the Welsh and their history; indeed, the fact that Wales, a classic 'unhistoric nation', had emerged as a community and as a nation but not as a nation state, made its history all the more fashionable. The historians' concern with regionalism and nationalism, with comparative cultural and linguistic pluralism, with the nature of *mentalité*, with 'history from below' penetrating beneath the formal veneer of the public archives and the records of government, made modern Welsh history appear fresh and relevant in quite new ways.

It was an intellectual development that interacted with the public in Wales, aware of massive processes of historical change with the closure of coal, new processes of secularization and the growing awareness of national identity. Movements of social and political protest loomed especially large in historical writing, perhaps reflecting the ideological preferences of most Welsh historians. Television and radio series in both English and Welsh, popular journals and magazines, well-attended day schools, the impact of the Open University, all spread the word amongst the general public. The history of Wales was entrenched, after a struggle admittedly, on the schools' core curriculum. Welsh history books, indeed, sold remarkably well (many of the volumes in the Board of Celtic Studies' monograph series, Studies in Welsh History, went rapidly into paper-back) perhaps because so many of them were attractively written in that extraordinary pungent literacy typical of so much Anglo-Welsh writing. Welsh history was, supremely, a branch of literature, not an arcane scholastic discipline for a limited group of specialists, still less an offshoot of computer science. A remarkable breakthrough had been made, and David Jones was one of the towering figures in its achievement.

This extraordinary renaissance, however, was the product of a remark-ably small group of scholars. Welsh historians were a thin red line of a few dozen at most; their very productivity masked their meagreness of numbers. Cuts into higher education in the Thatcher and post-Thatcher periods had their impact. They greatly reduced the number of graduate students in the humanities, cutting back almost to zero the researchers working for the Board of Celtic Studies, reducing severely the budgets of the university and school libraries which purchased the new books and journals, delaying technical electronic advances even in the National Library of Wales. The range of active scholars became smaller still. They were also growing old together. Diminishing human resources had been masked, in part, by the continuing industriousness and zeal of active Welsh historians who kept on producing major work into their seventies or even eighties. Welsh history had no real 'schools' since it was so much a minority interest.

3

Now this situation certainly has had its distinct advantages. Limited numbers have given historians of Wales a rare sense of fraternity, of intellectual and other comradeship. They have been a convivial (overwhelmingly male) group, enjoying each other's company in the National Library or the University, or in colloquia at Gregynog. Their attitude towards each other, informally and in the formality of book reviews, has always been supportive and encouraging; feuds of the Taylor *vs* Trevor-Roper type appear in Wales to be unknown. But the downside is that Welsh history has the problem sometimes of appearing too cosy and inbred. The scholars at work know and like each other almost too well, and perhaps review each other too often. When apparent disparities in interpretation appear – for instance between Gwyn A. Williams's depiction of south Wales as a revolutionary pressure cooker with the lid about to blow off, and Ieuan Gwynedd Jones's account of that same society twenty years later as stable and secure in reconstructing the basis of its institutional and religious life – there has been no open disagreement. It is very likely that both may be right, but at least the disparity is worth examination. A sign of the maturity of Welsh history, therefore, may be the emergence of argument, of dissent. The present writer is a peaceful man, as harmonious as his fellow members of the guild, with no wish to make war, even cold war, amongst his colleagues. But it appears not an inappropriate tribute to as creative a friend and as galvanising a scholar as David Jones to suggest at least one area where the contours of argument might begin.

A major theme of David Jones's work is that of conflict and consensus in modern Wales. It chimes in with the main features of all mature societies – the balance between change and continuity, between upheaval and stability. Historians of Britain since 1945 have especially been caught up in it, in considering whether post-war Britain was marked by an overall consensus about public priorities. Political scientists like Dennis Kavanagh have been well to the fore here.[1] The theme has especially attracted the attention of American historians, ever fascinated by present-day resonances or the usability of their nation's past. In the early years of this century, US historians tended to see their history in terms of sectional and class conflict. Quite apart from the momentous disjuncture of the Civil War and the gulf over slavery, American historians were heavily influenced by the Progressive movement and its positivist impact upon the humanities and the emerging social sciences. Thus men like Charles Beard and Frederick Jackson Turner saw the key to American history as lying in conflict – the struggle between creditor/mercantile elements in the north-east and a producer society, between an industrial-ising east and a debtor south and west. Perhaps one of the last studies of this kind was Arthur Schlesinger Jr.'s *Age of Jackson* (1945), the work of a young man who saw in Jacksonian Democracy of the 1830s a farmer–labour coalition that anticipated Franklin Roosevelt's New Deal a hundred years later. Indeed, Schlesinger's multi-volume *Age of Roosevelt* (1957–60) deliberately replayed some of the old tunes. It was American academia's inverted version of a Whiggish interpretation of history.

But from the 1950s onwards, this well-established view came to be seriously challenged. Scholars like Louis Hartz or perhaps a more con-servative figure like Dan Boorstin saw their nation's history as one of broad consensus. Hartz saw the key in an abiding liberal ideology reflecting the fact that America had no tradition of feudalism. Boorstin preferred the view that Americans were a pragmatic breed who had no real ideology at all.[2] By the sixties, some American historians, well aware of current tensions relating to black, gender and youth issues, and the war in Vietnam, were deeply alarmed at an anti-ideological brand of con-servatism that seemed to be capturing their discipline – seeing America, in John Roche's words, as 'a Quaker meeting moving through time'. It was, many feared, a backlash from the sterilities of the Cold War and the threat of McCarthyism.

Richard Hofstadter, my old mentor and perhaps the most intellectually dynamic of them all, somewhat hovered between the conflict and con-sensus scenarios. His *American Political Tradition* (1948) suggested long-term continuities, perhaps of an unattractive variety. His *Age of Reform* (1955) propounded conflict, at least between the rural Populists and the urban Progressives, a view shaped by Hofstadter's own reaction to racist, paranoid, rural McCarthyism. In his last major book, *Anti-Intellectualism in American History* (1963), Hofstadter focused on the topic more ob-liquely, namely the philosophical and political elements in American history that kept challenging radical intellectuals and placing them on the defensive. In an important essay published in 1968 shortly before his dreadfully premature death, Hofstadter reviewed the argument and tried to create a bridge between the two approaches.[3] He did, however, observe that a society marked by four years of terrible civil war and a fundamental ongoing rupture on the role of black Americans could hardly be deemed consensual in any firm sense.

American historians, then, reached a variety of conclusions. Not surprisingly, a consensus about consensus in their history was almost impossible to achieve. But at least they were debating and arguing amongst themselves. Now the history of Wales, in fact, implicitly raises many of the same themes. As noted, it is embedded in the very divergent view of early nineteenth-century Wales taken by Gwyn A. Williams and Ieuan Gwynedd Jones, a difference of temperament perhaps but also of scholarship. It has, however, been given spectacular public prominence. Again Gwyn A. Williams is the central exhibit. Indeed his writing throughout his career has been the embodiment of the conflict thesis. In *When was Wales?* (1985), as in many previous monographs and later television series, he saw Welsh history as the product of schizoid turbulence, social fractures and (a favoured phrase) 'brutal ruptures'. It was specifically put forward as an alternative, non-establishment interpretation. Welsh history for him was full of revolutionary moments, led invariably by unsuccessful revolutionaries, marginal men from Macsen Wledig through Owain Glyndŵr and Iolo Morganwg to Noah Ablett and David Irfon Jones in the last century. His thesis came out most vividly in *The Dragon has Two Tongues*, a series of memorable television confrontations (rather than programmes) with Wynford Vaughan Thomas.[4] They were to embody conflict and consensus in exaggerated form. Revolutionary turbulence and consensual inertia were personalised in the tiny, voluble valleys Marxist who argued with (or shouted at) the gentle elder pillar of the establishment. It reached almost absurd lengths of visual imagery. In the first programme, Williams physically embodied revolutionary movement as he was alternately thrust down the main shaft of Blaenavon's Big Pit and then hurtled aloft in a helicopter a few minutes later above the Uffington horse on the Berkshire Downs. Meanwhile, Thomas was to be observed chugging gently along the Neath canal on a sunny afternoon, apparently settling down over a gin and tonic.

It was in many ways a contrived study in joint exaggeration, and also unreal. Gwyn A. Williams, after all, was a distinguished and learned creative academic scholar; Wynford Vaughan Thomas was by trade a very distinguished radio outside broadcaster, but not a serious historian at all. The series was designed to entertain, provoke – perhaps shock – and it succeeded. It surely helped persuade a generation of Welsh school-children to find the history of Wales challenging, dramatic, intensely exciting; videos of the programmes were used for university recruitment by history departments. Williams, the marvellous illuminator of Madoc and other myths, found himself hailed as the source of a new myth, the diminutive apostle of 'impossible revolutions', lauded by radicals and nationalists as a 'people's remembrancer' in a way that other middle-class Welsh historians who appeared on television were somehow not. But, clearly, the series also opened up a wider theme of consensual and conflict images of Welsh history which are of great importance.

As it happens, David Jones himself embodies these two viewpoints throughout his work. He was a superb analyst of Welsh history as social protest. His work for most of his career concerned popular upheavals in both rural and industrial Wales – corn riots, enclosure protests, the Scotch Cattle and their 'black domain', the Merthyr rising and the martyr-dom of Dic Penderyn, the bloody suppression of Chartism, the Rebecca Riots. All of them he studied with impeccable scholarship, but also a quiet passion. He was aware always of the social and human roots of the movements he described. His study of the Rebecca disturbances and the attacks on the toll-gates was more emotionally and politically committed by far than that of his old Aberystwyth mentor, David Williams. The latter had indeed seen the riots as the product of a rural society in crisis, but his account of the troubles was detached, the work of a dis-enchanted disciple of the sceptic Voltaire, even ironic as he described 'the sordid events' with Shoni Sguborfawr and his mates weaving and wenching their way down the valleys. David Jones invested them all with humanity and a kind of heroism. Similarly whereas David Williams had cast doubt on the revolutionary intentions of John Frost and the

Gwent Chartists of 1839, David Jones saw them as intent on direct action, launching a mass uprising in south-east Wales perhaps to link up with Chartist groups throughout England. To him, 'moral force' and 'physical force' Chartism seemed to blend into one.

And yet there was another theme in David Jones's work. He was scrupulous in seeing these popular uprisings as all explicable and ultimately transient. He also documented the very rapid passing of the revolutionary moment of Wales's frontier years, amidst the Victorian respectability and self-help of Wales in the 1850s and 1860s. He noted how the Liberal pacifist, Henry Richard, looked back on Chartism in 1866 with 'undisguised repugnance and horror'.[5] In David Jones's later work, on crime and policing, indeed, the theme of consensus emerged all the more clearly. The rate of crime in nineteenth-century Wales was indeed relatively low by comparison with England. The crime-free land of the white gloves, 'gwlad y menig gwynion', while open to serious qualification, was not wholly a myth. This was partly because local crimes and misdemeanours were sorted out locally and informally, without involving the rigours of the criminal law, even amongst incorrigibly turbulent groups such as the coracle fishermen of the Tywi and Teifi. Police were thin on the ground in rural Wales and socially acceptable (the son of one of them became principal of Aberystwyth). There was an element of consensual social self-regulation which made the law almost redundant.[6] Self-advancement and greater prosperity in the later Victorian period strengthened the process. More and more of the Welsh had something to preserve.

David's posthumous work on crime and policing in south Wales in the twentieth century in its way further emphasised this theme of consensuality in Welsh society. David noted in passing the fierce eruptions of industrial conflict in Wales from the Penrhyn strike of 1900–3, through Tonypandy down to the unemployed marches of the 1930s, with a posthumous echo in the miners' strike in 1984. Yet in south Wales, too, there was something of Robert Reiner's English 'golden age of policing' down to the 1960s, dangers to public order were very few, and relations between police and public generally good. Despite the marked upsurge in criminal offences after 1960, the Welsh were still felt to be generally 'well-behaved', with less drinking than earlier in the century and with fewer indictable crimes than England as late as 1989.[7] By the 1990s, relations with the police were edgy as elsewhere, but the rapid growth in crime by individuals was explicable in social terms similar to those in England, and as abhorrent to the general community in Wales as elsewhere. David Jones, therefore, placed himself scrupulously on both sides of the consensus–conflict argument, according to his theme, and we may deal with each in turn.

The conflict thesis emerged amongst Welsh and other historians with particular force in the 1960s and 1970s. It was no doubt in part a product of the intellectual stimulus of movements in England, the impact of Marxist writers like E. P. Thompson and Raphael Samuel rescuing obscure popular movements, leaders and led, 'from the enormous condescension of posterity', and the rise of the History Workshop and other agents of radical scholarship. Intellectually, it was an attempt to assert the importance of ideas, a reaction to the 1950s, to Namier 'taking the mind out of history', and Oakeshott and the linguistic school doing the same to philosophy. It was an emphatic denial of Daniel Bell's pronouncement that the Cold War had meant 'the end of ideology'. It also reflected the wider social and cultural turbulence of the permissive 1960s, the 'youth revolt' so-called, and in Wales the particular impact both of class-conscious labour militancy and of a nationalist upsurge. It had a special impact on the earlier issues of the journal *Llafur* and the interest in labour and working-class history. Modern Wales, it seemed, should be viewed above all in terms of revolt and protest: a popular GCSE course with colourful documents attached was concerned with nineteenth-century Wales from the Merthyr rising in 1831 to the tithe riots in the 1880s. It was entitled 'People and Protest'. Less spectacular or more stable periods of Welsh history – such as the constitutionally-minded Liberal ascendancy of the years 1870–1914, the period of county councils and county schools, and the passion expended on the unlikely theme of the disestablishment of the Church of England – attracted less attention in the media, although Lloyd George perhaps bestrode both worlds to some degree.

Welsh history was seen, especially in the era since the advent of industrialisation, in terms of *Stürm und Drang*, class or sectional. It was a story of often violent confrontations, from the Scotch Cattle and the Merthyr rising through the labour troubles of 1910–26 down to the attempted arson of Penyberth aerodrome by Saunders Lewis and his fellow nationalists in 1936. Gwyn A. Williams's *When was Wales?*, following on a memorable charismatic BBC annual lecture under that title, brought many of those themes together. In particular, he focused on the marginal men, the Jacobins of the 1790s, the syndicalists of the Plebs League in 1912, the Marxist dissidents of National Left. Gwyn A. Williams's book, however, a product of the high noon of Thatcherism, was marked by a deep and growing pessimism as Wales's succession of impossible revolutions proved to be impossible indeed. His Wales was being destroyed by Toryism, capitalism and acid rain. All that was left was a fractured consciousness and a state of mind. On the other hand, a lively collective volume somewhat in the same vein, *A People and a Proletariat*, edited and with a sparkling introduction by Dai Smith (1981), was more pluralist and also more buoyant. Many of its contributions, perhaps a reflection of the comparative youth of many of the authors, were distinctly upbeat. Something of an exception is a Marxist lament on the management of the coal industry by Kim Howells, but he was the exception that proved a kind of rule.[8] He was later to emerge in the 1990s as a strongly Blairite MP and New Labour minister who called for the repression of ideas of socialism, indeed almost of ideology altogether.

The conflict thesis took hold amongst Welsh historians not only because it was colourful and dramatic but because in so many ways it was true. I was and am much drawn to it myself. The history of Wales in the past two hundred years has been shot through by confrontation at many different levels. There has been, for instance, ample evidence of political conflict, Liberal and Tory before 1914, Labour and Conservative thereafter. No doubt this is true of virtually all developed societies in the democratic era, but it has taken a particularly vehement, even virulent, form in Wales reflecting the class and other polarisation of Welsh society. The first county council elections in England in 1889, for instance, were not much of a change: in rural areas, respected landed gentry returned to head the new authorities. The success of descendants of the Marlborough dynasty in semi-feudal Woodstock, for instance, was only to be expected. But in Wales, from Anglesey to Monmouthshire, these elections saw a massive political revolution, with Liberals and non-conformists dancing on the political graves of a despised, fading squire-archy. More than other parts of the United Kingdom, the Welsh from the 1860s onwards drove on the left. It was not surprising that Keir Hardie, rejected successively by the voters of West Ham, Bradford East, North Aberdeen and Preston, should in 1900 find safe haven in the radical stronghold of Merthyr, where voters still cherished memories of Chartist clubs and the triumph of the pacifist Henry Richard. The fact that Hardie stood for Merthyr as an anti-war candidate amidst the jingoism of the Boer War, and shortly after Mafeking (defended by the allegedly Welsh Baden-Powell) was relieved, did his campaign relatively little harm.

Throughout the years of Liberal ascendancy down to the First World War and then the long march of Labour down to 1945, the Welsh found belligerent political champions. Lloyd George startled the English estab-lishment with the passion of his onslaught on the landlords and the Randlords: privately, he was a most pugnacious man, as is shown by the prevalence in his correspondence of the verb 'to smash'. Aneurin Bevan was in his day thought to be a socialist extremist; he notoriously cele-brated the launching of the National Health Service in July 1948 by declaring the Tories to be 'lower than vermin'. Of course, Welsh politics threw up many more moderate men, Tom Ellis or Jim Griffiths perhaps; but it was the more extreme practitioners who captured the public attention. In Wales, as in Clydeside in Scotland and most of Ireland, the tone of politics appeared to be particularly bitter. It was noticed in the 1930s that migrants from south Wales to Dagenham, Slough, Coventry or Oxford brought with them a new tone of class-conscious militancy, sometimes from within the Communist Party. It was the Welshmen in Oxford's car works who led the first strikes in Pressed Steel and Morris Motors in the early 1930s. Another car manufacturer, Herbert Austin in Longbridge, condemned the Welsh for their 'bloody-mindedness'.[9]

Political conflict was underpinned by its religious counterpart. As social life became politicised in the 1840s and 1850s, Welsh religious life was consumed by sectarian bitterness. Nonconformists began a pro-longed campaign against the Church of England for national equality.

So they did in England but, in Wales, the warfare was more intense and overlaid by national or nationalist overtones. Radical journalists like Samuel Roberts of Llanbrynmair and the especially pugnacious and dialectically unscrupulous Thomas Gee, publisher of *Baner ac Amserau Cymru* over many decades, drew on the latent passion once released in Chartism or the Rebecca disturbances. They openly encouraged acts of lawlessness like the Llanfrothen burial dispute which gave the youthful Lloyd George his first national platform, or the agitation and accompanying riots for the non-payment of tithe, or the clearly illegal non-implementation of the 1902 Education Act by the Welsh county councils, which foreshadowed the role of Clay Cross and other Labour local authorities in the 1970s. Welsh bishops like Bishop John Owen might proclaim the indissoluble role of the Church in the historical identity of the Welsh people from medieval times, but to nonconformists bent on civic status and political victory, this seemed antiquarian nonsense. Sectarian conflict poisoned prospects of consensus on other issues, for instance in university education where the inflexible approach of Lampeter kept it for seventy-five years removed from the national university. The long campaign for disestablishment of the Church, reaching its subdued climax in 1919 when a Welsh prime minister was otherwise engaged at Versailles, gave a virulent tone to Welsh denominational religion. The nonconformists and Anglicans seemed almost concerned more with undermining each other than with spreading the word: they focused more on statistics of each other's failing numbers in the religious census of 1906, rather than on the 55 per cent of the population who attended no place of worship at all. The tone was captured by Sir Henry Jones's verdict on the Commission on the Welsh Churches after his resignation in 1907: 'I learnt for the first time how much ill-feeling religious men can entertain towards one another. Such an atmosphere of distrust, suspicion and pious malice I never breathed before or since.'[10]

Linguistic conflict may seem a phenomenon of very recent years, since the formation of Cymdeithas yr Iaith Gymraeg (The Welsh Language Society) in the summer of 1962, and so in many ways it was. It was only after the First World War and especially after the Second World War that the Welsh language was felt to be under terminal threat: Liberals before

1914 were remarkably complacent about the clear evidence of growing anglicisation, especially in the industrial south. Yet it was their language and culture that underlay the Welsh campaign for national equality. It was the wholesale condemnation of both by the Education Commissioners of 1847, *Brad y Llyfrau Gleision* (The Treason of the Blue Books), which stung Welsh nationalism from its torpor. It first awakened the radical fires of popular publicists like S.R. and Gwilym Hiraethog. Cultural renaissance, the emergence of major new poets like T. Gwynn Jones and Silyn Roberts, the work of a popularising *littérateur* like Owen M. Edwards, the revitalisation of the National Eisteddfod, were pivotal to the Edwardian years prior to 1914. Cymdeithas yr Iaith, and even more the direct-action members of Meibion Glyndŵr in their arson attacks on English-owned property, drew strength from early traditions of Welsh law-breaking, often of a violent kind. Linguistic conflict, irresponsibly fanned by senior politicians like Leo Abse, underlay the tensions over devolution in 1979 and helped lead to its massive rejection. Without an accommodation and far greater tolerance, devolution would never have received even the very narrow endorsement it won in 1997. Wales could have been consumed by the linguistic violence of Catalonia, Belgium or French Quebec.

Social conflict of all forms has often taken a particularly frightening form in modern Wales. It need not be discussed at length here, since most of its manifestations have emerged in the work of David Jones. He and others focused on mass disturbances in both rural and industrial areas, on the Newport march, on the coordinated flouting of the law in the Rebecca disturbances, on the folk symbolism of the uprising of the Scotch Cattle or the significant ritualistic reappearance of the *ceffyl pren* (the 'wooden horse' as means of ritual humiliation). It should be added that conflict in the countryside returned in the 1880s, a period somewhat later than that in which David Jones chiefly worked. There was class tension comparable with that of Ireland in the confrontation between landlords and the Welsh Land League. It emerged fiercely in the Caernarfon Boroughs by-election in April 1890, fought between the youthful agrarian radical David Lloyd George, and Ellis Nanney, the squire of Gwynfryn Castle. Earlier, the protests against payment of tithe to an alien Church led to ugly incidents in normally tranquil farming communities in Clwyd and Powys. At Meifod in Montgomeryshire in June 1887, the county militia was brought in and the Riot Act had to be read. Fifty civilians, many of them farmers, and thirty-four police were injured. Wales, it seemed, had its own version of the Irish 'Plan of Campaign'.

After the turn of the century, this tradition spread to industrial areas. The south Wales coalfield, for micro-economic and also geological reasons, was the most torn by conflict and class hatred. In Tonypandy there was loss of life; contrary to his later disavowals, Churchill as Home Secretary (admittedly with much reluctance) had to send the hussars to the mining valleys. Troops dealt with demonstrators in Pontypridd with fixed bayonets. The trouble spread elsewhere in the coalfield to other industries. In the national rail strike of July–August 1911, several men were shot down and killed in Llanelli; detachments from the Worcestershire and Sussex regiments patrolled the town, but no inquiry followed. In the intensified industrial conflict after the end of the war, with mass unemployment rising especially fast in a traditionally exporting coalfield like south Wales, confrontations mounted. In the traditionally more peaceable anthracite coalfield of Welsh-speaking west Wales, there was massive violence between striking miners and the police at Ammanford in 1925, remembered for decades afterwards.[11] A similar story came with the 'stay-down' stoppages at Abertillery in 1935, and in the handling of demonstrators from south Wales in the means test and unemployed marches around the same period.[12] Even in the far less troubled years after 1945, the 1984–5 miners' strike replayed some of the old themes in south Wales. A passing motorist lost his life inadvertently, while Norman Willis, general secretary of the TUC, was greeted by an audience at Port Talbot with a gallows rope symbolically strung down from the public gallery. Nor was rural protest dormant either. Welsh farmers turned to direct action in the 1980s and 1990s as their livelihood collapsed around them, notably in furious protests over the handling of 'mad cow disease' in 1996, and picketing shipments of meat due to be landed at the port of Holyhead.

The continuing common theme was that of violence. In the coalfield the Welsh seemed to be in perpetual turmoil. In violent confrontation they led the way, from the Merthyr uprising and its brutal suppression, to the popular martyrdom of Saunders Lewis, another Dic Penderyn *avant la lettre*, in 1937 – which led even the anti-nationalist David Lloyd George to an explosion of wrath (admittedly from the safe and comfortable haven of Montego Bay).[13] Detailed study of aspects of Welsh society have reinforced this view. My late wife, Jane (a close professional associate of David Jones, who contributed a fine chapter to her memorial volume), found in her study of the police and industrial conflict that, even more than Liverpool or Glasgow, it was south Wales that provided her with the major examples of conflict.[14] She cited a contemporary account of Tonypandy when Churchill sent in the hussars: 'With a dervish yell and batons drawn they dashed out between 80 and 90 strong from the colliery yard . . . The two sides were in furious combat . . . Scores of the rioters were struck down like logs with broken skulls and left on the ground.'[15] One man (Samuel Rays) was left dead, five hundred were injured amongst the rioters, along with 40 per cent of the foot constables and sixteen mounted men. The rioting continued intermittently in 1911; meanwhile the local constabulary, the feared 'Glamorgans', turned their acquired experience of manhandling strikers to other fields, notably in battering into submission the clay workers of hitherto peaceful Cornwall in the St Austell area in 1913.

After 1920, things were just as bad. Captain Lionel Lindsay, long-term chief constable of Glamorgan who had first seen service in suppressing the Egyptian fellahin under Sir Garnet Wolseley, was fully embattled. The government used the Emergency Powers provision to send in troops, warships to patrol the port of Cardiff and even (for surveillance only!) the Royal Air Force to grind the miners in south Wales into submission. Nor was this violence confined to the industrial south. Just as the Chartist movement had first erupted in deeply rural Llanidloes, so the Penrhyn Quarry stoppage of 1900–3 was also marked by massive confrontations. As Merfyn Jones has shown,[16] Lord Penrhyn's regime (with its prohibition of trade unions which had originally provoked the strike) saw the massive use of auxiliary police, of cavalry and infantry in a manner astonishing to the quiet slate villages of Caernarfonshire. There was intense personal bitterness towards Penrhyn himself. For a generation or more of industrial conflict, from the turn of the century down to the mid-1930s, this pattern of physical confrontation was to continue. Violence, said in the 1960s to be 'as American as cherry pie', appeared rather to be as British as Welsh rarebit.

Is this, then, the true face of modern Welsh history? Were the Welsh always roaring boys, always a race apart? Was their social history a saga of rioting and striking, knocking down toll-gates and enclosure walls and burning down aerodromes, in eternal conflict with the official forces of the law? Has Wales since 1800 been in a state of continual sub-revolutionary turmoil simmering just below the surface, the cockpit of the western world?

Clearly this view would, in fact, be a parody. These episodes did indeed take place, but they were only part of the story, as David Jones's work recognised, especially when he wrote on the policed society. Compared, for example, with the multiple tragedies of modern Ireland, from the time of Cromwell down to atrocities such as that of Omagh in early 1998, Wales has been by contrast the model of constitutionality. Its representative folk symbol is not the nation in arms but the committee man in the council chamber, armed not with an Armalite but with his Bangor or Aberystwyth BA. There is nothing remotely like the Irish tradition of long-term communal violence. There was no Welsh Ulster, no Welsh Provisional Sinn Féin or IRA. The Welsh Land League was far less aggressive than the Irish, and the countryside infinitely more peaceful. There was no mass movement for a republic. There was no Welsh de Valera or Michael Collins, let alone Gerry Adams. In time, even social conflicts as intense as those of the Rebecca years in the 1840s or the industrial clashes of 1910–26 gradually faded away, and a more constructive phase took their place. Welsh history over the past two hundred years is one of conflicts, actual and potential, but then of their being invariably resolved.

There are many social explanations for this. Gradual economic prosperity neutralised points of conflict; unlike Ireland, labourers from the countryside, surplus to economic needs in marginal rural areas, found employment within Wales itself. Indeed, they found it possible to live harmoniously in the valleys with thousands of other immigrants from

England and Ireland (or, indeed, in Cardiff from North Africa and the Middle East). In rural areas, socio-economic unrest usually concerned small property-holders, conservative with a small 'c' if seldom with a large one. Welsh tenant farmers, politically antagonistic towards their landlords as they may often have been, were nevertheless small entrepreneurs, who owned their tools and stock and whose common interest with their labouring force was limited. At the turn of the century, as depression in the countryside eased and marketing and transport facilities improved, rural tension rapidly diminished. Lloyd George's land crusades seemed to be by 1914 somewhat out of date. Very few Welsh farmers endorsed the nationalisation of land advocated by the far-left Revd E. Pan Jones in *Y Celt*, published in Mostyn in deepest Clwyd. In any case, David Howell has argued, tenurial relations in rural Wales were never that hostile. Even in the worst depths of agricultural depression in the late nineteenth century, the social structure remained organic, closely knit and deep-rooted.[17] After 1910, Wales experienced its own 'green revolution' when tens of thousands purchased their freeholds. Their subsequent financial difficulties found them locked in conflict not with remote Anglican landlords (a pathetic rump by now) but with local banks.

In industrial Wales, revolt was neutralised by many factors. There was a robust strength to community life in the valleys, the product of a range of agencies from the nonconformist chapels to the mass of local rugby or other sporting clubs; the Tonypandy rioters in 1910 made a point of leaving alone the chemist's shop of Willie Llewellyn, a famous rugby international. One important element was the spread of house-ownership, a rapid development widespread in mining communities after the turn of the century.[18] 'Building clubs' and, later, building societies found profitable and harmonious fields for their operations in industrial south Wales, while the leasehold property owned by the Bute family and others in Cardiff, Barry and Newport did not create mass friction at this time. Here and elsewhere, Welsh society was becoming less polarised, especially as public education created a new generation of social leadership through the county schools and the national university. Even Welsh women, long subjugated, found professional and other openings, notably through the school-teaching profession. Bangor Normal and Trinity College, Carmarthen, entered after 1900 upon halcyon years.

Perhaps the most pivotal figures in Welsh life after the turn of the century are not the combatants but the bureaucrats. A new generation of bourgeois conquerors was created, the committee men who ran the new councils and commissions, public servants like Thomas Jones, Alfred Davies, John Rowlands, Percy Watkins or later Ben Bowen Thomas or Elwyn Davies.[19] Thomas Jones, a constructive Fabian, embodies the new ethos of 'administrative Wales' hailed as such in the monthly *Welsh Outlook* (which for a time he owned).[20] He was the supreme bureaucrat, running Welsh health and insurance, active in the university world, sponsoring local economic initiatives, launching adult education – most notably in Coleg Harlech in 1927. In Wales, as at Downing Street in the service of his fellow Welshman Lloyd George, he was 'the fluid person moving amongst persons who matter'.[21] In London this could seem an irritating symbol of close-quarter patronage; in Oxford, where Jones operated at All Souls alongside members of the 'Cliveden set' of appeasers of Hitler, stronger language could and would be used. In Wales, by contrast, Jones was a constructive, healing, idealistic figure, helping to bind the nation's earlier wounds, finding solutions and persuading his countrymen to pursue the path of peace.

A major factor in this move towards consensual approaches was without doubt the advent of democracy. Unlike Ireland, where democracy has so often foundered on irreconcilable social and sectarian divisions, especially in Ulster, Wales has found politics a panacea. It has spawned the triumphalism of the committee man. In the mid-Victorian era, that 'age of equipoise' so cogently analysed by Ieuan Gwynedd Jones, the years Walter Bagehot called the 'day after the feast',[22] modern Wales was reborn. New national and local institutions were created under the aegis of the new Liberal ascendancy. An almost unbroken string of peaceful victories followed – the capture of almost all the Welsh parliamentary constituencies at elections, the domination of the county councils (especially their crucial education committees), the ascendancy of a broad national/Liberal culture spanning chambers of commerce and trade unions, the nonconformist chapels, the editorial offices, the shops and the schools, even to a degree the local rugby clubs. In the Edwardian era, this consensual ascendancy had an immense variety of representative symbols, from the epoch-making victory over the New Zealand All Blacks in December 1905 to the subtly inclusive investiture of Prince Edward at Caernarfon castle in July 1911. Lloyd George and Bishop A. G. Edwards, two old polemical adversaries but two supremely serpentine Celts, were amongst the orchestrators. David Lloyd George was being denounced by Unionists in England as a wild man, a dangerous, divisive force, taxing the rich, threatening the Lords, threatening dire consequences like a latter-day John Knox for 'golfers, motorists and all those miserable sinners who happen to own anything'. In Wales, by contrast, he seemed to have transcended political divisions; he was the greatest living Welshman, the cottage-bred embodiment of *y werin* in power, the pride and joy of his countrymen.

At first, the First World War and his premiership made this supra-party symbolism all the stronger. After all, he could now appear as the ultimate champion of Liberal, national values, the passionate defender of gallant little Belgium, gallant little Serbia and Montenegro – and, by implication, gallant little Wales.[23] The old conflicts therefore simply melted away as somehow irrelevant. The martyred evicted farmers of 1868, turned out of their holdings for having dared to vote Liberal, had been avenged long before. The Welsh squirearchy had long held up the tattered flag of surrender, taking refuge in such activities as becoming lords lieutenant or high sheriffs, or else chairing local history societies. At the first sign of a Rorke's Drift or Little Big Horn, the squires turned tail. The bishops were to follow. The disestablishment of the Welsh Church in 1920, the age-old aspiration of nonconformists over the generations, thus seemed a monumental irrelevance. The long march of Welsh Liberalism ended not with an emotional bang but with the most anti-climactic of whimpers.

Democracy also helped to make consensual the Labour movement. Through social and political advance, Labour created its own constructive élite – in local government, in the world of the WEA and of adult education, in the deeply entrenched Co-operative Society, and always in the world of the trade unions. The miners and other workers created their own local leadership often as miners' agents. In place of firebrands like the proto-Fascist C. B. Stanton,[24] the Fed generated moderate leaders like Vernon Hartshorn or Charles Edwards or Arthur Jenkins, father of a famous Welsh centrist politician. The older pre-war Lib-Labs of the Mabon type passed away, but the militant advocates of direct action were gradually marginalised, too, especially after the general strike. Arthur Cook, the Somerset man who was the most charismatic of them all, ended his days sadly undermined by alcoholism, a feeling of class betrayal and fleeting sympathy for Sir Oswald Mosley.[25] Noah Ablett, the inspirational Marxist rhetorician of the Plebs League, also disappeared into the shadows. Meanwhile, Major David Watts Morgan, CBE DSO MP, 'Dai Alphabet', spoke of a new Labour respectability. The great Labour figures of twentieth-century Wales have all believed in the agency of democratic power. That was self-evidently true of Jim Griffiths, perhaps the most characteristic symbol of consensualism in the Welsh Labour movement. But it came to be true of Aneurin Bevan, too, who foreswore his early sympathy for forms of direct action like the Workers' Defence Corps and became dedicated to the pursuit and mobilisation of democratic power.[26] Both Griffiths and Bevan, different in personality and outlook as they were, ended up as Cabinet ministers with great social achievements to their credit, and as national statesmen. At the time of Suez, Bevan was hailed as a workers' patriot, morally superior to the Wykehamist traitor, Gaitskell. The Labour ascendancy after 1945, as deep-rooted as the Liberal ascendancy before 1914, defused any prospect of any kind of workers' revolt, even under the extreme provocation of Thatcherism in the 1980s. Great titans at the local level, of whom Llew Heycock in Glamorgan was the outstanding example, provided communal forces of stability and penetration after 1945, as they had fought to keep local services going during the harsh years of the means test and mass unemployment in the 1930s. For all its semi-revolutionary antecedents and occasional Marxist flourishes, Labour Wales was part of the consensus and of the establishment.

So, it may be remarked, was the Communist Party in its way. In the 1920s, it threatened to be a focus of radical and industrial protest of a quite new kind, as disillusion with parliamentary politics set in. Gwyn A.

Williams cast affectionate eyes on the role of David Irfon Jones, who had to seek refuge in South Africa in the end.[27] But in the 1930s, Arthur Horner, much the most important Communist, became president of the South Wales Miners' Federation; later on he worked closely with the National Coal Board in producing the Miners' Charter. The old poacher was close to becoming gamekeeper.[28] After his time, another distinguished Communist, Dai Francis, could move on from a career confined to the union to becoming an active participant in the movement for Welsh devolution.

Democracy had its emollient effect on nationalism also. Since the 1960s, Welsh Nationalists have become politicised. In effect, the irreconcilable outlook of Saunders Lewis has been replaced by that of Gwynfor Evans, and even more that of Dafydd Wigley. Instead of becoming instruments of protests, of expressionist politics, nationalists have mainly pursued consensual strategies, notably in enabling the two linguistic communities to work together in the setting up of Welsh-medium schools. Advocates of direct action, still more fringe movements such as the arsonists of Meibion Glyndŵr, have been totally marginalised, as Plaid Cymru has grown in confidence, the Scottish Nationalists have continued to thrive, and the prospects for inclusive co-operation within the Welsh Assembly have opened up. Plaid Cymru has certainly become far more politically aware than in the early 1960s, and also no doubt more aware of its opportunities as the heady possibilities opened up by strong by-election votes in Rhondda West and Caerphilly in 1967–8 later reappeared. But the main democratic achievements have lain not in political but in cultural nationalism, in the way that Welsh culture has become more harmonious and able to play a fuller part in the revival of popular culture, design and artistic life (notably in the cinema) that the period following the 1997 referendum result appears to have witnessed. Of course, in this nationalists have gone with the grain of the movement for national recognition in Wales, an urge for equality and fair treatment within the United Kingdom, rather than the separatism relentlessly sought by the Irish. But it is hard to see Welsh Nationalists as being more successful through militant methods under any circumstances. Even compared with the Scots, they have been subdued, in accordance with the modest nature of any kind of Welsh separatism. Owain Glyndŵr, potent symbol though he may be, is no Wallace or Bruce. He has never yet inspired a Welsh *Braveheart*.

The more rhetorical versions of conflict as the abiding theme of recent Welsh history must, therefore, be rejected. The Marxist diagnoses of Wales popular in some circles in the 1980s collapsed with the Berlin wall. The dominant tendency in Welsh history is not a militant tendency. On balance, during the twentieth century, elements of conflict within Welsh society have steadily diminished. The ideological extremes have not struck long-term roots. The Welsh Labour movement was solidly centre-right: Communism made only localised headway. Any form of Fascism found less receptive soil in Wales than elsewhere in the British Isles. There have been no anti-Jewish activities in Wales since 1911 – and those events in Tredegar may not have been anti-semitic at all.[29] Nor have there been any significant racial riots in the land since those in Cardiff in 1919.[30] For much of the century, Wales could be claimed to be more harmonious than England. In the years before 1914, George Dangerfield saw Liberal England in the process of undergoing a strange death, its civic culture undermined by violent strikes, militant suffragettes, near civil war in Ireland, and a widespread atmosphere of extremism. In Wales, at that very same period, there was a high noon of national unity and achievement. There was pride in the growth of the city of Cardiff, in the commercial development of the new port of Barry, in the eminence of cultural leaders like John Morris-Jones and Owen M. Edwards, and in the golden age of Welsh rugby. Even Lloyd George, as has been seen, played very different roles in Wales and in England. In England he was an extremist, but in Wales he was almost a reconciler. Indeed, similar contrasts can be made throughout the century if a comparative method is used and Welsh and English are posed face to face.

The conflict thesis, therefore, can be exaggerated. Yet consensus is hardly a satisfactory diagnosis of our historical experience either. In part, this may be simply a matter of semantics or of definition. Historians must consider such issues as consensus among whom, and at what level. Is it a consensus over the framework, over the policy, or is it a broader moral consensus? History in Wales, as elsewhere, is supremely the analysis of the process of change, of stress and its resistance. The study of the past is inherently a dialectic if not a materialist one.

Overt physical conflicts have been contained or set aside. But other forms of conflict keep emerging – even if historians, trained by their cloistered disciplines to seek harmonies in life, are sometimes too squeamish to acknowledge the fact. Even the gentle achievement of disestablishment of the Church in 1920, a wholly bloodless victory, was testimony to a major dislodging of traditional forms of authority. It helped to promote a wider disestablishment in Wales, notably that of the remnants of the landed gentry. Lloyd George, brilliant and brutal, was probably nearer the political realities than the gentle and philosophical Tom Ellis. And as one historic conflict was being resolved, it merely uncovered other forms of conflict based on class, culture, gender or generation. A new environmental radicalism, dimly prefigured in the Tryweryn controversies over water supplies in the 1950s, might transform the nature of Welsh protest yet again. And Wales is, of course, deeply affected by pressures from outside, especially in an age of televisual imagery and the revolutionary impact of information technology. Earlier conflicts down to the 1960s were moderated because of faith in the British social order and constitutional system, in the civil service, in local government, in the rule of law, so fascinatingly underlined in David Jones's later work on the police in south Wales. From that time on, Wales like much of the rest of Britain has seen an erosion in that earlier Fabian confidence, a declining faith in Parliament, in the justice system, in the monarchy itself. Just as the nationalist protests in Wales in the 1960s had links with events in the Sorbonne and Berkeley, so inherent conflicts at the end of the millennium reflected wider pressures from outside, notably a Europe with which Wales was inseparably entwined.

The Wales of whose history David Jones was the incomparable chronicler was, then, a complex society and a fluctuating concept. It is not surprising that parts of his work may be located in the camps both of the consensualists and of the apostles of conflict. It showed the difficulties with the simplistic dualism (created, it should be said, by the television series, not by the participants) of *The Dragon has Two Tongues*. Ultimately, though, David Jones depicts a people that has held together in the modern period, and indeed become more confident of its identity as the pressures have mounted. Richard Hofstadter spoke of a society like the United States keeping intact despite the massive disruption of a civil war because of what he called 'comity' – 'a sense that community life must be carried on after the acerbic issues of the moment have been fought over and won'.[31] He contrasted American society positively in this respect with Spain at the time of the Civil War in 1936.

In Wales, much of the comity of its recent history has come from the character of its nationhood. This has been expressed in terms of the idea of nationality rather than the aggressive doctrine of nationalism. It has thus been incremental rather than divisive. It could lead, as Rees Davies has brilliantly shown,[32] to Owain Glyndŵr becoming a protean figure in social memory, a looming hero for all moods and all seasons. It has not led to a Welsh Ulster, let alone a Welsh Bosnia being created from the fires. Welsh nationhood, however ill-defined, has thus enabled an inclusive form of self-expression to emerge. It has created a power of integration, in a form of Welshness increasingly acceptable to the English-speaking majority from the *eisteddfod* to S4C and Welsh-medium schools. Nor is it merely the cult of a bourgeois Welsh-speaking élite in the Cardiff suburbs. The Welsh trade unions, for long the class-conscious advocates of solidarity for ever, now flaunt their Welshness. This kind of nationhood had also encouraged an increasingly positive and intelligent response from outside over many decades. In that sense, to see the entire span of Welsh history from the 1880s to our own time as 'the rebirth of a nation', rather than a people crushed into embittered oblivion by the processes of global capitalism, is wholly justified. The advance of national equality for Wales is an erratic but consistent story from Gladstone in the late Victorian era down to politicians of all parties in the 1980s and 1990s. Even under Mrs Thatcher, that stern, unbending champion of British unionism, the Welsh Office developed mightily as the symbol of an active new Welsh territoriality. Even Thatcherism added an important ingredient to the awareness of identity. So, ironically, does an increasingly regional Europe, which the Mrs Thatcher of post-Bruges days regarded as anathema.

The impact of a devolved elected Welsh Assembly from May 1999 is hard to foresee. Its economic powers are very limited and this may lead

24

to friction. It may reproduce the kind of parochial bickering that has made the federal University of Wales less of a national institution than it could have been. It may, however, create a different style of inclusive social leadership which will both have wider implications for the work-ing of the British Isles and help evolve that sense of citizenship (perhaps in Europe as well as in Britain) that the Welsh have conspicuously lacked since the Tudor Act of Union. Nationality was not a theme in any of the social protests David Jones analysed: he was not Welsh-speaking and his view of devolution is not formally recorded. But it may be that its achievement could blur the disunities of his Wales. It could temper still further at least some of the stresses of a tormented society of which he was the wise and gentle remembrancer.

Notes

1. E.g. Dennis Kavanagh and Peter Morris, *Consensus Politics from Attlee to Thatcher* (Oxford, 1989).
2. Louis Hartz, *The Liberal Tradition in America* (New York, 1955); Daniel Boorstin, *The Genius of American Politics* (Chicago, 1953).
3. See particularly Richard Hofstadter, 'Conflict and consensus in American History', in Richard Hofstadter, *The Progressive Historians* (New York, 1968). It should be compared with the essay on Hofstadter by Arthur Schlesinger Jr., in Marcus Cunliffe and Robin Winks (eds), *Pastmasters: Some Essays on American Historians* (New York, 1969).
4. HTV television broadcast, January–March 1985.
5. David J. V. Jones, *The Last Rising* (Oxford, 1985), p. 228.
6. David J. V. Jones, *Crime in Nineteenth-Century Wales* (Cardiff, 1990), pp. 201ff.
7. David J. V. Jones, *Crime and Policing in the Twentieth Century: The South Wales Experience* (Cardiff, 1995), pp. 65ff.
8. Kim Howells, 'Victimisation, accidents and disease', in David Smith (ed.), *A People and a Proletariat* (London, 1980), pp. 181–9.
9. Kenneth O. Morgan, *Modern Wales: Politics, Places and People* (Cardiff, 1995), p. 16.
10. H. J. Hetherington (ed.), *The Life and Letters of Sir Henry Jones* (London, 1924), p. 95.
11. See Hywel Francis, 'The anthracite strike and the disturbances of 1925', *Llafur*, 1/2 (May 1973), 15–28.
12. See David Smith, 'The struggle against company unionism in the south Wales coalfield, 1926–1939', *Welsh History Review*, 6/3 (June 1973), 354ff.

[13] Lloyd George to Megan Lloyd George, 9 December 1936, in Kenneth O. Morgan (ed.), *Lloyd George: Family Letters, c.1885–1936* (Oxford and Cardiff, 1973), pp. 213–14.

[14] Jane Morgan, *Conflict and Order: The Police and Labour Disputes in England and Wales, 1900–1939* (Oxford, 1987).

[15] Morgan, *Conflict and Order*, p. 156, citing the contemporary account of the *South Wales Daily News* journalist, David Evans.

[16] Merfyn Jones, *The North Wales Quarrymen, 1874–1922* (Cardiff, 1981), pp. 246ff.

[17] Peris Jones Evans, 'Evan Pan Jones – land reformer', *Welsh History Review*, 4/2 (1968), 143–59; David W. Howell, *Land and People in Nineteenth-Century Wales* (London, 1977), esp. pp. 148ff.

[18] See P. N. Jones, *Colliery Settlement in the South Wales Coalfield, 1850 to 1926* (Hull, 1969).

[19] An invaluable work on this theme is the memoir, Percy Watkins, *A Welshman Remembers* (Cardiff, 1944).

[20] See the admirable biography by E. L. Ellis, *T.J.: A Life of Dr Thomas Jones CH* (Cardiff, 1992).

[21] Thomas Jones to his wife, 12 December 1916 (NLW), Thomas Jones Papers, X/7).

[22] Ieuan Gwynedd Jones, *Explorations and Explanations* (Llandysul, 1981), and Ieuan Gwynedd Jones, *Communities* (Llandysul, 1987). For Bagehot's view, see W. L. Burn's unjustly neglected book, *The Age of Equipoise* (London, 1964), pp. 55ff.

[23] Lloyd George's speech at the Queen's Hall, London, 19 September 1914, reprinted in *David Lloyd George, From Terror to Triumph* (London, 1915), pp. 1–15.

[24] Cf. Eddie May, 'Charles Stanton and the limits to patriotic labour', *Welsh History Review*, 18/3 (1997), 483–508.

[25] See Paul Davies, *A. J. Cook* (Manchester, 1987), pp. 159ff.

[26] Hywel Francis and Dai Smith, *The Fed* (London, 1980), pp. 192ff.

[27] BBC2 television broadcast, 'The Delegate for Africa: David Ivon Jones', 1992.

[28] See Arthur Horner, *Incorrigible Rebel* (London, 1960).

[29] A rare proto-Fascist was the Swansea businessman, W. Mainwaring Hughes: see Peter Stead, 'The Swansea of Dylan Thomas', in *Dylan Thomas Remembered* (Swansea, 1978), pp. 8–24. For the anti-Jewish disturbances, see W. D. Rubinstein, 'The anti-Jewish riots of 1911 in south Wales: a re-examination', *Welsh History Review*, 18/4 (December 1997), 667–99. The author concludes that, if anything, the Welsh were philo-Semitic. On the latter, see also Jasmine Donahay, *Whose People? Wales, Israel, Palestine* (Cardiff, 2012).

[30] Neil Evans, 'The South Wales race riots of 1919', *Llafur*, 3/1 (1980), 5–30.

[31] Hofstadter, 'Conflict and consensus', p. 454.

[32] Rees Davies, *The Revolt of Owain Glyndŵr* (Oxford, 1995), pp. 338–42.

2

Welsh Democracy, Revolution to Devolution

The Welsh enjoy many conceits. We thank the Lord, according to the Reverend Eli Jenkins, that we are a musical nation, christening our sons Haydn, Handel, Elgar and sometimes even Verdi. We think of ourselves as having once been a religious nation, with little Bethels sprouting up on every hillside, now perhaps replaced by unsightly wind turbines. We are surely a sporting nation, before whom even the mighty All Blacks have very occasionally to bow the knee, even if only once every fifty years or so. We say we are a classless nation, a model of egalitarianism and social mobility, free from a landed aristocracy, public schools or an established Church. The lead singer of Catatonia tells us that we are a proud nation, waking up each morning to thank the Lord (again) that we are Welsh. Above all, we cherish the thought that we are a democratic nation, by instinct and in practice, secular worshippers of the priesthood of all believers, celebrated as such from Henry Richard to Aneurin Bevan. No-one exalted our democratic ethos more eloquently than David Lloyd George in the 1910 elections: 'The spirit of the mountains, the genius of freedom that fought the might of the Normans.'[1]

But like all legends, our democratic instinct needs to be examined. As a term, 'democracy' was not much used before the 1920s (when the world was supposed to have been made safe for it). Politicians preferred to talk instead of 'the people', selectively defined. The Welsh word *gwerin*, with its essentially rural overtones, was even more imprecise. 'Democracy' was a word used perhaps when discussing American politics, or else, in the case, for example, of Professor Alfred Zimmern once of Aberystwyth, the ancient Greek Commonwealth. The Labour movement spoke of 'social democracy', transmuted by those further on the left into the term 'democratic socialism' – for an intellectual like R. H. Tawney, the democracy was quite as important as the socialism. Democracy was a hard enough term to define in English (as was another Greek concept – 'citizenship'). The Welsh really had no word at all for it. The word *gweriniaeth* could be applied equally to the Republicans and the Democrats in the United States. Democracy covered a multitude of meanings, as did popular government, all of which suggested in general terms the thrill of revolutionary ferment, a history consisting, in the vivid language of the late, great Professor Gwyn A. Williams, of those 'brutal ruptures'. David Marquand, in a fascinating account of British political ideas since 1918, has seen Wales as a model of 'democratic republicanism', which might yet influence or infect its larger neighbour over Offa's Dyke.[2] Yet, in Wales as perhaps in England (for all the impact of Milton or Tom Paine), the idea has had a somewhat fitful existence.

Even so, Welsh history over the past two hundred years has abundantly demonstrated key aspects of democracy as popularly understood – accountability to the people locally and nationally, free participation in public affairs, an atmosphere of reason and tolerance in which public debate may be conducted. The National Assembly, where these thoughts were originally delivered, is a legacy to the power of such ideas in the life and history of the Welsh people, just as its transparent style of architecture implies another basic idea – that of an essentially open democracy visible to all. The Richard Rogers firm of architects who designed it said that the *Senedd*, constructed of glass, steel and Welsh slate, was a 'transparent envelope', looking outwards towards Cardiff Bay, 'making visible the inner workings of the Assembly and encouraging public participation in the democratic process'.[3] Wales's democratic centrepiece had thus an implicit ideological message. But, in Wales as in Britain more generally, we have some fair way to go. It would be hard to claim that we have a democratic system of governance today: certainly supporters of proportional representation would not put that claim forward. Our constitution is based, as for centuries past, not on democratic citizenship or popular sovereignty, but on being subjects of the Crown. The American constitution proudly begins with the declaration 'We, the people of the United States.' Similar sentiments have been expressed in the many constitutions of France ever since 1789. But we are as yet unable to proclaim 'We, the people of Wales.'

The roots of the democratic debate in Wales emerged during the American Revolution which so excited radical thinkers like Richard Price and David Williams. Their debate was given momentum by the popular dynamism of the nonconformist chapels, then in a process of vigorous expansion, and by the social dislocation brought about by the advent of industrialisation, iron working and coal mining in the valleys of the south and, to a degree, around Wrexham in north Wales as well. All these came together during the American Revolution and, even more, the French Revolution of 1789. The radicals who responded embodied the prehistory of the democratic idea in Wales. They were a remarkable group of progressive thinkers. They included Richard Price, the dissenting Presbyterian minister-philosopher, who turned Deist and whose famous sermon memorably provoked Burke's powerful *Reflections* on the revolutionary events in France, and the rationalist David Williams, friend of the Girondins who actually attended the revolutionary Assembly in Paris and was offered French citizenship. The so-called 'Jacobinism' of dissent also drew in Morgan John Rhys, who exported Welsh communitarianism to 'Beulah land' in the United States as part of what Gwyn A. Williams memorably termed 'the Baptist International'.[4] The myth of the Welsh-speaking Indians made the story of Madoc a powerful vehicle for extending the message of liberty across the American continent.[5] More remarkable still was the maverick bard, Edward Williams, 'Iolo Morganwg', a progressive Unitarian and an admirer of Tom Paine, who grafted notions of modern democracy on to legends of druidic culture. His bizarre, but enduring and powerfully influential, legacy, the Welsh national *eisteddfod*, first held not in Wales but on Primrose Hill in London in 1792, embodied a democratic revolutionary concept, founded on the alleged 'Jacobinism' of the bards. That distinctly non-Welsh member of parliament for Merthyr, James Keir Hardie, was to see social-ism at work in the idea of an *eisteddfod*. It was originally created in the early middle ages, he claimed, to protect the bards against literary blacklegs.[6] These Welsh Jacobins were an outward-looking, if fragmentary, group. They saw their radicalism in a worldwide context, and their ideological influence was enduring.

Democracy in Wales was given a broader base in the era of Chartism in the 1830s. The Chartists operated at a time of much social dislocation in early industrial Wales – the violent riots at Merthyr in 1831, when more people were killed by troops than at Peterloo twelve years earlier; the Scotch Cattle troubles provoked by the social tyranny of employers in their 'Black Domain'; the Rebecca Riots directed against the toll gates in rural west Wales.[7] Chartism in Wales was a rough coalition of the dispossessed extending from rural Llanidloes in Montgomeryshire to the mines and ironworks of Gwent. Its key democrat was John Frost of Newport, a long-standing campaigner for radical political reform, much influenced by William Cobbett.[8] Frost's letter to Lord John Russell con-veyed the proud dignity of an angry democracy – 'by what authority' were decisions taken over the lives and activities of Welsh working people? He and others demanded the 'restoration of the ancient con-stitution', vaguely defined, which reflects the retro-radicalism of earlier generations of democrats. What Chartism added to Welsh democracy was the new, dangerous ingredient of class. Ideas such as the notion of a 'Silurian Republic', the product of the brain of that highly eccentric surgeon, Dr William Price, had profound revolutionary implications. In later years, Price was to underline his extremism by naming his illegitim-ate baby son Iesu Grist (Jesus Christ) and then attempting to burn his body after he died. In the end, following the shooting down of the work-ing men who had marched to Newport in 1839 to demand the release of Henry Vincent from the local goal, accusations that Chartism was a body prepared to use force divided its supporters, especially within the chapels. Welsh Chartism petered out in the socialism of Ernest Jones, later a close associate of Karl Marx. But Chartism was no failure. It left an enduring commitment to the conquest of power by the workers. It laid the foun-dations of mass democracy in Wales and beyond.

Chartism encouraged and helped to energise a myriad of individual democratic pressure-groups. It helped in the politicising of the chapels, hitherto politically cautious especially in the case of the numerically dominant Calvinist Methodists. In mid-century, there was now a vivid radicalism of the word, spread through vocal pressure-groups like the Reform League, the anti-slavery movement and the discreetly powerful Liberation Society committed to the disestablishment of the Church of England. The last had especial force in Wales, where the Church, *Eglwys Loegr*, was increasingly seen as anti-Welsh, the Church of England (especially of the anglicised landed gentry) in Wales. The growth of a vigorous press, especially after the repeal of the paper duties in 1861, was a powerful vehicle for dissent. The Welsh-language press had a particular radical tone, from *Yr Amserau* in mid-century down to Labour's *Llais Llafur*, published in Ystalyfera in the upper Swansea valley fifty years later. Nothing was more clearly to show the drift of *Llais Llafur* to the right during the early weeks of the First World War than when it transformed itself into an English-language pro-war weekly, *Labour Voice*. A man like the preacher-poet William Rees, Gwilym Hiraethog, was a democratic advocate of much importance now, a champion of the idea of democracy having cultural roots.[9] Hiraethog was also important in seeing Welsh developments in an international setting. He endorsed Mazzini's gospel of citizenship and corresponded with him. He worked closely with the anti-slavery movement in the United States and had a version of *Uncle Tom's Cabin* translated into Welsh. He saw the crucial importance of the victory of the anti-slavery North in the American Civil War. The outcome was the triumph of the Reform Act of 1867 which was to galvanise Welsh democracy as never before.

Lloyd George and others later claimed to see the dawn of democracy in the remarkable results of the 1868 election, *y lecsiwn fawr* (the great election) which established a half-century of nonconformist Liberal hegemony in Wales. How far this is true is debatable. The election certainly created images of key significance in future years, notably the eviction of tenant farmers in Merioneth and Cardiganshire turned out of their holdings by the landlords for daring to vote Liberal. This was a vital factor in the coming of the secret ballot in 1872. But popular

Liberalism was under middle-class leadership, dominated by men who distinguished themselves from *y dosbarth gweithiol* (the working class). The courageous Henry Richard, who dramatically captured a seat in Merthyr Tydfil, was not an extremist, other perhaps than in his total pacifism, the dominant element of his political creed. Although prepared to have the vocal support of Merthyr ex-Chartists in the 1868 election, he was careful to detach himself from Chartism as such. His attack was focused on 'feudalism', the territorial tyranny of Anglican landlords in the rural areas.[10] Nevertheless, the democratic impetus eventually provided by the Liberal triumphs of 1868 is beyond dispute.

Henceforth there was pressure on many fronts towards democratic objectives.[11] There were new issues, headed by disestablishment of the Church, a latimer for social equality, reform of the system of landed tenure, temperance reform, the abolition of tithe, a nationwide system of accessible, free education. There were new younger leaders, leaving behind older mid-century Liberals like George Osborne Morgan, Lewis Llewellyn Dillwyn (and, indeed, Henry Richard). Forceful young men like Tom Ellis and David Lloyd George, the latter still only 27 when he entered parliament in 1890, boldly compared the national grievances of Wales with those of Ireland. A new rhetoric appeared to identify Young Wales, Cymru Fydd, with the nationalism of Irish Nationalists and Michael Davitt's Land League. There were close links now with the newly militant nonconformist chapels, linking religious equality with national equality. It was a generation of change driven by the power of the ballot, of direct democracy. In the election of 1885, thirty of the thirty-four Welsh constituencies returned Liberal members. Even the fracture in the party over Gladstone's proposal for Irish Home Rule did not greatly undermine the party's ascendancy.

The transformation in local government was even more profound. The creation of county councils in the 1888 Local Government Act proved to be a powerful motor of change. The importance of local power was above all the message of the youthful Merioneth MP Tom Ellis, an intellectual figure but one of remarkable eloquence who could see the social revolution that the county councils would embody. Half a century ago, he declared in 1894, 'the political subjection of Wales was complete'.

The nonconformist majority were excluded from 'every post of civil responsibility or honour, every place of profit, every avenue of public merit'. Wales 'had no voice in Parliament, no advocate in the Press, no valorous friend to do battle for its honour outside its borders, no one to meet its enemies at the gate'.[12] But since then a transformation had taken place. Political democracy had come with the Reform Acts of 1867 and 1884, and the Corrupt Practices Act of 1883. The 1894 Parish Councils Act excited him in equal measure at the most local level. Educational opportunities had been provided by the Education Acts of 1870 and 1891, the University colleges of Bangor, Aberystwyth and Cardiff, and the new 'county' schools created by the Welsh Intermediate Education Act of 1889. Now the 1888 Local Government Act 'transferred the government of the counties of Wales from the Plutocracy to the people'. All save one of them were controlled by a Liberal majority.

Ellis championed the doctrine of subsidiarity, given voice within the European Union a century later. He drew parallels with Swiss cantons, with the Tyrol and Norway, small, mountainous communities, all of which he visited. Switzerland in particular he saw as the very embodiment of Mazzinian nationalist democracy. Lloyd George hailed the Swiss too, as a small people prepared to defend themselves with popular militias, a notion that lay behind his sympathy for the Boer farmers during the South African War in 1899. Later generations were not to see the Swiss cantons' vision as necessarily glorious, let alone democratic. They tolerated huge inequalities of gender. Women in Switzerland did not gain the vote until 1971 (it was as late as 1944 even in France for all past declarations of human rights since 1789), while racist and religious bigotry against Muslims and other Swiss immigrants found alarming and often violent expression. But in the passions of the late-Victorian democratic upsurge, Switzerland was an inspiring (and Protestant) exemplar of popular sovereignty in action, relatively close to home.

To a man like Tom Ellis, political democracy thus implied wider values, and brought their fulfilment in its train. It implied social equality by overturning a system under which a small class of anglicised landlords dominated society, the distribution of scarce land, the unjust exaction of tithe rent charge for a minority Church, control of the local schools and the personnel on the magistrates' bench. Democracy also implied cultural equality by providing institutions and resources to protect the language, literature, antiquities, and domestic and decorative arts in Wales. The National Library in Aberystwyth and the National Museum in Cathays Park, Cardiff, founded a few years after Ellis's sadly early death in 1899, would take these important objectives much further.

Crucial to the aspirations of nonconformists, there was religious equality. After decades of struggle, the disestablishment of the Anglican Church now seemed within their grasp. Indeed, a measure to achieve that was brought in, though ineffectually, by Asquith as Home Secretary during the Rosebery Liberal government of 1894–5. Church disestablishment appeared to Liberal democrats in Wales to bring all their many-layered aspirations together. It was a Celtic version of the Norman Yoke theory beloved of radical agitators in England. The historical ingenuity therefore brought to such arcane matters as the origin of tithe or the status of the Welsh dioceses after the Norman Conquest was thus of explosive political potential.[13] It reflected a growing mood that Wales and its national culture embodied a different sense of priorities and of heritage. This came out, too, in education, the belief that the rising elementary and intermediate schools should do more than replicate simply the educational traditions of the English. Hence the belief that the University of Wales, founded in 1893 on a federal basis with Anglican Lampeter choosing to exclude itself, was an institution with distinct roots in the community – *prifysgol y werin*, the university of the people, however defined. When the noted historian Sir Owen M. Edwards, brought up near Bala in rural Merioneth, left his post as a history don at Lincoln College, Oxford, to become Chief Inspector of Schools in Wales, he devoted much effort to ensuring that the curriculum and pedagogic style of the Welsh school should reflect the distinctive craft and skills traditions of the Welsh as a community; otherwise, a distinct Welsh system of popular education would betray its heritage. Edwards combined his work as inspector with running a famous children's magazine, *Cymru'r Plant*, to promote the national values of the young people of his land.[14]

Liberal democracy was outgoing and forward-thinking. Yet it had its limitations too. Labour and working-class aspirations were kept at arm's length, even by Ellis and his idealistic friends. It was extremely limited in its view on the democratic status of women, where the attitudes of the chapels had advanced little since doctrines laid down in the Old Testament. There were relatively few suffragettes in Wales, and they tended to meet with especially violent reprisals in the principality, as when suffragette sympathisers dared to interrupt the opening of a village institute in Lloyd George's home village of Llanystumdwy in 1910. One of the most active branches of the Women's Social and Political Union in Wales, significantly, was in highly anglicised Newport, close to the English border, where Margaret Mackworth, the daughter of the coal-owner MP, D. A. Thomas, himself a warm supporter of votes for women, briefly went to gaol for blowing up a letter-box.[15] A serious drag on the wheel for Liberal democracy was its dependence on the nonconformist chapels, politically adventurous but socially and culturally conservative, and slow to respond positively to the demands of labour. It was ironically within the chapel-going world that the most democratic, even anarchic upsurge of all occurred; *y Diwygiad Mawr*, the great Revival of 1904, which for two years carried all before it and made its young leader, Evan Roberts, a nationwide celebrity. It was, incidentally, a shrewdly media-conscious movement, and this added to its impact significantly. In fact, the Revival, emerging from the very epicentre of Liberal nonconformity, was to prove a revival in more ways than one, since it provided a powerful spark for early Welsh socialism with a remarkable group of young Welsh workers – Noah Ablett, Arthur Horner and S. O. Davies among them – following the aim of establishing the Kingdom of Christ upon this sinful, capitalist earth.[16]

The most powerful of the leaders of Welsh Liberal democracy in its most glorious era was without doubt David Lloyd George. He was the greatest popular tribune and demagogue of his day. He turned the campaign for his People's Budget in 1909 into little less than a class war. He had not anticipated that the Lords would so irrationally reject his budget, but he almost relished the fact when they did so. His speeches at Limehouse and Newcastle were of almost unprecedented belligerence for a minister of the Crown. He had shown this pugnacity many times before in Welsh politics, notably in urging on the Welsh councils unconstitutionally to resist the Education Act of 1902 and to make it unworkable. During the South African War he had been the most aggressive of anti-war campaigners in his complete opposition. The same qualities of populism were to be displayed in the opposite cause when urging popular support for the war effort, for a 'knock-out blow' and for 'unconditional surrender'. Lloyd George was socially always very radical. He not only supported land taxes to clip the economic power of the landowners; he was much attracted as a young man by the campaigns of the Irishman Michael Davitt, and of the radical nonconformist minister Evan Pan Jones, editor of the *Celt*, on behalf of land nationalisation. He himself was to proceed along this same startlingly radical path in his proposals for a state-assisted 'cultivating tenure' in the Green Book, Lloyd George's report *Land and the Nation* (1925). But as a political democrat he was far more variable. He tired of the parochialism of the Welsh local authorities, as he saw it. When his Cymru Fydd League was torn apart by regional and even linguistic rivalries in 1896, he dropped it in disgust. He wearied of Welsh disestablishment as a road-block in the way of social progress, and had private conversations with his old enemy, Bishop Edwards of St Asaph, to find ways of removing it from the public agenda, perhaps by making the Church an offer it could not refuse over the terms of disendowment of tithe and other assets.[17] After 1896, he was never really to be a Welsh nationalist again. Henceforth, he would set his heart on wider British and worldwide objectives.

After he became Chancellor in 1908, probably when he went to the Board of Trade three years earlier, his priorities and his vision changed a good deal. Dealing with deputations of businessmen and trade unionists gave him a far more corporate vision. At the Treasury he became the supreme advocate of national development, to promote Britain as the worldwide pre-eminent trading nation. He thus became an unofficial spokesman for the cross-party movement known as National Efficiency,[18] which included among its cross-party supporters personalities from the proconsular Lord Milner to the Fabian Webbs. Lloyd George himself became increasingly drawn to Milner: several of the young men in the latter's 'Kindergarten' of social imperialists, people like Philip Kerr, Lionel Curtis, Professor W. G. Adams and the very young Leopold Amery, were to serve in Lloyd George's so-called 'garden suburb' of special advisers in 10 Downing Street in 1917–18. In the summer of 1910, at the height of the bitterly partisan conflict over the Budget and the Parliament Bill, he brought forward the astonishing plan for a national coalition. It would focus on the supreme imperatives of social reform and national defence. Partisan issues like Free Trade, Welsh disestablishment, even Irish home rule – Lloyd George called them 'non-controversial issues' – would be passed over with compromises worked out in each case. Ireland would be fixed by a federal home rule settlement on lines advocated years before by Joseph Chamberlain, while Disestablishment would be decided by holding a referendum in Wales.[19] He met with much sympathy from leading Unionists like Balfour and coming men like F. E. Smith. But Asquith and the Liberal high command felt that these issues were indeed extremely controversial, and central to their Liberal beliefs. The coalition idea therefore led nowhere. In any case, it had not involved the rising Labour Party or the Irish Nationalists. But it was a most instructive episode, showing Lloyd George as a natural coalitionist and compromiser, who found his natural habitat in summit diplomacy, in a consensual but highly centralised government of national unity, narrowly defined. The First World War, his time as a dominant Minister of Munitions, and above all his premiership from December 1916 found Lloyd George in his element, factionalism put aside, even if it meant severing himself from half his own Liberal Party with Asquith as a distinctly uneasy leader of the Opposition.

Lloyd George's democracy, then, was always qualified. His historic heroes were the great national leaders – Cromwell, Napoleon, Lincoln, Theodore Roosevelt – whose 'New Nationalism' of 1912 he found most attractive and more inspiring than the so-called 'New Freedom' of Woodrow Wilson, whom Lloyd George was later to encounter in Paris in 1919. He admired men who transcended the party tribalism on which democracy commonly rests, and so got on well enough with a somewhat similar personality, Georges Clemenceau of France, during the war. In his memoirs, Lloyd George lavished praise on Lincoln, not only as a great human being and committed democrat of humble origins, but also as a statesman with the strength of character to stand up to his generals during the civil war, and also a man confident enough in himself to resist those calling for vengeance over the defeated South in 1865. Lloyd George tended to favour German solidarity – such as that endorsed by Bismarck, whose welfare measures were founded on the power of the German, more particularly the Prussian state – rather than the partisanship of the French which made for instability and disunion in the Third Republic. Lloyd George by 1918 was the consistent advocate of National Efficiency rather than grass-roots democracy. It was a creed successful in times of war, for which it was admirably suited, but which eventually brought about his downfall in 1918–22. The world of party, embodied variously by Baldwin on the right and MacDonald on the left, laid him low. The creation of the Conservative backbench 1922 Committee immortalised their role in bringing the great man down. As he himself said of Theodore Roosevelt, 'he should never have quarrelled with the machine'.[20] For all that, his voice was the most powerful force on behalf of the Welsh democracy. Welsh Liberalism has contributed precious little to Welsh democratic thought or action since his time.

Labour democracy was the most democratic of all in its origins. It was indeed a grass-roots movement, like the British Labour movement as a whole in which regional variations were exceptionally strong. The sense of class was overwhelming, and evident even in traditional chapel-going champions of the 'Lib-Lab' creed like 'Mabon' and William Brace. The workers organised themselves; their politics were founded on the idea of Welsh localism, which they took from Chartism and previous manifestations of working-class consciousness. Welsh Labour rejected the centralist creed of the Prussian Social Democrats, of Liebknecht, Bebel and Kautsky. Collectivist Fabianism was never strong within the world of the early Labour pioneers. By far the strongest ideological component was that of the Independent Labour Party. Elected for Merthyr in 1900, the ILP leader Keir Hardie advocated a creed of devolution, drawing on much of the earlier Liberalism, including the radicalism as well as the pacifism advocated by Henry Richard in 1868. The most important thrust of the ILP in south Wales was in local government, which was seen as the basis for devolution, a vision which would combine 'the red dragon and the red flag' in a socialist Wales.[21] This vision, emphasising strongly the community values of a truly democratic socialism was central to Hardie's vision, as it was in London for George Lansbury whose ideas developed in the local politics of Poplar. It was a vision that similarly captured the imagination of the historian and political thinker, R. H. Tawney when he worked for the Workers' Education Association in Wrexham, in the heart of the north Wales coalfield in the years before the First World War. It should be added that, unlike Edwardian Liberalism, it was far from being a movement for men only. On the contrary, the ILP had the closest links with the suffragette movement. I was told by the late James Griffiths, who was there, that the women's movement provided the party with its local machinery and publicity in the East Carmarthenshire by-election in 1912.[22] It was a close alliance symbolised by the relationship of Keir Hardie with Sylvia Pankhurst (though less so with the sternly anti-male Christabel) at the epicentre of politics.

Even after a nationally-run (if distinctly decentralised) Labour Party came into being in parliament in 1906, much of the most characteristic pressure in the Welsh labour movement concerned alternative models of mass democracy. During the massive and sometimes violent coal disputes of the 1910–12 period, there were passionate debates amongst the miners, now emerging fast from the cocoon of Victorian Lib-Labism. They concerned the very nature of socialism. Did it mean state-run nationalisation or local power based on the pit and the miners' lodge? *The Miners' Next Step*, published by the significantly-named Unofficial Reform Committee at Tonypandy in 1912, was the work of the charismatic Noah Ablett, Will Mainwaring (years later to become a right-wing Labour MP), Noah Rees and other young miners in the Rhondda area. Though often called syndicalist, it was ideologically distinct from that movement in France, but it clearly advocated industrial democracy – though for producers not for consumers. At a famous debate in the coalfield at Trealaw in November 1912, Noah Ablett (supported by Frank Hodges) spoke out strongly against the state control implied in nationalisation at the central level. 'In France the most servile and helpless section of the workers are the state employees.'[23] This localist tradition was kept up by the democratic élite of the Central Labour College during the war years and after. However, the nationwide character of the industrial disputes of the 1919–26, with the need for strong trade unions like the South Wales Miners Federation to defend the workers, saw it gradually fade away. The localist message was sustained in the post-war Minority Movement in the SWMF through young firebrands such as S. O. Davies, another product of the chapels inspired by the 1904 religious revival. The idea of workers' control filtered through to the early Communist Party, and leaders like Arthur Horner, in the 1920s; but it perished in the general strike of 1926. Henceforth, the nationally organised Labour Party, with its strictly constitutional approach, was the main focus of demo-cratic labour. Unlike the French or the Italian workers, there was no significant outlet further to the left. A supreme irony came in 1934 when S. O. Davies, that passionate Marxist voice of industrial democracy at the pithead and the shop floor, attacked the now declining ILP for sectarianism. Its attempt to affiliate with the Communist Party had made it 'an anachronism'.[24]

At the local level, the Labour commitment to the local authorities was of great importance in the 1930s. They were seen as providing an alter-native narrative to the right-wing government at Westminster, the govern-ment of the depressed areas which favoured 'the means test' and reduced benefits for unemployment insurance. The Welsh local authorities, often much maligned, came into their own in the thirties with a courageous determination to keep local welfare services and public amenities going somehow, and to feed their people. They had powerful models in England in Sheffield and from the early 1930s in Herbert Morrison's London County Council. The Clement Davies report on tuberculosis services in Wales in 1939 noted how Labour-run local authorities in Wales were far more active in housing and health programmes to ward off the scourge of tuberculosis than were more right-wing councils run by ratepayers anxious to keep down rate payments for wealthier citizens.[25] But a major transformation came during and after the Second World War. Under the influence of the mass unions (which saw, for example, the SWMF finally affiliate to the British-wide National Union of Mineworkers), and with the exemplar of wartime planning initiatives, for instance in coping with blitzed homes in Cardiff and Swansea, Labour now became strongly centralist and unionist. The idea of Britishness prevailed. The Attlee government adhered to Keynesian-style indicative planning and took a hostile view of ideas of devolution or localism. They revived the Welsh valleys through the regional strategies of the Board of Trade. In Douglas Jay's eternally memorable phrase, the gentleman from Whitehall knew best, and that all-wise mandarin lived and worked in London. This outlook was evident even in a sympathetic young Welsh MP in the 1945 parliament – Jim Callaghan in Cardiff.

Thus Aneurin Bevan changed his views, just as such an English social-ist as the academic G. D. H. Cole, who once advocated guild socialism, had also done. An early syndicalist attracted to Noah Ablett's ideas of workers' control, Bevan became an apostle of centralisation. He advocated this strongly in *In Place of Fear* (1952) and in the pages of *Tribune* which he edited. Labour now tended to blur social and democratic socialism. 'Parliamentary democracy is a sword pointed at the heart of property',[26] and it was effective in that ancient assembly where power was more effectively deployed, in the Houses of Parliament at Westminster. Bevan quoted the democratic creed of Colonel Rainsborough and the Levellers at Putney back in 1647.[27] Marxists, he wrote, were simply unable to under-stand the power of parliamentary democracy in overcoming the evils of capitalism. But democratic socialism now meant centralised planning and the imposition of uniformly civilised standards from Tonypandy to Tunbridge Wells. In the National Health Service, with the support of Attlee himself, Bevan argued successfully in Cabinet for the hospitals to be run as a national system, and overcame the resistance of Herbert Morrison, the champion of a municipal approach run by the local author-ities, cottage hospitals and all. In the Attlee years, younger Welsh social-ists like Cledwyn Hughes in Anglesey, Goronwy Roberts in Caernarfon and, in his own distinctive way, S. O. Davies in Merthyr Tydfil, all urging devolution within the nationalised industries or even a parliament for Wales, found the going hard. This continued to be the main thrust of Labour policy-makers in the 1960s or the 1970s. There is nothing about devolution in the writings of Tony Crosland or Dick Crossman. As in Pete Seeger's famous verse, all lived in little boxes, just the same. Then, of course, a decisive change in Labour thinking came in the later 1970s; and from Transport House in Cardiff to many, though far from all, local constituency parties, the old enthusiasm for democratic localism returned. Michael Foot, a stern, puritanical Bevanite advocate of centralisation in the 1940s, led the way in getting Scottish and Welsh devolution through the Commons, though not on to the statute book because of an amendment calling for a referendum.[28] Since 1999, Labour's commitment to devolution has become more and more emphatic. It could be said to have returned to its roots in the ILP and the gospel of Keir Hardie. Devolution, indeed, has been helpful to the party. After carrying through primary legislative powers for the Assembly in the referendum of March 2011, it was rewarded with an 8 per cent swing in the Assembly elections that May. It ended up with 30 seats out of 60 and its first Minister, Carwyn Jones, has led an all-Labour administration in the years since then. While the British general election of 2010 had shown a swing to the right in England, Labour, more than ever, could claim to be the dominant party of Wales.

Welsh Nationalist attitudes towards democracy, as expressed through Plaid Cymru, have been a tough march. Unlike their colleagues in Ireland, democrats in Wales scarcely thought of democracy in terms of Welsh self-government. A patient pioneer like E. T. John, once a Labour MP, introduced a number of Welsh home rule bills in the pre-war years but they got nowhere. When Plaid Cymru came into being, its key figures could hardly be said to be democrats at all. Saunders Lewis and W. Ambrose Bebb founded their party in 1925 in conscious rejection of the content and style of Welsh Liberal politics as it had existed before 1914. That was dismissed by Lewis as 'the spare-time hobby of corpulent and successful men'. He satirised their bogus 'nationalism' paraded at the National Eisteddfod, in denominational assemblies and at the annual dinner in London of the Honourable Society of Cymmrodorion.[29] He rejected what he and Bebb regarded as the fantasies of liberal parliamentarianism and every other aspect of post-1918 politics, indeed it might be said of post-1536 politics since Lewis's passionate Catholicism made him a fierce apostle of the organic universe of Christian medieval Wales before the secularisation and anglicisation brought about by the Reformation – not to mention Henry VIII's union with (that is, absorption of) Wales with the dominant English. The dominant features of Welsh history since then, the secularisation, the industrialisation, the immersion into an English imperial system, repelled Lewis fundamentally. He found comfort rather in the far right-wing views of French ideologues and journalists, notably Maurice Barrès, and of Charles Maurras, editor of *La Nation Française*, both anti-Dreyfusards and both fusing their French nationalism with intense anti-semitism. Lewis and Bebb also devoted much journalistic effort to praise for the corporate system of Mussolini's Fascism. One especially unfortunate observation by Bebb was that 'Mussolini influences the Nationalist Party in Wales. He influences every well-read and thinking man.' He also once observed that 'it is a Mussolini that Wales needs.'[30] Plaid's newspaper leaned towards Franco in the Spanish Civil War since the main threat to Europe came from atheistic communism. This made Plaid Cymru look like a strongly nationalist party but not at all a democratic one, somewhat to the embarrassment of liberal activists like D. J. Davies, a genuine social radical and an advocate of co-operative agriculture on Scandinavian lines. For Plaid Cymru, political democracy had meant Wales being swallowed up by the party system of England, and by extension swallowed up by the English state. In 1939, Lewis declared that there was a moral equivalence between the British Empire and the Axis powers. Some younger members of the party, like the distinguished Celtic scholar A. O. H. Jarman, were imprisoned for holding such views and declining to be conscripted. Thomas Jones was but one of many Welsh figures who denounced Plaid Cymru as anti-semitic and virtually fascist. It is, however, not a view that the historian can now easily support even if Lewis in particular sailed close to the wind in his enthusiasm for totalitarian regimes of the right.[31]

In the 1950s, after many years of political impotence, nationalist democracy underwent a considerable transformation. While he remained a charismatic figure for many young members of Plaid Cymru, especially those passionate for the Welsh language, Lewis was no longer the party's president and retired into the shadows, an embittered figure. His successor, Gwynfor Evans, was a very different, far more attractive personality.[32] He educated his party in the values of populist democracy. He practised E. F. Schumacher's view that 'small was beautiful', in which he was encouraged by an Austrian economist, Leopold Kohr, one-time lecturer at the University College of Swansea, and Schumacher's university tutor. Evans's democracy was unduly linked with the rural community and seemed to have little to say to industrial society. He was also too strongly identified with the Independent chapels and the Welsh-language world to be truly representative for a secular, urbanised, anglicised post-war Wales. But his idealism and humanity enabled him to straddle a variety of democratic traditions. His commitment to peaceful, constitutional means as opposed to the prospective violence of some youthful militants in the later 1960s, meant unpopularity for him in certain quarters; but in the long term his judgement was surely vindicated, and his party prospered accordingly. He committed Plaid Cymru firmly to the achievement of Welsh devolution while making it clear that he saw devolution only as a staging post on the route to full self-government. Plaid Cymru was thus enthusiastic about the historic report of the Crowther Commission in 1974, which called for governmental devolution for Scotland and Wales. Evans was elected to the Commons in the Carmarthen by-election of July 1966. By October 1974 there were three Plaid Cymru MPs, all elected in mainly Welsh-speaking rural constituencies. From that time onwards, the party has been a major participant in the Welsh democracy. It emerged as the main opposition to Labour after the election of the first Welsh Assembly in 1999, and it was a natural sequence that it formed a stable and successful coalition government with Labour from 2007 to 2011. Plaid Cymru joined the other parties in campaigning for a 'yes' vote in the 2011 referendum, but the outcome for the party was not encouraging. In the Assembly elections in May 2011, its tally of AMs fell from 15 to 11, and one of its leading figures, Helen Mary Jones, lost her important seat in Llanelli. The party then changed its mild-mannered leader, Ieuan Wyn Jones, for a younger, more combative and more left-wing figure, Leanne Wood. Nevertheless, the experience of devolution has been a positive one for the party. Political nationalism in Wales is marginalised no longer.

The advent of devolution and the election of a Welsh Assembly have led to another phenomenon, one previously hardly taken seriously by commentators on the Welsh scene: the emergence of Conservative democracy. For many decades since the 1832 Reform Act, the Conservative

Party had been associated with non-democratic, even anti-democratic elements in Welsh society, with a tattered backwoods squirearchy, with a heavily anglicised Church of England, then in industrial areas with hated coal-owners whose heartless treatment of the colliers during the depression years made them a byword for reaction. The Conservatives were also saddled with past experience and attitudes such as those of Bishop Basil Jones of St Davids, who had declared in the 1870s that Wales 'was but a geographical expression'.[33] This was a view associated with the notorious entry in the *Encyclopædia Britannica*, 'for Wales, see England'. In more recent times, there had been episodes damaging to the Conservatives such as the deeply unpopular decision of Henry Brooke, the maladroit Minister for Welsh Affairs, in 1958 to flood the valley of Tryweryn in Merioneth to create Llyn Celyn, a reservoir of unlimited water supplies for the sole benefit of the English city of Liverpool.[34] Conservatives also appeared indifferent to foreign owners of second homes in rural areas, and slow to respond to demands by the Welsh Language Society for Welsh schools and other institutions (though they did yield to demands for a Welsh-language television channel after Gwynfor Evans threatened to go on hunger-strike). They doggedly opposed devolution in Wales in 1979 and again in 1997. John Redwood, a right-wing and strongly anti-European Secretary of State in 1993–5, following two very sympathetic pro-European Secretaries in Peter Walker and David Hunt, was another unpopular figure. His hapless attempts to sing the Welsh national anthem made him a target for ritual derision. In the general elections of 1997 and 2001, not one Welsh Tory was elected.

But the advent of devolution in Wales in 1999 meant a considerable change in fortune. It is not only that the list voting system, designed to help minorities, has inevitably meant that several Conservatives are elected as Assembly Members; it has also, with the consensual atmosphere in which the Assembly conducts most of its business, given the Conservatives a positive and constructive role to play, which they have assumed with enthusiasm. Although they have not yet entered government, and seem unlikely to do so in the immediate future, they have manifestly embraced devolution and played a far more valuable role than in parliamentary politics, where they were effectively marginalised from 1868 onwards. The born losers are now influential players in the game. Conservative Assembly members like David Melding, Glyn Davies (now an MP) and Nick Bourne (now sitting in the House of Lords) yield to none in their support for devolution. The Conservatives in Wales now speak with a far more confident voice. They joined all the other parties in supporting the granting of primary legislative powers to the Welsh Assembly in the referendum in March 2011, and thus shared in the acclaim for the 63 per cent majority in favour of such powers. When the coalition government announced in the autumn of 2013 that they accepted the thrust of the Silk Commission to give the Assembly the right to have its own financial powers, including power to raise income tax (subject to a referendum at some stage), Lord Bourne of Aberystwyth, the former Conservative leader in Wales Nick Bourne, spoke warmly of the decision. The prime minister, David Cameron, declared in Cardiff that 'this is a government that believes in Welsh devolution', a view totally unimaginable from Margaret Thatcher in previous years.[35] Ironically, as a sign of changing political moods there was a different challenge that might lie ahead in 2015, not from a traditional Labour Party but rather from UKIP, which had a member returned in Wales in both the 2009 and 2014 European elections, and which showed how an encroaching anti-Europeanism was transforming the course of Welsh politics as it had existed for several decades past.

The National Assembly, indeed, had in part come about because of a sense of democratic outrage at the policies of the Thatcherite Conservatives, carried out by a party for which only a fairly small minority of Welsh electors had voted in the first place. There was less outrage in evidence than in Scotland, especially after the poll tax fiasco, where nationalist sentiment against the ties with England, and against the Tories in particular, was especially strong. Even so, the Assembly was a major democratic step forward as part of a more general regional development in the European Union at this time. At least the Conservatives' revised approach towards devolution, and willingness to extend the powers of the Assembly, an Assembly which had been created by Tony Blair's Labour government, suggested that the broad attitude towards Wales's enhanced political status was the product of consensus.

After the creation of the Assembly, many key questions about Welsh democracy, however, remained. Despite the strong vote in the 2011 referendum and growing support for devolution in opinion polls, in 2014 the Assembly was still not yet a fully-functional law-making institution. Its authority lagged behind that of the Scottish Parliament. Peter Hain's Government of Wales Act of 2006 had been a major step forward, but the system for giving the Assembly primary legislative power was too complicated, especially the orders for legislative competence which had to be approved by both houses of the Westminster parliament. It seemed absurd, for example, that the unelected House of Lords should decide on whether the Cardiff Assembly had the competence to consider policy on the Welsh language, of all things. Despite the grant of legislative powers, the role of the Assembly was still very much a work in progress. The legal functions of the Assembly were further constrained by there not being a separate Welsh jurisdiction, despite the growing body of Welsh-centred law that emerged after devolution. There were renewed calls for a Welsh judicial system, as there had been prior to the abolition of the Court of Great Sessions back in 1830. Secondly, for years the Welsh Assembly, unlike the Scottish Parliament, had no financial power. There could, surely, be no genuine representation without taxation for any elected assembly worthy of the name. The Coalition government's decision in October 2013 to accede to the Silk Commission's view that the Assembly should have taxing and fiscal powers was somewhat limited by its cherry-picking of which taxes other than income tax the Assembly should be permitted to collect. Legislation was promised after the second Silk report published on 1 March 2014. That report was to propose extending devolution in Wales by replacing a conferred with a reserved powers model and would devolve powers on policing and youth justice. Silk also suggested increasing the size of the National Assembly from sixty to 'at least eighty' members.

Another crucial and unresolved issue was that of which resources the Assembly with its new tax powers would actually receive. As long as the notoriously unfair Barnett Formula continued, reducing Welsh funding according to a scheme based on population devised back in 1978, then the Welsh government would find its revenue getting smaller, which would make a mockery of the new-found power the British government wished to grant it. The defects of the Barnett Formula were mercilessly exposed by the report of Gerald Holtham for the Assembly in 2009, and again by a House of Lords committee containing such powerful figures as the former Chancellor Nigel Lawson, and the former Scottish secretary Michael Forsyth. The formula was 'unfit for purpose'. But both Gordon Brown's Labour government and David Cameron's coalition were equally evasive; neither wanted to risk being seen reducing the funding for Scotland, an inevitable result of giving fair funding to Wales. Carwyn Jones, Wales's First Minister, was understandably hesitant in 2013 about accepting taxing powers if that meant locking in the Barnett injustices within the tax system. Another important aspect was devolution not for Wales, but within Wales. The status of local government had not been made more robust, and more devolution within a devolved Wales was highly desirable.

Yet, despite these issues, the Welsh Assembly had clearly been accepted as a plausible landmark of Welsh democracy. Scotland was surging ahead, with a key referendum on possible independence organised by its Nationalist government for September 2014. England, by contrast, had been accorded nothing, and growing English complaint was to be heard on issues such as the Barnett Formula for Scotland and the continuance of the controversial 'West Lothian' question. While Scotland and Wales advanced, England was left unreformed, in the words of University College London's Constitution Unit, as 'the black hole of the constitution'. It was a situation that could not rationally endure. Yet it seemed inconceivable that English regional government would play any part in the 2015 general election despite the obvious social inequalities in the various regions of the English nation.

Devolution is not the same as democracy. Asymmetrical devolution was entrenched as part of a wider piecemeal process of constitutional reform, not as a coherent planned scheme of democratic governance. There remain such oddities as an unelected House of Lords, while the Coalition government since 2010 has added its own eccentricities such as the virtual erosion of collective responsibility within government. The constitution, devolution and all, needs to be much more than a patchwork of convention, tradition and guesswork. As the Chartists demanded back in the 1830s, there should be a written, codified constitution, in which the organic relationship between an elected government and a sovereign people needs to be set down. The opportunity is now there, and it is good that the Commons Constitution Committee, in liaison with a distinguished team of scholars in King's College, London, is now working out the feasibility of a codified constitution. The present dissatisfaction with our system of governance was enhanced by the parliamentary expenses scandal in 2011, but there are more profound roots to current anxiety than the trivial details of glamorous duck-houses and gilded bath plugs. Since 1997 the classic, largely informal and relentlessly deferential constitution of Bagehot, Dicey, Anson and Jennings has been disappearing. Lord Irvine, Tony Blair's reforming Lord Chancellor, proved to be our greatest governmental revolutionary since Oliver Cromwell. The standard textbooks on our constitution are now all out of date. Yet we remain legally subjects of the Crown, not citizens in control of our destiny. Only when this is clearly understood, and reversed, can democracy in Wales, and the hopes of radicals across the years be properly fulfilled. Only then can we move on from Wales in British Politics to the Rebirth of a Nation.

Notes

[1] Lloyd George's speech at Falmouth, 10 January 1910, in David Lloyd George, *Better Times* (London, 1910), p. 296.

[2] David Marquand, *Britain since 1918: the Strange career of British Democracy* (London, 2008).

[3] Statement by Richard Rogers Partnership (RRP), 2005.

[4] Gwyn A. Williams, *Madoc* (London, 1979), p. 112.

[5] The definitive account is provided in Williams, *Madoc*.

[6] *Labour Leader*, 24 November 1900, 17 August 1901.

[7] David J. V. Jones, *Before Rebecca: Popular Protests in Wales 1793–1835* (London, 1973).

[8] David Williams, *John Frost* (Cardiff, 1939).

[9] See below, pp. 53–4.

[10] Henry Richard, *Letters on the Social and Political Condition of the Principality of Wales* (London, 1866).

[11] See Kenneth O. Morgan, *Wales in British Politics 1868–1922* (Cardiff, 1970), *passim*.

[12] Tom Ellis, *Speeches and Addresses* (Wrexham, 1912), pp. 181–2.

[13] See Kenneth O. Morgan, 'The Campaign for Welsh Disestablishment', in *idem, Modern Wales: Politics, Places and People* (Cardiff, 1995).

[14] See Hazel Walford Davies (gol.), *Llythyrau Syr O. M. Edwards ac Elin Edwards 1887–1920* (Llandysul, 1991).

[15] Angela V. John, *Turning the Tide: The Life of Lady Rhondda* (Cardigan, 2013), pp. 99–105.

[16] Kenneth O. Morgan, *Rebirth of a Nation: Wales 1880–1980* (Cardiff, 1981), pp. 96, 134–5; Robert Pope, *Building Jerusalem* (Cardiff, 1998), pp. 97ff.

[17] A. G. Edwards (Archbishop of Wales), *Memories* (London, 1927), pp. 193–4.

[18] See Geoffrey Searle, *The Quest for National Efficiency: a Study in Politics and Political Thought* (Oxford, 1971).

[19] Lucy Masterman, *C. F. G. Masterman* (London, 1968), pp. 170–2.

[20] See below, pp. 65, 112.

[21] Kenneth O. Morgan, *Keir Hardie, Radical and Socialist* (London, 1975), p. 118; Keir Hardie, *The Red Dragon and the Red Flag* (1912, pamphlet).

[22] Conversation between the author and the Rt. Hon. James Griffiths, *c.*1973.

[23] Kenneth O. Morgan, 'Socialism and Syndicalism: the Welsh Miners' Debate, 1912', in *idem, Modern Wales*, pp. 137–8.

[24] Robert Gruffydd, *S. O. Davies: A Socialist Faith* (Llandysul, 1983), p. 95.

[25] Report of the Committee on the Anti-Tuberculosis service in Wales and Monmouth (non-parl.) (London, 1939).

[26] Aneurin Bevan, *In Place of Fear* (London, 1952), p. 25.

[27] 'Celticus' (Aneurin Bevan), *Why not trust the Tories?* (London, 1944), pp. 87–8.

[28] Kenneth O. Morgan, *Michael Foot: A Life* (London, 2007), pp. 351ff.

[29] Saunders Lewis, in *The Welsh Nationalist*, January 1932, 1.

[30] Ambrose Bebb, in *Y Ddraig Goch*, August 1935.

[31] But see Richard Wyn Jones, *The Fascist Party in Wales? Plaid Cymru, Welsh Nationalism and the Accusation of Fascism*, trans. Richard Wyn Jones and Dafydd Jones (Cardiff, 2014).

[32] See, among many other works, Rhys Evans, *Gwynfor Evans: Portrait of a Patriot* (Talybont, 2003).

[33] Bishop Basil William Tickell Jones, charge to St Davids diocese, 1886.

[34] An engaging recent account of the Tryweryn affair may be found in Wyn Thomas, *Hands Off Wales: Nationhood and Militancy* (Llandysul, 2013), chapters 1 and 2.

[35] Article by David Cameron in the *Western Mail*, 1 November 2013, and press conference by him and Nick Clegg in the Assembly building on the same day.

Kentucky's cottage-bred man: Abraham Lincoln and Wales

The Welsh, like other small nations, delight in praising famous men (famous women far less often). In 2009, three particular heroes had key anniversaries commemorated – President Lincoln, Mr Gladstone and George Frideric Handel. The last may be left to Messianic celebration elsewhere. Gladstone's celebrity resulted from the overwhelming Liberal ascendancy in Wales from the 1868 general election onwards. After all, he married a Welsh woman and lived in Wales, in Hawarden Castle, Flintshire.[1] Abraham Lincoln, born and bred in the far-away American mid-west, is a more surprising hero, but perhaps the most emblematic of them all. Long before his assassination, he had become an iconic figure for many in Wales. For nonconformists, he was the very embodiment of their libertarian values. After his death, *ein Lincoln* (our Lincoln) was close to being sanctified.[2] Both Old and New Testament were seen as offering parallels as he was variously depicted as another Moses leading his people towards the promised land, and a second Christ at Gethsemane. The man and his gospel seemed indivisible. For the chapel-going, male, Liberal-voting majority of Wales down to the First World War, he symbolised their ideological and moral creed. For two generations, he was created and re-created in their image.

The Welsh had been closely involved with American liberal ideas long before Lincoln's time. Radical Welsh groups of nonconformists had been drawn there by the excitement of the American Revolution. One such was the Baptist Jacobin radical Morgan John Rhys, who migrated to the new American republic in the 1790s and briefly set up a Welsh *gwladfa* (settlement) in Beulah in western Pennsylvania in 1794.[3] Others followed on at Paddy's Run in Ohio and near Utica in New York state. In the first half of the nineteenth century, as elsewhere in Britain, a steady stream of Welsh people crossed the Atlantic in search of a better world. Many of the first settlers were from rural areas; increasingly, others were miners and ironworkers. They settled in the anthracite coalfield of western Pennsylvania in the Schuykill and Susquehanna valleys, and in the bituminous field of that same state, and in Ohio, Indiana and Illinois. A Welshman, David Thomas, set up the first American hot-blast furnace in Pennsylvania in 1839.[4] Bill Jones has finely described the largest Welsh settlement of all, in Scranton and Wilkes-Barre in north-east Pennsylvania.[5] But many, too, found new homes in rural America, from Utica in the north of New York state, where the first Welsh newspaper, *Y Drych* (the Mirror), launched in 1850, moved to in 1860,[6] down to scattered prairie towns like New Cambria in Missouri and Arvonia and Bala in Kansas in the 1850s, as gravestones still bear witness today.[7] By the 1850 census, there were almost 30,000 Welsh-born residents of the United States, making an impact beyond their numbers through their skills and presence within an older English-speaking migration. Many more were to follow: indeed, during the years of civil war, Welsh emigration to America increased. There were said to be 384 Welsh-language chapels in America in 1872. By the 1890 census, the Welsh-American population was to be recorded as 90,000.

They were from the first politically and ideologically active, above all through the nonconformist chapels. After the early heady enthusiasm of what Gwyn A. Williams has called 'the Baptist International' of the 1790s,[8] there were strong links between chapels in Wales and America on behalf of such themes as temperance, land tenure reform and cutting down the privileges of the established Church. The political awakening of the Welsh chapels in the 1840s made the United States ever more appealing. Radical journalists like Gwilym Hiraethog, editor of the newspaper *Yr Amserau* (The Times), drew simple parallels between the 'feudal' dominance of landlords in the Welsh countryside and the power of the plantation owners in the American South. A natural kindred transatlantic theme was the anti-slavery movement. In Wales, as in England, it had lost some impetus after the achievement of the abolition of slavery in the Empire in 1833, but the progress of the abolitionism in the US in the 1840s gave it new life. Welsh emigrants like the family of the Revd Benjamin Chidlaw in Ohio played their own aggressive part.[9] It was a natural transition for Lincoln to provide a spearhead for this kind of passion later on.

No novel made a greater impact upon Welsh-speaking Wales than did *Uncle Tom's Cabin*.[10] Much was made of the Welsh great-grandmother of Harriet Beecher Stowe herself. The novel was, as is well known, a huge publishing success in England with 1,500,000 copies in circulation. Less well-known is its importance in kindling political passions in Wales. It was, in fact, the first novel translated into Welsh, even Dickens himself being denied that honour. A version of it, much adapted and relocated to a Welsh setting, appeared in the newspaper *Yr Amserau* from September 1852, around the time of its publication in England, under the title *Aelwyd f'Ewythr Robert* (Uncle Robert's Hearth). It was published as a book in Denbigh in 1853 and had a huge and enduring impact. The present writer recalls reading it at Sunday School in Aberdyfi as late as the 1940s. Several other Welsh translations followed around this time: with its strong moral tone, Stowe's work helped to weaken the resistance of Welsh nonconformists to the novel as an art form. *Uncle Tom's Cabin* appeared at a key moment in Welsh public sensibility, soon after the uproar caused by the report of the Education Commissioners in 1847, the so-called 'Treason of the Blue Books'.[11] All the chapels, the Calvinist Methodists last of all, now moved into forceful political mode. This followed the pattern of similar movements in England, but the starker class division in Wales and the cultural-nationalist overtones made Welsh radicalism always distinct in nature as the later career of David Lloyd George was to indicate.

A key figure in Wales at this time was indeed Gwilym Hiraethog, properly the Revd William Rees, born in a remote farm on the Denbighshire moors, auto-didact preacher-poet, crusading editor and, above all, powerful journalist whose columns 'Llythyrau 'Rhen Ffarmwr' (The Old Farmer's Letters) were widely read and discussed.[12] He had a major impact in stimulating the new democratic radicalism of a part of the United Kingdom hitherto (according to another preacher-politician, the pacifist Henry Richard) sunk in 'feudalism', with 'clansmen struggling for their chieftain'. Gwilym Hiraethog had strong views on most topics. He advocated universal suffrage, votes for women, temperance, dis-establishment of the Church, penal reform, an end to landlordism; and he courted republicanism. He is most notable in Welsh history, perhaps, for his strong international sense. He met and corresponded with the celebrated Italian nationalist Guiseppe Mazzini during his time in Britain, and lauded the exploits of Garibaldi and Kossuth. He had strong personal links with American abolitionists and, in 1844, launched a powerful 'Address to the Welsh in America', published in most Welsh-American newspapers, which condemned slavery as a sinful offence against American ideals of liberty. Gwilym Hiraethog, as noted earlier, masterminded the publicising of *Uncle Tom's Cabin* in Wales, and made it known to the wider public. In public lectures, he became the most passionate of Lincoln's champions and inspired the movements that made him a unique Welsh hero.

Lincoln's eminence in Wales was, naturally a product of the Civil War. The Welsh were at first uncertain about the strength of his commitment to ending slavery but, after the Proclamation of Emancipation, his stature was assured. Most of the Welsh-language newspapers formed at this time – the monthlies *Y Dysgedydd* (1821) and *Diwygiwr* (1835), both Independent, *Y Drysorfa* (Calvinist Methodist) and *Yr Eurgrawn Wesleyaidd* (Wesleyan), the bi-monthly *Seren Gomer* (Baptist), the non-denominational weekly *Yr Herald Cymraeg* and, most importantly, *Baner ac Amserau Cymru*, the major weekly founded and edited by Thomas Gee at Denbigh in 1859 – gave him full and favourable coverage. As I will be discussing later, English-language newspapers were less ecstatic. From the start, Lincoln was claimed to embody Welsh values – social mobility, the free ethic of the democratic republican ideal. He was, more dubiously, also hailed for his devotion to religious principle. His flirting with Unitarian-ism and the fact that he was said not to be 'technically a Christian at all' was not revealed, and indeed would have dented his image more than somewhat in relentlessly orthodox Protestant Wales.[13] Here and elsewhere, he is a classic example of what has been called 'reputational entreneurship' where a former leader, such as Churchill, is used subsequently used to strengthen communal solidarity.[14] Lincoln was thus seen as a Welsh hero. Even more, amongst filio-pietistic sentimentalists, it was claimed that he was actually Welsh. Through his mother, Nancy Hanks, it was believed that he could claim descent from medieval Welsh princes. His maternal grandmother was said to have come from Ysbyty Ifan on the Caernarfonshire/Denbighshire border. The Scranton Welsh in 1909 referred hopefully to 'our Welsh president'. There were also claims that Mary Todd Lincoln was of Welsh descent. Sadly, the evidence for all this appears to be speculative and is not accepted by genealogical scholars.[15] The more precisely Welsh-linked presidents remain Thomas Jefferson (who appears to have read Welsh) and, more bleakly, Richard Nixon.

Lincoln's standing was sustained by overwhelmingly strong Welsh support for Union cause. This was wholly predictable. Of the 45,763 Welsh-born in the United States, over 90 per cent lived in the northern states.[16] There was a strong new settlement in the new territory of Wisconsin, which materially helped the Union armies. Perhaps 10,000 Welsh-born men served in the Union armies in such regiments as the 5th Wisconsin and the 56th Ohio. There were Welshmen in the 5th Wisconsin when they finally stormed the Confederate defences at Petersburg on April 1865. Ministers like the Revd Benjamin Chidlaw became recruiting sergeants for the Union armies. *Y Drych*, like the Welsh-American community generally, was zealous on behalf of the Union cause and fierce in its condemnation of defeatists or Copperheads. After the war was over, it sponsored *Hanes y Gwrthryfel Mawr* (History of the Great Civil War) in 1866 which set the great conflict against the background of earlier US history in highly partisan terms.[17] Hardly any Welsh were to be found in the Confederate armies. One remarkable exception was John Rowlands of Denbigh, born in the workhouse in that small town. He was captured at Shiloh in 1862 and then turned his coat and fought for the Union cause; he seems to have had no principled view and to have had been little more than a mercenary. He was to follow a similar course later on in life in his travel around Africa under his adopted English name, Henry Morton Stanley.[18]

A rare Welsh backer of the South was the famous radical journalist, S.R., Samuel Roberts of Llanbrynmair in Montgomeryshire.[19] He had unwisely set up Brynffynnon, a Welsh settlement in Tennessee, as a refuge from landlord rule in Wales, in 1856. His previous views had been impeccably radical; they also, significantly, included pacifism. When the war began in 1861, Roberts became a stout defender of the Southern cause. Beyond his pacifism, he defended the right of the Confederate states to secede and defend themselves, and condemned northern aggression. Worse still for S.R., his brother J.R., John Roberts, in his own newspaper *Y Cronicl*, kept up a stream of aggressive invective directed against the North and of insults directed against Lincoln in particular, whom he accused of unconstitutional, tyrannical rule, and of poor mental and moral qualities. Lincoln's re-election in 1864 was greeted by J.R. with a mixture of incredulity and derision.[20] His eccentric stance did his brother no favours. When S.R. returned to Wales after the Civil War, he seemed a broken man, discredited, his influence destroyed. Unwisely, a volume of lectures and sermons of his published just after Appomattox included much harsh invective against Lincoln. His hostility to the great Emancipator ruined his career. His attempted settlement in Tennessee was widely condemned as a treacherous beachhead on alien soil. By total contrast, Y Wladfa, the later Welsh settlement in Patagonia in 1865, inspired by the radical nationalist the Revd Michael Daniel Jones, has always been seen as embodying the noblest of Welsh virtues.

Lincoln's reputation built up as the war took its course. At first, his apparent caution and anxiety to distance himself from the abolitionists somewhat lessened his reputation in Welsh political circles. Even at the time of his nomination in 1860 *Baner ac Amserau* had speculated whether Seward or even Sumner might not have been a more effective candidate.[21] There were three particular causes for doubt about Lincoln. The Emancipation Proclamation in October 1862 was received less than ecstatically. It was seen as a military stratagem to put pressure on the cotton plantations of the south rather than a moral gesture: as things stood, not a slave would gain his freedom in areas where Federal troops were in occupation. Lincoln, it was said, was unduly swayed by his own origins as a product of a slave-holding state and his own resultant sensitivity to border states such as Delaware, Kentucky and Missouri. Much attention focused on his famous response to Horace Greeley that his object was to save the Union, rather than either save or destroy slavery as such.[22] Secondly, his use of executive power to make inroads into traditional civil liberties such as freedom of the press met with much criticism.[23] And, thirdly and significantly, there was what seemed to be American aggression in the *Trent* case. Here, the Southern envoys Mason and Slidell being taken by Wilkes's *San Jacinto*, while travelling on the British steamer, the *Trent*, was condemned by many in Wales. The Welsh, after all, were British, and had their meed of sympathy with the Palmerstonian jingoism of the time.[24] Throughout the century down to 1914, the attitude of the Welsh and the Irish towards union and empire were sharply divergent. Something of a wedge appeared between the Welsh community in American and sentiment in the mother country over the *Trent* affair. In the end, Lincoln's role as a pacifying element in preventing any outbreak of war (as again with the depredations of the British-built *Alabama* on Northern shipping) was said to resound greatly to his credit.

The coming into effect of emancipation at the start of 1863 turned the tide. From then on, for almost all Welsh political and religious leaders, the Union cause had an unquestioned moral integrity. Newspapers like *Baner ac Amserau Cymru* and *Yr Herald Cymraeg* now hailed his wisdom and idealism in giving full effect to the process of emancipation.[25] Nonconformist ministers addressed meetings around Wales strongly supporting Lincoln's unequivocal approach. All earlier reservations about the president were dispelled. His re-election as president in 1864 was almost universally hailed in the Welsh press and pulpit as a powerful blow for the ideals of liberty.[26] He was now seen as embodying, in his own person as a country lawyer of humble origins, the democratic principles which Welsh reform movements now proclaimed. He symbolised the triumph of the legendary *gwerin*, the Welsh common folk. In this, Welsh radical and Liberal opinion mirrored that of England, with the huge surge in support amongst the Reform League and, indeed, the nascent trade unions, for Lincoln and the Union cause. It is interesting that in England the popular hero, the Quaker John Bright, a friend of Charles Sumner, had passionately defended Lincoln throughout.[27] His close associate in Wales, Henry Richard, who wrote powerful articles on behalf of parliamentary reform in the *Morning and Evening Star*, had as a pacifist taken a somewhat similar stand towards the war to that of the unpopular S.R. Henry Richard openly justified the South's right to secede but his reputation remained untarnished, and in 1868 he was to be triumphantly returned as radical member for Merthyr Tydfil.[28]

One feature of press coverage is the almost universal enthusiasm for Lincoln amongst Welsh-language newspapers. By contrast, the English-language daily, the *Cambria Daily Leader*, founded in Swansea in 1861, was consistently sour. It denounced the Emancipation Proclamation in starkly reactionary terms:

> Unrestricted liberty, in the hands of those who do not understand the privilege, may be found inconvenient, if not dangerous; and a legion of uneducated slaves, with a guiding intelligence little above the brute, is not the sort of thing to be let loose upon society, without proper provision being made for its reception.[29]

It was cold in its judgement on Lincoln after his assassination. He had been intolerant and oppressive towards the press. 'America could probably have found a better President.'[30] A similarly harsh view had been offered to a prominent Welsh landowner politician, Sir George Cornewall Lewis of Harpton Court, Radnorshire, Home Secretary in Palmerston's Cabinet, who had been given absurdly one-sided comparisons of Jefferson Davis and his vice-president, with Lincoln. The latter, Lewis was told in 1861, was 'destined to great and inevitable degradation'.[31] Like *The Times*, his grief at Lincoln's death was somewhat muted. This patrician detachment contrasts sharply with the anguish and sorrow of almost all the Welsh-language journals after the tragedy. Perhaps something of the same phenomenon may be found as in the South African War in 1899–1902, when the Welsh-language press was overwhelmingly anti-war and 'pro-Boer' whereas English-language newspapers (including, again, the *Cambria Daily Leader*), whether Liberal or Conservative, were mostly imperialist and jingo.[32] No doubt the imperatives of Welsh nonconformity offer one major explanation. More generally perhaps, the rhetoric and emotional thrust of Welsh-language publication and thought seemed then, as earlier, a more natural outlet for the immemorial grievances of a marginalised small nation.

After the war, Lincoln's 'martyrdom' had powerful emotional impact. The passing of 'Our Lincoln' was viewed as another crucifixion.[33] The cult of Lincoln grew steadily. He was now regarded as perhaps the very greatest of all American presidents, with the exception of the near-sacred George Washington. The Welsh community in America in particular venerated his memory. It was noted that, more than most immigrant groups, they identified totally with the values of post-bellum society; since 1856 they had voted solidly Republican, with much effect in newer mid-west states like Wisconsin and Iowa. Scranton and Wilkes-Barre, with their thriving anthracite mines and steelworks, their vigorous chapel life, local *eisteddfodau* and *cymanfaoedd canu* (singing festivals) were very epitomes of all-American Welsh republican values.[34] Walter Johnson has shown that William Allen White, a shrewd critic of the excesses of the Gilded Age, viewed from his editorial offices in Emporia, Kansas, noted that the Welsh seemed to him very models of that sober, honest industrious civic involvement which American democracy most needed.[35] A Welsh-American like Samuel 'Golden Rule' Jones, the Mayor of Toledo, embodied this spirit as the executive instrument of progressive municipal reform.[36]

Wales itself after the 1868 election moved into a long period of Liberal hegemony that lasted until the end of the First World War, when the most famous Welshman of them all was resident in 10 Downing Street. Wales made an impact on the British political scene as never before and achieved considerable success in pushing for Church disestablishment, land and educational reform, temperance and modest devolution. Its middle-class professional spokesman naturally revered Lincoln as an inspirational model, though not all looked immediately to him. An important Welshman like Tom Ellis, chief whip in 1894–5, a man perhaps more nationalist than Liberal, found his inspiration in the patriotic gospel preached by Mazzini and the Irish nationalist of the 1840s Thomas Davis, rather than in movements across the Atlantic.[37] But, otherwise, Lincoln was a dominant figure. Ellis's close friend, D. R. Daniel, wrote a glowing essay on Lincoln as 'the first American'. The Emancipation of 'the American negro' he saw as 'the downfall of the most accursed and degrading system of human bondage that ever dishonoured the name of a nation'.[38] By now, Lincoln's portrait hung in many of the humbler Welsh homes, often next to another popular hero, Gladstone, 'the people's William' standing proudly alongside 'honest Abe', for all Gladstone's illiberal and effectively pro-Southern views during the earlier part of the Civil War. There were plays about Lincoln, and eisteddfodic prizes awarded for compositions about him. He provided a subject for a drama competition in the Pontypool Eisteddfod as late as 1925.[39] Lincoln became a recognised Welsh Christian name, as with the steel workers' leader Sir Lincoln Evans, and the Cardiff politician, Sir Lincoln Hallinan. One especial enthusiast for Lincoln was William Williams, 'Carw Coch' (1808–72), eisteddfodic bard and man of letters, an Aberdare Unitarian who owned the Stag Hotel in that town and actually held *eisteddfodau* in it ('Carw Coch' is the Welsh for stag). His passion for Lincoln knew no bounds. His hotel had a map of the USA on its wall, where supporters of Lincoln would foregather to discuss the latest developments in the war. Williams received a large portrait of Lincoln (allegedly from the US) which was hung 'in the most honourable place in the house'. Of all devotees of the Lincoln cult, Carw Coch was the most fanatical.[40]

One exotic visitor to Welsh political life had seen the great man at first hand. This was Major Evan R. Jones, a Cardiganshire man elected Liberal MP for Carmarthen Boroughs in 1892.[41] He had fought bravely in the 5th Wisconsin in the Army of the Potomac for four years, distinguishing himself at the battle of White Oak Swamp in 1862, in the siege of Petersburg and the battle of the Wilderness generally in 1864. He served at Gettysburg and was wounded at Spottsylvania, but later returned to front-line duties. He was made captain in February 1864 and later rose to Major. He returned to Britain as the US consul in Newcastle before entering Liberal politics. Major Jones wrote four books, a worthless novel, a handbook of advice and information for would-be emigrants to America, his own quite vivid war diary, *Four Years in the Army of the Potomac*, and a volume of three historical sketches on Lincoln, Stanton and Grant. Jones's views of Lincoln convey a conventional admiration; his essay on Stanton, whom he regarded as unjustly neglected, is rather warmer. His services were said not to be inferior to those of Lincoln and Grant 'for the salvation of the country and the overthrow of slavery for ever'.[42] Lloyd George, a colleague and rival of Jones in parliament in 1892–5, was derisive about 'the little Major',[43] really because they took different views of political tactics over Welsh disestablishment, but he was a courageous man who deserves better of posterity. Unfortunately for Jones, whereas a link with America might have seemed very popular in 1892 at the time of his election, by 1895, when the next general election was held, America was largely identified in Carmarthen Boroughs with the catastrophic effects of the McKinley tariff on the local tinplate industry, in Llanelli above all. 'The curse of McKinley' was fatal, not least because McKinley was a Republican, the party for which Jones had voted in the United States.[44] He lost his seat to a Liberal Unionist in 1895 and his brief political career was over.

The Welsh links with Lincoln and his reputation, however, continued to flourish. The Lincoln centenary in 1909 saw much reverent celebration of the hero, as in a long analysis in *Baner ac Amserau Cymru* in which he was hailed as a unique pioneer of human equality. It also drew the contrast between Lincoln's selfless ideals and the segregation and 'lynch law' currently operating in the post-bellum South.[45] The Welsh devotion to Lincoln extended to the United States itself. There was the case of the Revd Jenkin Lloyd Jones, a Unitarian minister who had fought in the war and who published his war diary in 1913. In his retirement, he founded the Abraham Lincoln Center near Louisville, Kentucky, Lincoln's birthplace, while his son Robert was much involved in saving the famous log-cabin for the nation.[46] Welsh-Americans participated in the huge commemoration in July 1913 to mark the fiftieth anniversary of Gettysburg, seen by President Wilson as part of a nationwide movement of reconciliation and harmony.[47] Whether the Welsh, however, responded so cordially to the southerner Wilson's declaration of the effective moral equivalence of North and South in a 'a quarrel forgotten' is another question. For Welsh-Americans, waving the bloody shirt was a tradition not easily set aside.

By far the most important Welsh champion of Lincoln, however, was Woodrow Wilson's close wartime collaborator, the most famous Welsh politician of them all, David Lloyd George. From the very start of his career, when he read about the recently-fought Civil War battles in the *Examiner*, and lapped up tales of Grant, Lee and Stonewall Jackson, all heroes of his, Lloyd George was Lincoln's most passionate and eloquent champion.[48] He was an ardent worshipper of great men – Gustavus Adolphus, Cromwell and Napoleon were among his favourites. But Abraham Lincoln was unique; he was for Lloyd George a lifelong hero with qualities all his own. Years later, his secretary-mistress Frances Stevenson and his daughter Megan would become resigned to hearing yet another eulogy of the great American's qualities.[49] It began practically at birth, since Lincoln was a great hero also for Lloyd George's shoe-maker uncle and mentor, his Uncle Lloyd. To this day, the portrait of Lincoln may be seen on the wall of the parlour of 'Highgate', the shoe-maker's home in the village of Llanystumdwy, where Lloyd George was brought up. From the start, Lloyd George hailed Lincoln as a unique popular tribune – indeed, it was Lincoln the democrat rather than Lincoln the emancipator that he chose to emphasise, as will be seen. As a small-town lawyer of limited education, who moved into high politics and conquered through his own talents, Lincoln had obvious resemblances to 'the little Welsh attorney' that could be usefully exploited. J. Hugh Edwards, an early biographer of Lloyd George's in 1908, entitled his volume *From Village Green to Downing Street* an obvious 'log cabin to president' evocation of another populist leader.[50] His subject liked to refer to Lincoln as a combatant in the age-long contest between the common rights of humanity and the divine right of kings.[51] Lloyd George himself was not averse to pointing out parallels of a more personal kind. He referred to Lincoln's difficult marriage on more than one occasion, and also his alleged attraction to pretty women. He quoted Lincoln's comparing his views of women with his love of gingerbread – 'I like it very much but I never get any.'[52] Throughout, Lloyd George always placed particular emphasis on Lincoln's humanity as a man of the people. He was 'the biggest man thrown up by the United States – far bigger than Washington who was always so correct that he was uninteresting. He never did anything wrong!'[53]

If Lincoln was a background influence for Lloyd George in his career as a democratic radical before 1914, the First World War added enormously to the relevance of his career as a liberal leader in war. This, of course, became a more powerful influence still when Lloyd George himself became leader of the nation in December 1916. His *War Memoirs* afford some important insights into his conduct as war leader and also wider themes in his career more generally. Lincoln is seen as a great British hero, a revered name with 'its amplitude and equality of opportunity for all those who toiled and wrought intelligently.'[54]

Several aspects of Lincoln's greatness appear in Lloyd George's conversations and speeches at the time and in his *War Memoirs*, and subsequently *The Truth about the Peace Treaties* published in the 1930s. First, there is Lincoln the uncompromising defender of the Union against secession (Lloyd George could use this analogy to justify his own resistance to Irish nationalist republicanism during the 'troubles' in 1921).[55] Second, Lincoln is praised as a civilian with no personal knowledge of warfare who involved himself to great effect in the running of the war. This was obviously a helpful argument for Lloyd George in justifying his own position in disputes with his generals in 1917–18. He cites Lincoln's wise judgement in removing McClellan and then Meade from command, the latter after the victory at Gettysburg, and then retaining Grant despite much criticism. In 1922, Lloyd George was to tell Thomas Jones, 'When Lincoln found a general in Grant he had no desire to interfere. When I found Foch I had no desire to interfere.' The *Memoirs* emphasise how often Lincoln was proved right. Lloyd George's own prolonged contests with Haig and Robertson over strategic decisions on the western front are naturally brought into the account, with the implication that here was another Lincoln at the helm. Haig he later compared most unfavourably with Stonewall Jackson. His men always followed Jackson devotedly because he never gave them an impossible task. Unlike Haig at Passchendaele, he never ordered an attack until he was convinced that the object was attainable.[56] Third, Lincoln is commended for being uncompromising in his fight for victory. His policy in adopting conscription and restrictions on civil liberties and freedom of the press were proved right, just as Lloyd George believed his own policies were in the use of the Defence of the Realm Act and stern treatment of dissenters. Lincoln in 1864–5, like Lloyd George in 1917–18, is seen as the symbol of unconditional surrender, doing what had to be done in a supreme crisis.[57] And, finally and crucially for Lloyd George's vision of his own post-war role, Lincoln is praised as the great magnanimous reconciler, who rejected a settlement based on vengeance, but who wanted to bring the defeated South back into a more perfect union. His statesman-like approach is contrasted with the bigoted partisanship of radical republicans, anxious to wreak vengeance on the South in 1865, the equivalent of those in 1918 who wanted a punitive peace and squeezing the defeated Germans until their pips squeaked.

There is, fascinatingly, one Lincoln whom Lloyd George does not mention. This is the great Emancipator. Lloyd George's account conforms fully to David W. Blight's of the 'reconciliationist' view of the Civil War, seeing moral equivalence between North and South, and setting aside the ideals of racial equality and multicultural citizenship which had inspired the abolitionists prior to 1861.[58] Lloyd George's emphasis on the need for reconciliation in 1865, steering clear of ideological extremes, in effect saw the attempt to turn the war into a crusade for civic equality as misguided. Lloyd George, for all his liberalism, would not have embarked on any reconstruction of the South, he would have bound up the nation's wounds without attention to the social evils that had led to war coming about. He was a supreme democrat, but not a crusader for racial equality. He had opposed the Boer war because of the evil deeds of the men who had caused it, and out of some sympathy for Protestant Boer farmers, not because he aspired to an equal future for the black majority in South Africa. Indeed, the settlement of the Union of South Africa introduced by the pre-war Liberal government, and brought into effect in 1910, actually made the status of black people in Natal and Cape Colony far worse by dragging them down to the same level of powerlessness as those in the Boer republics of Transvaal and the Orange Free State.[59] In this, Lloyd George was thus all too typical of the tenor of British politics at that time. It is a significant, if surprising, lacuna in his outlook.

Lincoln and his message hovered above the three peace-makers at the Paris peace conference in 1919. On one memorable occasion, Lloyd George, Wilson and Clemenceau had a private discussion concerning Lincoln and his career. Wilson, a Southern Democrat who held con-servative views on race issues, and Clemenceau, who first went to America in 1865 shortly after Lincoln's funeral and married an American woman, had their varying perspectives. In their different ways, they all hugely admired Lincoln. But Wilson was dogmatic on race questions. He introduced segregation into the social arrangements of the White House as president, while as an academic historian he had actually changed his historical writings on the Civil War so as not to offend southern readers. Lloyd George, as previously noted, was not passionate on the issue of slavery. Perhaps, therefore, it was Georges Clemenceau, the old French 'tiger' who had backed Andrew Johnson's impeachment, and not the 'Anglo-Saxons' (*pace* the Welsh prime minister) who was closest in sympathy to the old president.[60]

Lincoln was always a factor in Lloyd George's lack of confidence in, or regard for, Woodrow Wilson. A more recent personal comparison was with Theodore Roosevelt, the great exponent of the 'New Nationalism' against Wilson's 'New freedom' in the famous 1912 presidential election. Lloyd George and 'T.R.' much admired each other: they met briefly in 1910 when Roosevelt was *en route* to shoot lions in Africa. Roosevelt's Bismarckian blend of social reform and a strong foreign policy was closer to Lloyd George's own vision of political leadership.[61] In *The Truth about the Peace Treaties*, Lloyd George described his own shock and anger when Wilson responded without emotion to the news of Roosevelt's death. 'I was aghast at the outburst of acrid detestation which flowed from Wilson's lips . . . There is the story of a famous American politician who, on being asked whether he proposed to attend the funeral of a rival whom he cordially detested, replied, "No, but I thoroughly approve of it".'[62] But there was also the historic comparison of Wilson with Lincoln. The comparison of the two in *The Truth about the Peace Treaties* is wholly in favour of Lincoln. He was 'a man of genius who had the practical common sense of a son of the soil'. Like many of Lloyd George's heroes, he embodied the wisdom of the common man rather than the arid learning of the scholar. Lincoln was also far more human, whereas Wilson 'completely lacked the human touch. The hand was too frigid. It gave you the impression that Wilson's philanthropy was purely intellectual, whereas Lincoln's came straight from the heart.'[63] Lincoln was not only much the greater man, but also the more effective president. Wilson dithered about throwing all his energies into battle, whereas Lincoln never hesitated about using all legitimate methods to win the war, and showed far better judgement than his generals in so doing. By these standards, Wilson was mediocre.

Lloyd George had one great opportunity to proclaim Lincoln's qualities to the world during his premiership. He unveiled Lincoln's statue in Parliament Square in 1920. The ceremony had been preceded by a bitter argument about which statue to have, a debate in which Lloyd George took no part. The original statue by Barnard, which was thought 'uncouth' and demeaning to Lincoln, was sent to Manchester instead. Augustus Saint-Gaudens's more dignified if more conventional sculpture was erected in London. But Lloyd George's address on Lincoln, delivered in pouring rain on 28 July 1920, added nobility to the occasion. 'He is one of those giant figures, of whom there are very few in history, who lose their nationality in death. They are no longer Greek or Hebrew, English or American; they belonged to mankind'. These remarks were greeted with 'loud and prolonged cheering'. Lloyd George's rhetorical passion was never more memorably deployed.[64]

Lloyd George's love-affair with Lincoln reached its climax after his premiership had come to an end. This was in October 1923 when he paid his one visit to the New World, including a journey to Springfield, Illinois, to speak on Lincoln.[65] In a sense, Lincoln's ideals, as interpreted by Lloyd George, provided the very core of his speaking tour in the New World. It was arranged in large measure by the new Welsh-American 'Gorsedd', notably through a newspaper, *The Druid*, in Pittsburgh.[66] Lloyd George travelled six thousand miles in Canada and the United States; it was, he told his secretary-mistress Frances Stevenson, 'one triumphant procession'. By any standards it was a gruelling experience for a man in his sixties, and he came close to losing his voice towards the end. Mrs Lloyd George had to deputise for him at Chicago on 16 October when her husband had a 'slight fever'.[67] He was greeted everywhere by huge crowds and respectful journalists. One asked Lloyd George what it felt like to be the most famous man in the world. The reply was, 'it makes me very shy'. He arrived at New York on 5 October on the *Mauretania* and, among other excitements, met Charlie Chaplin at the Music Box Theatre. He went on by train to Canada where he spoke at Montreal, Ottawa, Toronto and Winnipeg, before entering the USA at Niagara Falls where he was given a biography of Lincoln (probably that by Nicolay and Hay). He then spoke at Minneapolis, Chicago stock yards (to twelve thousand people when he first encountered a new invention called 'the Radio or Broadcasting'),[68] St Louis, Indianapolis (audience of twelve thousand), Cleveland (twenty-five thousand, the largest crowd yet, including many Welsh Americans), Pittsburgh, Washington, Philadelphia, and New York again in the Metropolitan Opera House with an overflow audience of twenty thousand in Central Park hearing the speech from loudspeakers, before sailing for home (and an imminent general election) on 3 November.

There were major political highlights, a meeting with ex-president Wilson in Washington, then meetings with Secretary of State Charles Evans Hughes (a fellow Welshman) and President Coolidge. He spent time with Hughes discussing, and agreeing with, a proposal for a committee of experts to work out German's capacity to pay reparations (in effect, putting the issue out into the long grass).[69] As a diversion, he was given by a scroll by Jewish organisations for his work in Palestine and also, for less obvious reasons, was inducted into the Sioux tribe in Minnesota as 'Wambli Napa' (Eagle of War and Peace). But there was plenty of time for Lloyd George's Civil War enthusiasms. He visited Gettysburg on 27 October, Chancellorsville the next day (when he spoke about Stonewall Jackson who met his death there), and Richmond to see the site of the Seven-Day Battle and meet some Confederate veterans.[70] But the highlight, and fulcrum, of the entire tour was the focus on Abraham Lincoln. He visited Lincoln's home in Springfield and visited his tomb. Here he laid a wreath with the inscription, 'A humble and reverent homage to one of the world's greatest men.' He also met Abraham Lincoln's elderly son, Robert, 'a man fragile and worn with a faint resemblance to his father'.[71] Robert Lincoln had had a notable career himself, serving as minister to England during the presidency of Benjamin Harrison in 1889–93. Lloyd George's daughter, Megan, who accompanied him, wrote how 'Father was overcome with joy to meet the son of the man he has always hero worshipped.' He was greatly moved by discussing his father's personal qualities with Robert Lincoln, to whom he observed how a civil war was far more harrowing than even his own wartime experiences.[72]

Then at Springfield, Illinois, on 18 October, Lloyd George spoke, under the modest auspices of the Mid-day Luncheon Club. He spoke, movingly, of Lincoln's ageless qualities. 'He was one of those rare men whom you do not associate with any particular creed, or party . . . not even with any country, for he belongs to mankind in every race, in every clime and in every age.' Lincoln was a great man of all time for all parties, for all lands. He was the choice and champion of a party, but 'his lofty soul could see over and beyond party walls the unlimited terrain beyond'. He was 'misrepresented, misunderstood, maligned, derided, thwarted in every good impulse, thought or deed', but he triumphed in the end. He was 'the finest product in the realm of statesmanship of the Christian civilization, and the wise counsel he gave his own people in the day of their triumph he gives today to the people of Europe in the hour of their victory over the forces that menace their liberties'.[73]

Lincoln, in Lloyd George's view, had a vivid message for the present time. Lincoln stood, he argued, for two great principles. The first was 'clemency in the hour of triumph'. Lincoln's doctrine was to 'reconcile the vanquished'. The second was to 'trust the common people' – he believed in their sincerity, their common sense, their inherent belief in justice. Thus the two great conclusions that Lloyd George drew from the Great War he linked to Lincoln's ideas – the need for reconciliation and reconstruction of a shattered continent, and for faith in democracy. A time would come 'when the principles of Abraham Lincoln will have to be fought for again'.[74] One stated implication was that the United States should modify its isolationist stance towards Europe to help give them effect. At the Biltmore hotel, New York, in his final speech on 1 November, he drove the point home. Lincoln had called for reconciliation in 1865, in opposition to 'vindictive men after the war who wanted to trample on the defeated South'. This was 'the Lincoln touch, a policy of conciliation not of vengeance'. That was precisely what was needed now, moderation in dealing with reparations and German frontiers, refraining from imposing humiliating terms, working for European reconstruction.[75] Lincoln's approach was the very converse of the belligerent French prime minister, Poincaré, currently sending in troops to occupy the Ruhr.[76] The Lincoln touch, therefore, magnanimity in the hour of victory, was precisely the answer to mankind's problems at the present time. In a series of well-publicised (and very well paid) newspaper articles, Lloyd George, the champion of reconciliation and a fundamental revision of the peace treaties in a way that finally commanded the approval of Keynes, drove Abraham Lincoln's message home. His visit was to be long remembered, and was recalled by Franklin Roosevelt and John F. Kennedy in future years.

Lloyd George's passionate evocation of Lincoln and his ideals, however, was perhaps the final chapter in this story. Lincoln's fame in Wales really amounted to a cult status among the Liberal nonconformist forces which had dominated the nation since the 1868 election. The Welsh working class, who emerged increasingly powerful in the Labour Party after 1918, never shared the same passion. They did not respond to the views of the early German Social Democrats who saw Lincoln, as Marx had done, as a kind of working-class hero.[77] The left in Wales, as elsewhere in Britain, increasingly saw in America not the last, best hope of democracy, but the linchpin of capitalism (even though the American section of the International Brigade during the Civil War in Spain called itself the Abraham Lincoln battalion – it included many black Americans).[78] Aneurin Bevan illustrates this precisely: Lincoln never featured in his oratory. The present writer noted this when writing on Bevan's biographer, Michael Foot, and the British labour movement. Isaac Foot, Michael's father, regarded Lincoln as supreme among statesmen and among human beings. In a remarkable lecture before the Royal Society of Literature in London in April 1944, he compared Lincoln with Oliver

Cromwell as a colossus in both peace and war – and for Isaac, founding father of the Cromwell Association, there could be no more honourable standard of comparison.[79] Isaac was not only a huge admirer of Lincoln but also of the United States. In Isaac's case, this was partly nurtured by his strong sense of the history of his native Plymouth, whence the Pilgrim Fathers had famously set sail to the new world. His socialist son, Michael, by contrast, for all his devoted loyalty to his father, had no especial regard for Lincoln whom he saw as a conservative figure. His American heroes were Thomas Jefferson, friend of Tom Paine and enlightened architect of revolution, and the novelist Ernest Hemingway.[80] In similar vein, the black American singer, Paul Robeson, became a cult figure among the Welsh miners, especially after taking part in the radical film *The Proud Valley* (1939) about the Welsh mining valleys.[81] But this may have been because of his Marxist socialism as much as his being a symbol of black ethnicity. So the new era of Labour dominance in Welsh political and social life from the 1920s saw Lincoln retreat from centre stage, perhaps only re-emerging when slavery returned to the public agenda in commemoration of the abolition of the slave trade in the bicentenary year of 2007.

Still, it is right that Wales should be represented here. Welsh politics in the nineteenth century were different in substance and style from those of England. There was, therefore, a distinctive Welsh perspective on Lincoln. He towered over the Welsh democracy in its most formative period. The Welsh, like free citizens the world over, could claim him as one of their own, and some of us still do.

Notes

[1] Kenneth O. Morgan, 'Liberals, Nationalists and Mr. Gladstone', in *idem*, *Modern Wales: Politics, Places and People* (Cardiff, 1995), pp. 322–38.
[2] Jerry Hunter, *Sons of Arthur, Children of Lincoln: Welsh Writing from the American Civil War* (Cardiff, 2007), pp. 484ff.
[3] See Gwyn A. Williams, *The Search for Beulah land* (London, 1980).
[4] Rowland T. Berthoff, *British Immigrants in Industrial America* (Cambridge Mass., 1954), pp. 62ff.

[5] William D. Jones, *The Welsh in America: Scranton and the Welsh, 1860–1920* (Cardiff, 1993).

[6] For *Y Drych*, see Aled Jones and Bill Jones, *Welsh Reflections: Y Drych and America 1851–2001* (Cardiff, 2001).

[7] The present author confirmed this while exploring cemeteries in Emporia, Kansas, in 1999.

[8] Gwyn A. Williams, *Madoc* (London, 1980), p. 114.

[9] Chidlaw served as chaplain to the 39th Ohio. See the autobiography, Revd Benjamin Chidlaw, *The Story of My Life* (Philadelphia, 1890).

[10] See Daniel G. Williams, 'Uncle Tom and Ewythr Robert: Anti-Slavery and Ethnic Reconstruction in Victorian Wales', *Slavery and Abolition*, 33/2 (2011).

[11] See Prys Morgan, *Brad y Llyfrau Gleision* (Llandysul, 1991).

[12] The biography by T. Roberts and D. Roberts, *Cofiant y Parch. William Rees* (Dolgellau, 1893), is useless on these matters. There is an excellent discussion of Robert Everett and other Welsh anti-slavery figures in Jerry Hunter, *Sons of Arthur, Children of Lincoln*, pp. 49ff. I am greatly indebted to Dr Hunter for advice in this area.

[13] Richard J. Carwardine, *Lincoln* (London, 2003), pp. 35ff. The description comes from Mary Todd Lincoln.

[14] Richard Toye, 'The Churchill Syndrome: Reputation, Entrepreneurship and the Rhetoric of Foreign Policy since 1945', *British Journal of Politics and International Relations*, 10/ 3 (August 2008), 364–78.

[15] See William E. Barton, *The Lineage of Abraham Lincoln* (New York, 1929). I am grateful for information from Mr Tom Schwarz and Professor Richard Carwardine here. Cf. also letters of Thomas Jones (NLW, MS 11004C) on Lincoln's alleged Welsh ancestry.

[16] Alan Conway, *The Welsh in America* (Cardiff, 1961), pp. 283–9.

[17] Jones and Jones, *Welsh Reflections*, pp. 24–5.

[18] See Dorothy Stanley (ed.), *The Autobiography of Sir Henry Morton Stanley* (New York, 1909), for a veiled account.

[19] See Glanmor Williams, *Samuel Roberts, Llanbrynmair* (Cardiff, 1950).

[20] *Y Cronicl*, 1863, 78–86; 1865, 27 and 168.

[21] *Baner ac Amserau Cymru*, 28 November 1860.

[22] *Baner ac Amserau Cymru*, 17 September and 15 October 1862.

[23] *Y Dysgedydd*, XLIII (1864), 341; *Y Traethodydd*, XX (1865), 478ff.

[24] Robert Huw Griffith, 'The Welsh and the American Civil War, c.1840–1865' (University of Wales, unpublished Ph.D. thesis, 2004), pp. 143ff.; Dean B. Malin, *One War at a Time: The International Dimensions of the American Civil War* (Washington DC, 1999), pp. 58ff.

[25] *Baner ac Amserau Cymru*, 21 January 1863; *Yr Herald Cymraeg*, 11 and 18 October 1862.

[26] *Baner ac Amserau Cymru*, 7 December 1864.

[27] James G. Randall, *Lincoln the Liberal Statesman* (New York, 1947), pp. 135–50.

[28] Richard's biography by C. S. Miall (1889) omitted any discussion of his views on the Civil War.

[29] *Cambria Daily Leader*, 7 October 1862.

[30] *Cambria Daily Leader*, 27 April 1865.

[31] Sir Edmund Walker Head to Sir George Cornewall Lewis, 24 February 1861 and 25 March 1861 (NLW, C1555. 1556).

[32] Cf. Kenneth O. Morgan, 'Wales and the Boer War', in *idem, Modern Wales: Politics, Places and People* (Cardiff, 1995), pp. 46–58.

[33] Hunter, *Sons of Arthur, Children of Lincoln*, pp. 474ff.

[34] Jones, *The Welsh in America*, chapters 3 and 4.

[35] Walter Johnson, *William Allen White's America* (New York, 1947), p. 235.

[36] For Samuel Milton ('Golden Rule') Jones, see Russell B. Nye, *Midwestern Progressive Politics* (Ann Arbor, 1959), pp. 175–8. Jones, a Christian Socialist, was a brilliant mayor of Toledo after 1897. He was born in Caernarfonshire and it is curious that he is always ignored in accounts of the American Welsh.

[37] See Neville Masterman, *The Forerunner* (Llandybïe, 1972).

[38] 'Essay on the First American', D. R. Daniel Papers (NLW), 591.

[39] *Y Dysgedydd*, CIV (1925), 160.

[40] See his entry in the *Dictionary of Welsh Biography*.

[41] For a sketch of him, see *The Welsh Members of Parliament* (Cardiff, 1894).

[42] E. R. Jones, *Lincoln, Stanton and Grant: Historical Sketches* (London, 1875), pp. 130ff.

[43] Kenneth O. Morgan (ed.), *Lloyd George: Family Letters c.1885–1936* (Oxford and Cardiff, 1973), pp. 69–73.

[44] Kenneth O. Morgan, *Wales in British Politics 1963–1922* (Cardiff, 1963), p. 159.

[45] *Baner ac Amserau Cymru*, 17 February 1909.

[46] Merrill D. Peterson, *Lincoln in American Memory* (New York, 1994), pp. 178–80.

[47] David W. Blight, *Race and Reunion: The Civil War in American Memory* (Cambridge, MA, 2001), pp. 11 ff.

[48] W. R. P. George, *The Making of Lloyd George* (London, 1976), pp. 179–80.

[49] e.g., A. J. P. Taylor (ed.), *Lloyd George. A Diary by Frances Stevenson* (London, 1971), p. 252 (entry for 12 February 1934).

[50] J. Hugh Edwards, *From Village Green to Downing Street* (London, 1908); J. Hugh Edwards, *David Lloyd George*, vol. 1 (London, 1929), pp. 45–9, makes explicit comparison between the two leaders and their humble backgrounds.

[51] Edwards, *From Village Green to Downing Street*, p. 393.

[52] Colin Cross (ed.), *A. J. Sylvester: Life with Lloyd George* (London, 1975), pp. 82–3 (entry for 10 November 1932).

[53] Lord Riddell, *Intimate Diary of the Peace Conference and After* (London, 1933), p. 226.

[54] David Lloyd George, *War Memoirs* (London, 1938 edn), vol. 1, p. 999.

[55] Keith Middlemas (ed.), *Thomas Jones. Whitehall Diary*, vol. 3 (Oxford, 1971), p. 60 (entry for 27 April 1921).

[56] Keith Middlemas (ed.), *Thomas Jones. Whitehall Diary*, vol. 1 (Oxford, 1969), p. 203 (entry for 13 June 1922); Lloyd George *War Memoirs*, vol. 2, pp. 2014–15.

[57] Middlemas, *Thomas Jones. Whitehall Diary*, vol. 1, pp. 232–3.

[58] Blight, *Race and Reunion*.

[59] Kenneth O. Morgan, *Keir Hardie* (London, 1975), p. 198. Hardie was one of the very few to criticise the Union of South Africa Bill.

[60] Peterson, *Lincoln in American Memory*, p. 199.

[61] See Morgan, *Lloyd George Family Letters*, p. 164 (Lloyd George to Mrs Lloyd George, 16 October 1912).

[62] David Lloyd George, *The Truth about the Peace Treaties* (London, 1938), vol. 1, p. 232.

[63] Lloyd George, *War Memoirs*, vol. 1, p. 233.

[64] *The Times*, 29 July 1920; F. Lauriston Bullard, *Lincoln in Marble and Bronze* (New Jersey, 1952) p. 85; TNA, WORK 20/106 for government correspondence on the statue.

[65] There is a file on this visit in the Lloyd-George of Dwyfor Papers, Parliamentary Archives, House of Lords, Box G/165.

[66] Jones, *The Welsh in America*, pp. 184ff; *The Druid*, 15 October 1923 (Lloyd-George Papers, G/259).

[67] *The Times*, 17 October 1923; Lloyd George to Frances Stevenson, 22 October 1923: A. J. P. Taylor (ed.), *My Darling Pussy* (London, 1975), p. 72.

[68] Lloyd-George Papers, Box G/165; Ffion Hague, *The Pain and the Privilege: the Women in Lloyd George's Life* (London, 2008), pp. 419–24.

[69] *The Times*, 26 October 1923.

[70] *The Times*, 31 October 1923.

[71] Notes by Megan Lloyd George, NLW, MS 23265D, 93.

[72] Notes by Megan Lloyd George; material on the career of Robert Lincoln may be found on the internet at the Abraham Lincoln research site. He died in 1926.

[73] Text of speech in Lloyd-George of Dwyfor Papers, Box G/165.

[74] Text of speech in Lloyd-George of Dwyfor Papers.

[75] *The Times*, 3 November 1923.

[76] *The Times*, 3 November 1923. Philip Kerr had urged Lloyd George not be too abusive about France in his speeches (Kerr to Lloyd George, 1 September 1923, Lloyd-George Papers, Box G/259).

[77] Uwe Luebken, 'A Humanitarian as broad as the World: Abraham Lincoln's legacy in International Context', *German Historical Institute Bulletin*, 42 (Spring 2008), 135.

[78] See Edwin Rolfe, *The Lincoln Batallion* (New York, 1939). There was later formed the George Washington Batallion, headed by a Yugoslav.

[79] Isaac Foot, *Oliver Cromwell and Abraham Lincoln* (Royal Society of Literature, 1944), inscribed copy in the author's possession.

[80] Conversations between the author and Michael Foot, 2002 onwards.

[81] David Berry, *Wales and Cinema: The First Hundred Years* (Cardiff, 1995), pp. 166–70. Robeson had first come into contact with the Welsh miners when singing in Wales to raise money for the Popular Front government in Spain: see Hywel Francis, *Miners against Fascism. Wales and the Spanish Civil War* (London, 1984), p. 249. Important is Daniel G. Williams, *Black Skin, Blue Books: African Americans and Wales, 1845–1945* (Cardiff, 2012), pp. 151–207. Of much interest is the same author's *Aneurin Bevan and Paul Robeson: Socialism, Class and Identity* (Cardiff, 2010), a lecture delivered at the 2010 National Eisteddfod in Ebbw Vale.

4

The Relevance of Henry Richard

The issues of the twentieth-first century make it particularly appropriate to reflect on the long and controversial career of Henry Richard. Born in rural Tregaron, in southern Ceredigion, more than two hundred years ago in 1812, the priories which he championed have a remarkable contemporary relevance. Since one of Richard's famous slogans was *Trech gwlad nag Arglwydd* (A land is mightier than its lord), it may appear paradoxical that his career should be re-evaluated by a member of the present (still unelected) House of Lords. For all that, this provides an opportunity to recall one of the most remarkable and courageous Welshmen of the modern world. He was associated with great causes – notably as the proclaimed *apostol heddwch* (apostle of peace) in the crusade for world peace, which took him from the Peace Treaty of Paris in 1856 to that of Berlin in 1878, and into a challenge to militarism and imperialism which led to confrontations with both Gladstone and Disraeli. In Wales itself, he is most celebrated as the radical victor in the important electoral contest in Merthyr Tydfil in 1868, 'the cracking of the ice' in the old neo-feudal political and social order, and an immense landmark in the achievement of democracy in our nation.

Richard is now a largely forgotten figure, other than in the annual Richard memorial lecture faithfully maintained by the United Nations Association in Wales. After his triumph in 1868, he turned into a kind of revered licensed rebel, the doyen of Welsh members, a national treasure honoured, acclaimed and usually ignored. Although he stayed on as member for Merthyr until his death in 1888, he seemed marginalised by the new currents of radicalism after 1880, and was swept aside by far younger, more glamorous and charismatic nationalist figures like Tom Ellis and David Lloyd George. Stuart Rendel (himself a middle-aged Englishman with an Eton and Oxford background) wrote in his memoirs of Richard as 'the leader . . . of a section of the House which was exceedingly English', for all his accepted chairmanship of the Welsh MPs. He did not sympathise with agrarian agitation in Wales, nor in pursuing disestablishment of the Church for Wales on its own, separately from England. He was bracketed with other 'old hands', senior Welsh Liberals like Lewis Llewellyn Dillwyn, Sir Hussey Vivian and Fuller-Maitland. In language reminiscent of Tony Blair a hundred years later, Rendel saw Richard as 'old Wales', aiming at 'respectability above all things' and 'very "middle class"' (this from Rendel who made millions from armaments manufacture and kept a comfortable residence on the French Riviera). The alternative to Richard's 'old Wales', contrary to Tony Blair's formulation, was felt to be 'young Wales' rather than 'new Wales'.[1]

This characterisation of Henry Richard endured, with his being seen as kind of beleaguered backwater from a previous age. Despite the massive upsurge of interest in the social and political history of modern Wales, he has remained a surprisingly neglected figure. The work of an historian like Matthew Cragoe treats him unsympathetically, almost dismissively. Despite the existence of a goodly collection of Richard's political papers in the archive of the National Library of Wales, the only biography since C. S. Miall's extraordinarily old-fashioned work of 1889, a 'life and letters' of traditional Victorian piety, is Gwyn Griffiths's study in 2012.[2] In his entries in both the *Oxford Dictionary of National Biography* and the *Welsh Encyclopædia*, Richard has not been well served, perhaps in part because his strain of anti-separatist Welsh radicalism does not relate easily to the historical antecedents of Plaid Cymru.

However, Richard represents something of much importance in the spectrum of nineteenth-century Welsh Liberalism, so often seen purely introspectively – its internationalist dimension. In this, he emulated William Rees, Gwilym Hiraethog, the inspirational bard/publicist who met and corresponded with Mazzini, who worked closely with the American anti-slavery movement and who championed Abraham Lincoln and made him a Welsh popular hero – and who also lacks a decent modern biography.[3] Richard, like Gwilym Hiraethog, operated on a world stage. In the peace movement, he collaborated with great Frenchmen like Lamartine, Tocqueville and particularly Victor Hugo who addressed the 1848 Peace Congress in Paris. Henry Richard, more than most Welsh radicals, was a citizen of the world. This was acknowledged by another great internationalist, Keir Hardie, when he was himself elected MP for Merthyr in 1900 during the mass jingoism of the South African War. Hardie was elected primarily as a socialist, on class grounds, though he gained wider radical support in Liberal circles. But he paid his full tribute to Merthyr Tydfil's unique political tradition, and to the followers of Henry Richard in 1868 'who were then uncorrupted'.[4] A seamless tradition of radical, pacific internationalism and fraternalism had been restored. It is therefore of much importance to Welsh historians to re-investigate both the central themes of Richard's long career in his own day and their later relevance, because the crusades in which Richard so willingly enlisted, far from dying with him, have been ongoing and remain of deep significance in Wales and the world at present.

There were four Henry Richards whom we should define and celebrate. First, of course, there was Henry Richard the Welshman. The son of a Calvinist Methodist minister in Tregaron, the Revd Ebenezer Richard, he became a Congregationalist after entering Highbury Congregational College, and became a minister of Marlborough chapel in the Old Kent Road in 1835. From then on, he lived primarily in England. He seemed destined for an active career spent primarily in the world of English dissent. But it was Welsh issues that began to call him. He wrote in the English press offering social and religious explanations of the factors lying behind the Rebecca Riots of the early 1840s with their assault on toll-gates. More powerfully, he became one of the leading opponents of the notorious Blue Books of 1847, that 'treasonous' publication which traduced Wales in its culture, language, religious and moral probity.

Richard was appalled and his highly effective retaliatory articles in the *Daily News* and elsewhere gave him a new status in his native Wales.[5] Richard's view of Welsh nationhood linked it indissolubly with nonconformity. All the many positive features of the Welsh he identified with the values of the chapel – its populist democracy, its vibrant Welsh-language culture, its love of music and poetry, the absence of crime. Wales was *gwlad y menig gwinion*, 'the land of white gloves', a place unpolluted by violence with few of its people in prison, where judges were presented with white gloves at the assizes to celebrate a crime-free, respectable community, and where policemen hung around looking for something to do. Here, Richard was far from wholly wrong, though he did focus on 'Proper Wales', and tended to ignore the ports and larger towns of the industrialising south where 'the population had long ceased to be distinctively Welsh'.[6] He vindicated Wales most eloquently and effectively in a famous series of articles on the social and political condition of Wales in the *Morning and Evening Star* in 1866, in which emphasis was laid heavily on Wales as a 'nation of nonconformists', shown in Horace Mann's 1851 census of religious worship to be 78 per cent nonconformist and only 22 per cent Anglican. It was on this basis, as the voice of Welsh nonconformity, that he became Liberal candidate for Merthyr Tydfil in 1868, its electorate having been massively expanded by the Reform Act of the previous year. His very adoption made it plain that it was as a nonconformist that he offered himself to the electors. The body that put itself forward described itself as 'The Henry Richard or Nonconformist Committee'.[7] When, in this two-member constituency, he came top of the poll, out-polling his fellow Liberal, the ironmaster Richard Fothergill, and ousting the Liberal industrialist, Henry Austin Bruce, shortly to become Gladstone's Home Secretary, it was widely perceived that, in a nation hitherto conspicuous for its political unimportance, a new more democratic era had dawned.

Richard's view of his native Wales was thus defined by his religious background. His *Letters* in the English press had depicted Wales as a deeply divided country, with a small, privileged landlord class, English in speech and sympathy, and, crucially, Anglican in religion fundamentally separated from the nonconformist mass of the population. There was a profound inequality entrenched within its society, and therefore his political priority henceforth, throughout his two decades in parliament, was the disestablishment and disendowment of the Church of England in Wales. He had the enormous encouragement in his very first session in parliament of Gladstone's measure to disestablish the Church in Ireland. This set down, he wrote, several important principles. It acknowledged that where the established church was not the Church of the nation, its position was anomalous. It recognised that ecclesiastical property was national property as it had endured since the Middle Ages. Above all, it disposed of the fallacy of a collective state conscience which imposed its own beliefs as an established creed on resistant dissenters. Along with other favourable measures, such as the repeal of the Test Acts for Oxford and Cambridge, Richard and his allies in the Liberation Society could see an irresistible onward momentum for the various nonconformist causes.

Welsh disestablishment, however, was not at all a straightforward matter. In the first place, there was an urgent need for leadership and direction in pressing the matter home. Only since the 1868 election, had the issue gained a clear overwhelming priority in Wales.[8] Even then support for disestablishment among Welsh MPs was only limited. Thirty of the thirty-three members were Anglican, and twenty-four were landowners – that is, all the ten Conservatives and fourteen of the Whig-Liberals who formed the bulk of the Gladstonian ranks. Only three Welsh MPs were nonconformists – Richard himself, Evan Matthew Richards (Cardiganshire) and Richard Davies (Anglesey). There was significant bickering when Watkin Williams, Liberal member for Denbigh District and an Anglican, put forward a motion for Welsh disestablishment and disendowment in August 1869 without consulting his colleagues. This led to much protest. Many doubted whether the maverick Watkin Williams was really a Liberal at all, and it was darkly murmured that he had voted against John Stuart Mill in the Westminster constituency at the recent general election. Henry Richard himself thought the motion ill-advised and badly-timed. The issue of the secret ballot should have been dealt with first with a commission of inquiry to collect data on the strengths of the various religious bodies in Wales. The influential journalist John Griffith ('Gohebydd') considered Williams's *démarche* to be 'a very great misfortune'.[9] When Williams's motion was finally debated on 24 May 1870, Richard inevitably spoke and voted for it, but it gained only 47 votes. Only seven Welsh MPs voted for it, eight Welsh Liberals voted against, and ten others were absent or abstained – including the nonconformist E. M. Richards and E. J. Sartoris (Carmarthenshire) who had been advised not to vote for it for fear of jeopardising his seat.[10] Perhaps most seriously, Gladstone himself felt impelled to deliver an *ex cathedra* statement opposing Welsh disestablishment (one which was to embarrass him greatly in later years). The Welsh Church, he declared, had 'a complete constitutional, legal and historical identity with the Church of England' and it was impossible to legislate for it separately.[11] This was not the way in which intelligent would-be disestablishers ought to proceed, in Richard's view.

But his dissenting position went beyond matters of parliamentary tactics. He did not favour pressing for disestablishment for Wales alone. His roots were in the London-based Liberation Society, of which he was a leading officer and which had been a powerful force on his behalf at the polls in 1868. Richard was no kind of nationalist or home ruler. In a parliamentary debate on international arbitration in 1873, he asked rhetorically, 'Is not England our country?'[12] He saw a fundamental difference between Wales, an intrinsic part of the United Kingdom albeit one with grievances and priorities of its own, and Ireland, where many saw disestablishment as a precursor to home rule. To Richard, by contrast, disestablishment was an alternative to home rule. He felt it was dangerous to press the case on quasi-nationalist grounds, and it also risked the possibility of Wales losing valuable Church endowments in the process. This was also the view of his colleague, Sir George Osborne Morgan (Denbighshire): 'I entertain strong doubts whether it is possible to separate the question of disestablishment in Wales from that of England – Wales being, politically at least, as much a part of England as Yorkshire or Cornwall.'[13] Richard agreed with Sidney Buxton that the general case for disestablishment in England, Wales and Scotland together 'would be of greater interest and command a much larger circulation' than if it were confined to Wales on its own.[14]

In spite of this, Richard's role as an advocate for Welsh causes was a powerful one, and his speeches in the Commons, often of great length, commanded much respect. By the 1880s, his outlook on the basic rationale on the Welsh church question was clearly shifting. In a debate on a further motion to disestablish the Welsh Church, he and his fellow veteran Liberal, Lewis Llewellyn Dillwyn (Swansea District), took a clear national stand. The Welsh Church was now briskly dismissed as an 'alien Church'; it was *Eglwys Loegr*, 'the Church of England in Wales'. Richard's own exceedingly lengthy speech, which took up eleven columns in Hansard, focused on the historical alienation of the Church from the Welsh nation over the centuries.[15] He was now far more emphatic on the distinctive cultural and political features of Wales as providing the basic arguments for Welsh disestablishment. The primacy of the Church in Wales should be removed because the people of Wales wanted it, and demonstrated the fact with large Liberal pluralities in successive general elections from 1868 to 1886. Richard and his Liberationist colleagues also recognised the historic importance of the Welsh Sunday Closing Act of 1881 as setting a precedent for solely Welsh legislation, even though his support for this measure stemmed mainly from his temperance rather than his nationalism.[16] He was turning his attention also to the Welshness of the Church of England in the appointment of its bishops, and also to retaining the Meyricke endowments at Jesus College, Oxford, for the Welsh scholars for whom they were intended. Principal Harper of Jesus seemed on the verge of frittering them away. Richard worked to this end with sympathetic Welsh Anglicans such as Dean Henry T. Edwards, the Liberal brother of the ferocious defender of the Anglican establishment, Bishop A. G. Edwards of St Asaph.[17]

Over a wide range of issues, Richard was recognised over a generation as the most authoritative voice on behalf of the religious, civic and educational demands of Welsh Liberals. In the 1880 general election, Gladstone's aide Lord Richard Grosvenor was to urge Richard to speak on behalf of William Rathbone, the Liberal candidate in Caernarfonshire. 'You have a peculiar faculty of raising the enthusiasm of Welshmen and Mr Rathbone labours under the disadvantage of not being able to speak one word of Welsh'.[18] Richard was also urged to lend his vocal support to the Liberal the Hon. G. C. Brodrick in his unsuccessful contest in highly anglicised Monmouthshire.[19] He was thus able to draw attention to the needs and historic identity of Wales as no politician had previously been able to do. In particular, he had a clear impact on the ideas of Gladstone who made plain in a speech at the Mold Eisteddfod in 1873, near his Hawarden home, that Richard's *Letters* had made a profound impression upon him. 'A countryman of yours – a most excellent Welshman – Mr Richard MP did a great deal to open my eyes to the facts.'[20] It was Richard, as much as Rendel, who helped Gladstone to become in time a great Welsh hero, 'the people's William' in a special sense in the principality – not to mention becoming the people's disestablisher. It might be added that it was very much to Gladstone's advantage that in 1886 Richard, somewhat reluctantly in view of his powerful commitment to Protestantism, declared his support for Irish Home Rule, in contrast to such nonconformist comrades as the Revd R. W. Dale and (for a time) Thomas Gee.[21] The secessions to the Liberal Unionists in Wales were kept to a minimum. With regard to Welsh affairs, Richard's outlook was different from the younger nationalists of *Cymru Fydd* like Tom Ellis in 1880s. He endorsed nationality not nationalism. Thus to them he was cautious, behind the times. After his death it was noticeable that the Welsh MPs immediately formed a 'Welsh Parliamentary Party' (chaired by Stuart Rendel), an idea which Richard had always resisted as unofficial chairman. But in his own time he was an essential bridge between the British-wide radicalism of the sixties and the more pluralistic, more socially aware Liberalism of the late Victorian period. On issue after issue he proclaimed the needs and identity of Wales. He used debates on the appointment of Welsh-speaking judges in 1872 and 1874 to spell out the validity of the culture and its language, no mere patois as he eloquently demonstrated.[22] This nonconformist non-nationalist, therefore, was clearly a godfather of the growing sense of Welsh nationhood that evolved in the decades down to the First World War. In that sense, he is also a godfather of devolution.

Secondly, Richard was a great democrat. His *Letters* passionately attacked political landlordism in Wales. He declared that Welsh politics were servile and dependent. Wales was 'feudal', not a democracy at all,

but a land where 'clansmen battled for their chieftains'.[23] Thus he campaigned vigorously in the Reform League for manhood suffrage and the
secret ballot. He regarded the 1867 Reform Act as a first instalment of a
wider enfranchisement. In time, he became an eloquent advocate of
women's suffrage as well. His own election in Merthyr and Aberdare
had an inspirational, revivalist quality. He said to the electors in Aberdare that they tell the landlords, 'We are the Welsh people not you. This
country is ours not yours.'[24] He went on to battle for the reform of the
franchise in the county constituencies, which duly happened in the
Reform and Redistribution Acts of 1884–5, and this served to make the
Liberals' strength in Wales all the more impregnable.

Richard's first major speech in the House in 1869 was on a great
democratic theme. He and other Liberals declared that there had been
much evidence of intimidation by landlords at the polls, with the eviction
of many tenant farmers for voting Liberal.[25] He raised the issue in a
debate on 6 July 1869, when in a highly personal way he referred to
forty-three cases of political eviction in Cardiganshire and many others
in Carmarthenshire and Caernarfonshire. Colonel Powell, the former
Conservative MP for Cardiganshire, was identified as one egregious case
of a bullying landlord. A recent account of this episode is somewhat
grudging and perhaps influenced by an inability to read the Welsh-
language press.[26] There is no doubt in fact that Richard's motion brought
a serious political scandal to public attention. A Liberal colleague noted
the particular delight with which Gladstone listened to his speech. A
nationwide fund organised by the radical journalist John Griffith,
'Gohebydd', raised around £4,000 to compensate some of the victimised
farmers.[27] More importantly, a Select Committee was appointed under
the chairmanship of Lord Hartington which received powerful evidence
from the Revd Michael Daniel Jones and other leading Liberals about
the nature of rural intimidation. Jones had written to Richard on the
extent of rural persecution – 'in the next election we shall lose ground if
the farmers have no protection'.[28] Its findings were a major factor in the
passing of the secret ballot in 1872. It was a great democratic triumph
for Richard. Perhaps in grim retaliation, in the 1874 general election
Welsh Conservatives recaptured seats in Carmarthenshire, Cardiganshire

and Caernarfonshire, those counties where rumours of landlord coercion in 1868 had been most vivid. Landowners such as Viscount Emlyn of Golden Grove, heir to the 70,000 acres of the Cawdor estate, and the Hon. George Douglas-Pennant, the son of Lord Penrhyn in his castle, now represented the Welsh-speaking farmers and labourers in those rural communities. As yet, the novelty of the secret ballot had had little impact. After 1880, however, democratic Liberalism prevailed.

In the longer term, the memory of political pressure and intimidation became what the great French historian, Pierre Nora, would call a *lieu de mémoire* for Welsh Liberals, as Taff Vale and Tonypandy would become for the Welsh Labour movement. Welsh Liberals had acquired the popular martyrology without which no popular movement can thrive. It was Wales's Amritsar or Sharpeville. Lloyd George gave it imperishable prominence in his speech at the Queen's Hall in London on 23 March 1910 on behalf of his People's Budget. Referring to the evictions in 1868, he declared that 'they woke the spirit of the mountains, the genius of freedom that fought the might of the Normans for two centuries. There was such a feeling aroused amongst the people, that, ere it was done, the political power of landlordism in Wales was shattered as effectually as the power of the Druids.'[29] Lloyd George's language was florid and overdrawn, perhaps, but it was in broad terms an accurate testimony of the democratic upsurge which Henry Richard had generated.

As a democrat, Richard was no socialist. However, he was able to identify with the working class movement of the day: he was thus a bridge between the worlds of Cobden and Bright and of Keir Hardie. He recognised, of course, that Merthyr and Aberdare were working-class communities, composed largely of miners and ironworkers, and Richard's campaign acknowledged the fact. The Reform League in 1868 deliberately placed working-class representatives, including several survivors of the last Chartist revival in 1848, on Richard's platforms. He proclaimed himself as the poor man's candidate, without the resources to buy his way into a constituency, and contrasted his own relative poverty with the affluence of the bourgeois industrialist Henry Austin Bruce. He was also skilful in taking up such issues as pit safety and the imposition of the 'northern' or double-shift system of working in the mines. John

Beynon, secretary of the local Double Shift Committee, campaigned for him. Recent wage reductions in the pits also helped Richard's cause. He claimed that his election victory was a triumph for the property-less, disinherited working-class man.[30] In the 1874 election, Richard shrewdly declared his sympathy for much of the programme of the Amalgamated Association of Miners which had grown rapidly in the Welsh coalfield, and whose secretary, Thomas Halliday, ran against him in the election. Halliday polled remarkably well, obtaining 4,912 votes (25.3 per cent), and Richard's vote fell on a much smaller turn-out of voters than in 1868. Even so, his established credentials as a working-class candidate and a proven champion of labour legislation still made him impregnable and he easily headed the poll. Following another comfortable victory in 1880, in 1885 and 1886 he and his Liberal running-mate, C. H. James, were returned unopposed. Richard, then, was not an inappropriate hero for the social democracy, as well as the political democracy of a later era. As noted, he was an inspiration for the socialist Keir Hardie in the 'khaki election' of 1900. Over a century later, in March 2010, his name was mentioned (by Monsignor Bruce Kent) in the roll-call of left-wing heroes at the funeral service of another great Welsh democratic representative, Michael Foot. In the long line of democratic dissenters, Alan Taylor's 'trouble-makers', Richard takes his honoured place.

Third, Richard was a considerable educationalist. At first, his concern seemed largely an outgrowth of his religious views. He was a leading figure among the nonconformists within the Liberal Party who attacked the Forster Education Act of 1870 for its subsidies to Church schools from public funds. Thus he led a public outcry against the Cowper-Temple clause in the 1870 Act, since it would have led to increased rate aid to denominational schools. There was, he wryly observed, 'no conscience clause for ratepayers'. However, his amendment in committee obtained only 62 votes, with nonconformist MPs divided.[31] His own stance was a minority one within the world of Protestant dissent, since, unlike most of his brethren, he was a passionate advocate of a purely secular education.[32] This was wholly consistent, of course, with his support for disestablishment and the general broad principle of the separation of church and state. However, his educational views are often misrepresented.[33] He did not object to the state being involved in education as such, but simply to its being used to promote denominational instruction and clerical special interests. His views were far more progressive than simply a rehearsal of the anti-clericalism that coloured debates on education in Britain, France and many other countries at the time. He wanted a new, national system of education, primary and secondary, sustained by central government. It would be uniform and universal; also it would be compulsory and free of charge. He saw it as a particular key to progressive change within Wales where educational provision was recognised as being weak. A secular system of primary education, via the Board schools without religious involvement, and a new network of non-denominational secondary or 'intermediate' schools were essential to his objectives, and they form a major part of his legacy. Even though his amendment to the Forster Act failed badly in 1870, he had the satisfaction of seeing Clause 25 of the act, which allowed School Boards to finance the school fees of voluntary denominational schools from the rates, repealed by Lord Sandon's Education Act of 1876, passed by Disraeli's Conservative government.

Richard thus became a major pioneer of Welsh education. On higher education, he played a major part with the energetic if controversial Sir Hugh Owen in building up the new 'college by the sea', the college at Aberystwyth first established in 1872. He battled hard with Gladstone for a public subsidy in 1870 and 1871, but at first without success. In 1870, the prime minister took the line that he had already refused grants to various English colleges and would hardly be able to make an exception in the case of Aberystwyth. Significantly, though, he did concede that 'it was impossible to place Wales, with its clearly marked nationality and its inhabitants divided from by strong line of demarcation, both of race and language, upon the same footing as an English town or district'.[34] The following year, Gladstone took the different line that it would raise a religious issue and would commit the state to a new principle in aiding colleges from the exchequer on the basis of teaching only 'an undenominational education'. After failing to help Owen's College, Manchester, the government could hardly help Aberystwyth.[35] The 'college by the sea' on the seafront opened in October 1872 with most of the £10,000 purchase money still owing, and only twenty-five initial students. But Richard's campaign went on and in 1882 Aberystwyth did receive an annual grant of £4,000.

He served in 1881 on a committee of immense importance for Welsh education, the Select Committee on Higher Education chaired by his old election adversary, Henry Bruce, now Lord Aberdare.[36] Richard himself, now an elderly man, proved to be a most effective member of it, full of energy and attested facts. The Committee advocated the setting up of two new colleges in Wales, one in the north and one in the south. Gladstone, now strongly committed to Welsh causes, lent his authoritative support, and the Aberdare Committee's proposals went ahead. In time, after much public campaigning, these institutions turned out to be located in Bangor and Cardiff respectively. It was also proposed that a new state-supported structure of 'intermediate schools' be created throughout Wales to provide students for them as well as to promote professional opportunities more generally. It was an issue on which Richard had spoken in the Commons. This was a progressive, forward-looking agenda for Welsh education. But it also left Aberystwyth high and dry, with the prospect that it would lose its annual grant and see it transferred to Bangor. Richard now re-doubled his efforts on behalf of Aberystwyth, applying particular pressure on the minister in charge of education, A. J. Mundella. Here his efforts finally bore fruit. Mundella wrote, in somewhat panicky fashion to Richard in 1884, 'I wish you would come and see me about Aberystwyth. We had better settle this question before you turn us out, as the Tories will not help you. If we subsidize a third College, we must do it on the same conditions as the other two.'[37] In the event, Mundella managed to prise only £2,500 out of the Exchequer for Aberystwyth, but in August 1885 the incoming Salisbury government, for somewhat unexplained reasons,[38] generously raised the Aberystwyth grant to £4,000 as well. All three of the new Welsh university colleges, therefore, could regard Richard as a highly important ally.

In his old age, in 1886–8 Richard served on the Cross Commission on elementary education, of which he was again an effective member.[39] Some of his time was taken in fending off bombardments from the Welsh Language movement about whose activities Richard was less than enthusiastic, like many senior Liberals of the day. He found pressure from Beriah Gwynfe Evans, the energetic secretary of the 'Society for the Utilization of the Welsh Language' to be 'rather embarrassing'.[40] In general, however, his educational activities were valuable and creative. He was undoubtedly a major figure in the social revolution that transformed Welsh education, and indirectly social mobility, in the last decades of the century. A year after Richard's death, the 1889 Welsh Intermediate Eduction Act, passed by the Salisbury government, saw another of his dreams come into effect, the new intermediate schools. For decades to come, the 'county schools', free and unsectarian, were a decisive instrument of social change. The Welsh could even pride themselves in having a state-run educational system in advance of England, and without its paralysing social divide created by the private schools. In 1893 there followed another landmark for which Richard had campaigned, a federal national University of Wales, created to crown the edifice of Welsh higher education, and destined to last for the next hundred years.

Fourth, and finally, there is Richard the internationalist and peace crusader, perhaps the area in which his reputation was most generally created. He always operated within other reformist movements across the world, notably with the anti-slavery movement in the United States. A committed pacifist, in 1848 he was appointed secretary of the Peace Society and he retained this position when he retired, on grounds of age, in 1885. He played a prominent part at the peace congresses at Brussels and Paris in the year of revolutions, 1848; the latter thrilled to an inspirational address from Victor Hugo. 'France, England, Germany, Italy, Europe, America, let us proclaim to all nations. "You are brothers"!' Richard campaigned inexhaustibly against war. He vehemently condemned the Crimean War, along with his close friends Richard Cobden and John Bright, and crusaded against the wars variously waged by Britain against the Boer Republics, the Zulus and the Afghans in the late 1870s, that era of aggressive imperialist militancy. He also condemned Gladstone's invasion of Egypt in 1882, declared by the prime minister to be a temporary policy but in fact inaugurating a lengthy British occupation that endured until 1954. Richard's major demands were forward-looking in the extreme. He called for an international tribunal to be set up, for the arbitration of disputes between nations. He visualised beyond that a kind of league of nations to administer such a system and to provide an effective and workable regime of international law.

Even in the warlike atmosphere of the mid- and later Victorian period, Richard and his associates in the Peace Society were not without success. They managed to have a protocol inserted in the Treaty of Paris of 1856 that wound up the Crimean War in favour of international arbitration and, more surprisingly, another included in the Treaty of Berlin in 1878 when it was rumoured, however improbably, that Bismarck himself showed some interest in the notion.[41] These were no more than paper successes, but Richard found great encouragement in Gladstone's decision to go to arbitration with the United States to adjudicate on the American claims against Britain following the activities of the British-built *Alabama*, operated by the Confederate navy, during the American Civil War. In the event, despite some domestic disgruntlement, the British accepted the tribunal's claims and paid damages of three and a quarter million pounds, a significant sum but much less than the Americans had asked for. This episode could, perhaps, only have taken place in the context of the particular relationships between Britain and the United States at the time, but it did offer Richard's proposals some practical encouragement.

Richard took several opportunities to bring the cause of peace before the House of Commons. The first, on 8 July 1873, was a motion on behalf of a general and permanent system of international arbitration.[42] He deplored the horrors of war and 'the bottomless pit of military expenditure', and called for an effective system of international law. Gladstone replied in amiable and respectful terms, and spoke warmly of the arbitration between Britain and the United States at Geneva, but called for 'a step by step' approach. Richard's motion was lost by 98 votes to 88.

On 15 June 1880, Richard tried again, calling for international disarmament, but now adding a new theme: namely, that foreign wars and the concluding of foreign treaties should always require the consent of parliament.[43] This again made no headway. His most important effort came in an amendment to the Address on 19 March 1886. He urged that no wars should be embarked upon, no treaties concluded, and no territories annexed to the empire without 'the knowledge and consent of Parliament'. He pointed out that the royal prerogative in these matters was a total fiction. A war was already in being before parliament was asked to vote supplies. He contrasted the totally different system of control exercised in the French Republic and by the Congressional House of Representatives. 'We never get the information before war breaks out', Richard declared, with total accuracy. 'Is it not a monstrous thing that the blood and treasure and moral responsibility of a great nation like ours should be pledged for all time behind our backs?' The British governments had, all of them, a mania for annexation. Henry Richard concluded in moving fashion: 'My hope is in the Democracy. I have lost faith in Governments. They seem to have delivered themselves up, bound hand and foot, to the power of rampant militarism which is the curse of Europe'.[44] Gladstone's reply reads weakly and evasively now. He argued the difficulty in distinguishing between war and 'warlike operations'. James Bryce, who wound up for the government, was even worse. Absurdly for so great a scholar of American issues, he replied to Richard's point about the US House of Representatives by claiming that the American system was very different since 'it had no foreign policy this side of the Atlantic anyway'. Richard's motion was lost by 115 votes to 109, but it is difficult not to believe that he won the argument, even against the combined learning of Gladstone and Bryce.

At times, Richard's uninhibited pacifism could lead him into difficulty. Nineteenth-century Britain had a warm sympathy for the efforts of 'nations rightly struggling to be free', such as the Greeks and Italians who appealed to those of classical bent. Garibaldi, leader of the famous red-shirted 'thousand' during the battles for Italian unification, had been a great popular hero on reformist platforms during the campaign for a Reform Bill in the 1860s. Richard himself got into trouble during the civil war when, unlike most Welshmen, he rebelled against the cult of Lincoln and defended the South in the American Civil War since he claimed it was a victim of Northern aggression. When asked about slavery, this pillar of the anti-slavery movement responded that it would die out in time through peaceful means. What is interesting, however, is that this is much the same line of argument adopted at the time by another pacifist and radical, Samuel Roberts, 'S.R.' of Llanbrynmair, who actually set up a Welsh settlement in the slave state of Tennessee, intended to escape landlord persecution in Wales. That decision virtually ruined Roberts' reputation and career.[45] Richard, by contrast, endured no such fate. It was testimony to how uniquely robust his reputation had become.

What remained of Henry Richard's campaigns after his death? It is striking in the early twenty-first century that all his causes have a powerful contemporary resonance. With regard to his commitment to the advancement of Wales, there has been an ongoing process of evolution. Despite the apparent tone of more emphatic nationalism in the Cymru Fydd movements of the 1890s, associated with Ellis and Lloyd George, Welsh political ambitions down to 1914 remained within the parameters of the age of Henry Richard. While progress was made on disestablishment, education, land reform and temperance, there was only limited concern with anything resembling separation, or even devolution. E. T. John's efforts prior to the First World War to promote a movement for Welsh home rule led nowhere.[46] There was only limited administrative devolution – in education in 1907 and in agriculture after the war in 1919. The emphasis was still on extending equality for Wales within the United Kingdom – and also the Empire, which the Welsh warmly endorsed during the First World War, under the leadership of a Welsh prime minister. The old national movement of post-1868 had clearly run its course; when Welsh disestablishment and disendowment, Richard's old dream, was finally achieved in 1919, there was an atmosphere of relative indifference, even of impatience that such an ancient cause could still take up parliamentary and political energy. After the First World War, politics in Wales drifted away from the priorities of Henry Richard. It was an era of unionism in which all parties, fortified by the Second World War, participated. The Labour Party, especially in the case of such figures as Aneurin Bevan and Ness Edwards, mirrored Henry Richard in seeing the problems of Wales as part of a wider theme – in Labour's case, that of class, as for Richard it had been of nonconformist unity. Only with the creation of a Welsh Secretary of State in 1964 did there seem to be change of direction, and the new Welsh Office was significantly limited in its powers. The real advance from the Henry Richard legacy came with the pressure for devolution in Scotland, and to a lesser degree Wales in the 1970s. That followed, variously, the unexpected upsurge of Plaid Cymru, the campaign for the Welsh language (only a relatively minor theme in Henry Richard's day), and especially the introduction of Scottish and Welsh devolution bills in the Commons by the Callaghan government following the Kilbrandon Commission. Devolution eventually followed in 1999, winning support by the tiniest of majorities, but it gradually gained in popular support. In 2009 the Jones-Parry report called for the law-making powers and financial authority of the Welsh assembly to be put to a popular referendum. Henry Richard was not a forgotten figure here – I personally had an interesting exchange about Richard when giving evidence to the Richard Commission and being interrogated by Ted (now Lord) Rowlands, the former member for Merthyr Tydfil as it happened. The priorities today clearly see the role of the Assembly to be the key to the future of Wales in British and European politics, and we have moved on far from Henry Richard. Even so, he played a significant role earlier on, in pressing for Welsh legislation, for Welsh parliamentary priorities distinct from those of England, and a firm Welsh presence in the political agenda. Richard, and abiding memories of the triumphs and suffering of 1868, still remain important in the making of modern Wales.

Richard's concern with democracy is, even more, a work in progress. The constitutional and political system in which he operated, based on parliament and strong centralist governance, are now transformed. All the textbooks which described the democratic fabric of Richard's day, works by Bagehot and his successors, are now scarcely relevant. There were significant reforms introduced by the Blair government after 1997, including reform of the Lords, human rights legislation, freedom of information legislation, and of course devolution for Wales, Scotland and Northern Ireland. Further reforms, some though not all in a democratic direction were proposed by the Conservative-Liberal Democrat coalition after its creation in May 2010. But Henry Richard would note the sluggish progress made towards some of his objectives. In 2010 there was still an unelected House of Lords; it still contained bishops as a symbol of the Church establishment. The authority of the Commons was still inadequate in relation to the executive, and its prestige as a reputable assembly had recently declined. Above all, Richard, who liked to cite the written constitutional arrangements of the Americans and the French, would not accept that British citizenship was still constrained. With a largely unwritten constitution, the British remained subjects, not full citizens. They remained subjects of the Queen. Richard felt that power should flow from below and independent free citizens should be empowered as he saw them being in Wales after 1868. A committee (of which the present author was a member) began work on the prospects for a written constitution. The agenda for democracy that Henry Richard proposed is still to be pursued.

Richard's work as an educationalist has taken a very different form. The denominational conflicts of his day have largely been superseded, although the debate about faith schools and their encouragement may revive his priorities as regards the value of secular education. His vision of a secular, comprehensive free system of primary and secondary is still hampered by the existence of a dual system of education, public and private, based on private funding and on class. His ideas still resonate. Perhaps it is in successful campaigns for access and for the pursuit of lifelong learning that Richard's objectives have made most progress.

Finally, and crucially, there is Richard the apostle of peace. As noted, his campaigns for the Peace Society were not wholly fruitless. The idea of international arbitration gained more support after the Anglo-US settlement of the Alabama claims. By 1914 there were arbitral agreements between twenty governments, and over a hundred arbitral agreements in force. The United States was especially active through such figures as Secretary of State Elihu Root, President Woodrow Wilson and through the steel capitalist, Andrew Carnegie who set up his Endowment for International Peace, and in 1910 called for a League of Nations. The Hague Peace Congress of 1899 set up a Permanent Court of Arbitration at the Hague, and another, larger peace congress followed there in 1907. But these yielded very little. It was indeed ironic that they honoured a strongly militaristic US president, Theodore Roosevelt, champion of 'the big stick' in foreign affairs, the voice of gunboat diplomacy in Latin America and the advocate of a strong navy. Roosevelt himself celebrated a 'peace of righteousness', achieved by fighting the good fight in a just war.[47] It was symbolic of the hypocrisy of the times that Roosevelt in 1910 became a recipient of the Nobel Peace Prize – though he has been followed by even more improbable people since.

The ending of the First World War encouraged brave new world hopes of the creation of a new world order, something approaching the peaceable ideals of Henry Richard. In fact, the Treaty of Versailles was met with much disillusionment. The League of Nations set up to promote the peaceful resolution of disputes and world disarmament soon proved to be a disappointment. Welsh internationalists and advocates of peace moved on smartly beyond Richard's pacifism now, as when David Davies, an idealistic champion of the League, called for an international police force to impose order. The Woodrow Wilson chair of International Politics Davies had set up at Aberystwyth to promote the idea of the League was, in 1936, occupied by E. H. Carr, whose *Twenty Years' Crisis* (1939) poured massive scorn on 'utopians' who wanted international arbitration.[48] Carr cheered Hitler on in his demolition unilaterally of the peace settlement of Versailles. In both world wars, the Welsh were as belligerent as any and recruited heavily both times. They endorsed a Welsh prime minister (a youthful associate of Henry Richard) who called for 'a knock out blow' and 'unconditional surrender'. There was a brief flourish of Richard's legacy in the 1923 general election when the Christian Pacifist, George Maitland Lloyd Davies, who had spent time in Wormwood Scrubs and Winston Green prisons as a conscientious objector during the war, was elected MP for the University of Wales.[49] But this was a strictly temporary phenomenon. Davies upset some of his supporters by unexpectedly taking the Labour whip and lost his seat in 1924 to Ernest Evans, one of Lloyd George's former (male) private secretaries.

Yet despite all this, and the warlike episodes that have chequered the history of the post-war world in Korea, Vietnam, the Middle East and many other places, the issues ventilated by Henry Richard retain their validity. Richard would have surely approved of those in Britain in 2003 who protested against the invasion of Iraq as he protested against that of Egypt. He would have joined them in deploring the by-passing of the

United Nations, and war being planned in order to impose 'regime change' far away without the sanction of the international community. He would have campaigned against war in Afghanistan in 2010 as he did even in 1880 when the British army was commanded by the Welshman Lord Roberts. Gladstone's response to Richard in the Commons over Egypt is paralleled by the 'liberal interventionism' governing Tony Blair's responses over Iraq and Afghanistan. The same questions arise over the status of an international organisation and the nature of its authority.

Richard's approach was essentially one of pure and simple pacifism. That has had no impact since his death any more than Gandhi's doctrine of non-violent resistance was decisive in winning India its independence. George Lansbury's Christian appeals in the 1930s to both Hitler and Mussolini to desist from force now appear tragic and pathetic. But Henry Richard's call for international arbitration is still far from redundant. The Permanent Court of International Justice set up under the League of Nations in 1922 gave way to the more authoritative International Court of Justice, also at the Hague, in 1946. There was also the International Criminal Court set up in the 1990s. The World Court has not been very active, since it hears only two or three cases a year. In key cases it has had much difficulty in making its decisions effective, notably when it vainly ordered the Israel government to destroy the wall it had created in Palestine in 2004. The Criminal Court has been undermined by some of the great powers, including the United States and China. Even so, the writings of authorities such as Philippe Sands and Lord Bingham have served to show that, especially since the Pinochet case in the 1990s, international law is now a more coherent entity, and that the United Nations is a more credible instrument in enforcing it. Bingham has even seen the Iraq invasion as leading to aggressor nations being more readily 'arraigned at the bar of world opinion, and judged unfavourably, with resulting damage to their standing and influence'.[50] Compared with Henry Richard's day, it is perhaps less of a lawless world.

One of Richard's practical themes still is very attainable. He called for parliamentary sanction to be required both for conducting treaties and for going to war. The Brown government did respond and seemed prepared to advocate what would have been a clear diminution of the royal (i.e. the prime ministerial) prerogative. Its Constitutional Renewal Act passed just before the general election in April 2010 would have pleased Henry Richard in one respect, since it did require parliamentary sanction for treaties to be approved. This met an old demand, not only from Richard's generation but from those in the Union of Democratic Control in 1914 who opposed 'secret treaties'. The old Ponsonby Rule dating from MacDonald's first government in 1924 were recognised as inadequate. However, the previous draft bill of 2008 had also included a proposal that the war-making power be determined by affirmative resolution of parliament. The Joint Select Committee, on which I sat, decided by one vote in private session not to support a statutory sanction.[51] Many problems remain in resolving the war-making power – the precise meaning of the term 'war', the problem of 'mission creep' (as demonstrated in Afghanistan since 2001), the problem of revealing the legal justification and the role of the Attorney-General, the government's source of supposedly independent legal authority who is himself or herself a member of that government. All this means that Richard's agenda is still very relevant. He would have been as surprised as others were that the Royal Air Force should be flattening Baghdad or Basra in the name of a wholly innocent resident of Windsor. The Commons' narrow rejection of an armed assault on Syria in August 2013 would have delighted him, of course. But that demonstration of independence, especially by Conservative backbenchers such as David Davies, was the fortuitous product of political accident not of the unambiguous rule of law.

Henry Richard's crusades, then, limited or perhaps confused as some of them may have been, were certainly not a failure. They retain their validity in a still undemocratic, violent age. Reformers may still regard him as a prophetic figure. They may still honour the red flame of radicalism that inspired him as it has inspired internationalists and idealists in later generations. The apostle of peace may lie a-mouldering in the Abney Park cemetery,[52] but his truths perhaps go marching on.

Notes

1 *The Personal papers of Lord Rendel* (London, 1931), pp. 304–5.
2 Matthew Cragoe, *Culture, Politics and National Identity in Wales, 1832–1886* (Oxford, 2004). For a helpful reference to the Richard Papers, see J. Graham Jones in NLW Political Archive, *Newsletter*, 5 (Spring 1988). The most recent biographical works are Gwyn Griffiths, *Henry Richard: Apostle of Peace and Welsh Patriot* (London, 2012), and a translation, *Henry Richard: Heddychwr a Gwladgarwr* (Caerdydd, 2013).
3 See Kenneth O. Morgan, 'Lincoln and Wales', in Richard Carwardine and Jay Sexton (eds), *The Global Lincoln* (New York 2010).
4 *Labour Leader*, 13 October, 1900; Kenneth O. Morgan, 'The Merthyr of Keir Hardie', in Glanmor Williams (ed.), *Merthyr Politics: The Making of a Working-class Tradition* (Cardiff, 1966), p. 80; and Kenneth O. Morgan, *Keir Hardie, Radical and Socialist* (London, 1975), pp. 116–17.
5 C. S. Miall, *Henry Richard MP* (London, 1889), pp. 17–18.
6 D. J. V. Jones, *Crime in Nineteenth-Century Wales* (Cardiff, 1992), p. 45.
7 Ieuan Gwynedd Jones, 'The Election of 1868 in Merthyr Tydfil', in *Explorations and Explanations* (Llandysul, 1981), p. 201. This is much the best analysis of the 1868 election in Merthyr.
8 Kenneth O. Morgan, *Wales in British Politics 1868–1922* (Cardiff, 1963), p. 25.
9 Henry Richard to Thomas Gee, 17 August 1869 (NLW, Thomas Gee papers, 8308D, 297); 'Gohebydd' (John Griffith) to Gee, 9 August, 11 August 1869 (NLW, Thomas Gee papers, 8310D, 506, 507).
10 'Gohebydd' to Gee, 11 August 1869 (NLW, Thomas Gee papers, 8310D, 507). In fact, Sartoris did lose his Carmarthenshire seat at the 1874 general election.
11 *Parl. Deb.*, 3rd ser., CCI, 1295.
12 *Parl. Deb.*, 3rd ser., CCXVII, 73 (8 July 1873).
13 J. Carvell Williams to Thomas Gee, 25 September 1869 (NLW, Thomas Gee papers, 8311D. 583), citing Henry Richard's view. Williams was secretary of the Liberation Society. Also George Osborne Morgan to Richard, 20 August 1869 (NLW, Richard Papers, 5505C).
14 Sidney Buxton to Henry Richard, ?17 January (NLW, Richard Papers, 5503C); George Osborne Morgan to Richard, 20 August 1869 (NLW, Richard Papers, 5505C).
15 *Parl. Deb.*, 3rd ser., CCCIII, 305 ff. (9 March 1886).
16 Minutes of the Liberation Society, 12 September 1881 (Swansea University Library).
17 Henry Richard to Gladstone, 8 March 1870 (BL, Gladstone papers, Add. MSS 44424, ff. 226–30). Richard pressed the case of John Griffiths, rector of Neath, a Liberal. Dean H. T. Edwards to Richard, 6 March 1879 (NLW, Richard papers, 5503B).

[18] Lord Richard Grosvenor to Richard, 17 November 1880 (NLW, Richard papers, 5504C).

[19] Lord Aberdare to Richard, 22 March 1880 (NLW, Richard papers, 5503C).

[20] Speech at Mold National Eisteddfod, *The Times*, 20 August 1873.

[21] Revd R. W. Dale to Richard, 20 July 1886 (NLW, Richard Papers, 5503C).

[22] *Parl. Deb.*, 3rd ser., CCIX, 1664–6 (8 March 1872), and *Parl. Deb.*, 3rd ser., CCXX, 535 (26 June 1874). Also, see T. R. Roberts ('Asaph'), 'Welsh-speaking Judges', *Young Wales* (January 1900), 18–21.

[23] *Letters on the Social and Political Condition of the Principality of Wales* (London, 1867), p. 80; *Parl. Deb.*, 3rd ser., CXCVII, 1294ff. (6 July 1869), where the term 'feudalism' appears.

[24] *Aberdare Times*, 14 November 1868.

[25] *Parl. Deb.*, 3rd ser., CXCVII, 1294ff.

[26] Cragoe, *Culture, Politics and National Identity in Wales*, pp. 166–7.

[27] Michael Daniel Jones to Richard, 13 April 1869 (NLW, Richard papers, 5504C).

[28] Morgan, *Wales in British Politics*, p. 38.

[29] David Lloyd George, *Better Times* (London, 1910), p. 296.

[30] Jones, 'The Election of 1868 in Merthyr Tydfil', pp. 206–12.

[31] Speech on second reading, *Parl. Deb.*, 3rd ser., CC, 269, and amendment in Committee, 20 June 1870. He urged that the state confine itself to providing only literary and scientific education, with even the Bible excluded from state schools. See also Revd R. W. Dale to Revd J. B. Paton, June 1870, in A. W. W. Dale, *The Life of R. W. Dale* (London, 1905), pp. 278–80.

[32] Revd John Thomas to Richard, 9 August 1886 (NLW, Richard Papers, 5505C).

[33] e.g. in his entry by Matthew Cragoe in the *Oxford Dictionary of National Biography*.

[34] Minutes of Richard's interview with Gladstone, 28 May 1870 (NLW Richard Papers, 5509C).

[35] Gladstone to Richard, 14 April 1871 (NLW Richard Papers, 5504B).

[36] *Report of the Committee appointed to inquire into the condition of Intermediate and Higher Education in Wales* (C.3047, 1881).

[37] A. J. Mundella to Richard, 17 March 1884 (NLW, Richard Papers, 5505C).

[38] E. L. Ellis, *The University College of Wales, Aberystwyth, 1872–1972* (Cardiff, 1972), p. 83.

[39] Cf. *Third Report of the Report of the Commissioners appointed to inquire into the Elementary Education Acts* (C 5158).

[40] Richard to Gee, 1 November 1886 (NLW, Gee Papers, 8308C, 304).

[41] Goronwy J. Jones, *Wales and the Quest for Peace* (Cardiff, 1969), pp. 81–2.

[42] *Parl. Deb.*, 3rd ser., CCVII, 52ff. (8 July 1873).

[43] *Parl. Deb.*, 3rd ser. (15 June 1880).

[44] *Parl. Deb.*, 3rd ser., CCCIII, 1395 (19 March 1886).

[45] See Morgan, 'The Global Lincoln'.

[46] Morgan, *Wales in British Politics*, pp. 255–9, and entry on E. T. John in the *Oxford Dictionary of National Biography*.

[47] Theodore Roosevelt, *An Autobiography* (New York, 1913), pp. 575ff. Good accounts of Roosevelt's attitude appear in John Milton Cooper, *The Warrior and the Priest: Woodrow Wilson and Theodore Roosevelt* (Harvard, 1983), and James Chace, *1912* (New York, 2005). Roosevelt acquired his reputation as a man of peace through his mediation efforts at the Treaty of Portsmouth to wind up the Russo-Japanese war in 1905 and taking part in the Algeciras conference during the Moroccan crisis of 1906.

[48] See Kenneth O. Morgan, 'Alfred Zimmern's Brave New World: Liberalism and the League in 1919 and after', below, pp. 175ff.

[49] Kenneth O. Morgan, 'Peace Movements in Wales, 1899–1945', in *Modern Wales, Politics, Places and People* (Cardiff, 1995), pp. 98, 103.

[50] Tom Bingham, *The Rule of Law* (London, 2010), p. 129; Philippe Sands, *Lawless World* (London, 2005), *passim*.

[51] The present author voted in the minority on this motion put forward by Martin Linton MP.

[52] A bicentennial commemoration was held at Abney Park cemetery on 2 April 2012, addressed by Monsignor Bruce Kent, Diane Abbott MP and the present writer.

5

Lloyd George as a Parliamentarian

In recalling the momentous passage of the Parliament Act over a hundred years ago, and in celebrating the influence and authority of parliament over our national life, no-one in the twentieth century illustrates that more emphatically than Lloyd George, 'the little Welsh attorney', whose epoch-making People's Budget brought the Parliament Act into being in the first place. The seventeen-year-old trainee solicitor first set eyes on parliament in November 1880 on his first visit to London. He gave it a somewhat mixed review. 'Grand buildings outside but they are crabbed, small and suffocating', especially the House of Commons. But, significantly, he went on, 'I will not say that I eyed the assembly in a spirit similar to that in which William the Conqueror eyed England on his visit to Edward the Confessor, the region of his future domain.'[1] The young man was already thinking in terms of conquest of that great institution, 'the great assize of the people', and over the next half century that is manifestly what he achieved.

He was, of course, a uniquely controversial parliamentarian, both in his public career and his private life, and it was a long while before parliament gave him his due. Back in the 1930s, the French put up a statue of Lloyd George's wartime ally Georges Clemenceau in the Champs Élysées. He stands tall there with his cape, his cane and his black leather boots, and was universally hailed as *Père la Victoire*.[2] It was not until

November 2007 that Lloyd George's appropriately dynamic statue was unveiled in Parliament Square by Prince Charles. He was the first radical to feature there, alongside five Conservative prime ministers and a conservative king. I note that Winston Churchill's statue there was decorated by anti-capitalist demonstrators and latterly some protesting student demonstrators. It is agreeable to think that Lloyd George's statue may some time be adorned by the pheasant-shooting wing of the Countryside Alliance.

He was a parliamentarian almost from birth. At the age of five, he was carried on the shoulders of his Uncle Lloyd to hail the great Liberal victory in Caernarfonshire in the general election of 1868. He was an intensely political young schoolboy at Llanystumdwy National school, where he led a strike of his schoolfellows to prevent them reciting the Anglican Creed before the headmaster. He began professional life as a country solicitor in Porthmadoc, an ideal platform for engaging in assault on the Anglican 'Unholy Trinity' of the Bishop, the Brewer and the Squire, who dominated the rural scene in nonconformist Wales. His boyhood hero was the recently assassinated Abraham Lincoln – indeed the image of another country lawyer who went on from log cabin to become president of the United States was made much of by his admirers. *From Village Green to Downing Street* was the evocative title of one early biography.[3] He was thought of as a possible Liberal candidate for Merioneth in the 1885 election when he was a mere twenty-two; he entered the Commons in 1890 when he was twenty-seven. His victory in Caernarfon Boroughs was actually a Liberal gain. Down to 1906 he conducted a bold and brilliant start to his parliamentary career in a highly marginal constituency. The Anglican influence in the cathedral city of Bangor was always a looming threat.

From the start of his time in the Commons, he emerged as a speaker of extraordinary power and charisma. His maiden speech on 13 June 1890, on the congenial topic of temperance and the prospect of compensation for publicans, included bold satire of two parliamentary giants, Joseph Chamberlain and Randolph Churchill (the latter something of a hero for the young Lloyd George) whom he compared to two contortionists who set their faces in one direction and their heads in the opposite.

He told his young wife back in Caernarfonshire, 'There is no doubt I scored a success and a great one' – no false modesty about Ll.G. He also told his wife that he would take time in making a second speech to give it the more impact.[4] Soon he was established as one of the most admired and feared members of the House.

It is worth examining why his speeches were so effective. Clearly there was the influence of the nonconformist pulpit – the lyrical language (in Welsh quite as much as in English), the compelling rhythm, the Biblical imagery and the use of homely metaphor (such as, famously, his reference to picking up firewood in greater abundance after stormy weather). But he was also moved by another late-Victorian institution – the music hall. He also made much use of humour, not commonly a feature of nonconformist chapel sermons, especially in Wales. The prime minister of Great Britain reflected something of the style of George Robey, the Prime Minister of Mirth. Lloyd George was always infinitely adaptable as an orator. He could move easily, effortlessly, from the slapstick to the sublime, from partisan knockabout to supra-party moral consensus.

There were great figures in the Commons when he entered it in 1890. He was most impressed by the titanic personality of Gladstone – 'Head and shoulders above anyone else I have ever seen in the House of Commons.'[5] Lloyd George marvelled at his power of 'gesture, language, fire and, latterly, wit', also the transfixing power of the Grand Old Man's 'terrible eye'.[6] His one criticism was that, at times, Gladstone would go on too long, seldom something for which Lloyd George himself could be criticised.

Lloyd George's speaking style, in the Commons and elsewhere, depended heavily on communion with his audience. He was always subtly responsive to his listeners, in parliamentary debate and in meeting deputations as a minister. He was also outstanding at listening to others. In the famous phrase, he could charm a bird off a bough. He loved heckling and, like his countryman, Aneurin Bevan, fed off it richly. He could be exceptionally devastating and ruthless in personal attack. On the platform he would describe Herbert, Viscount Gladstone, as 'the finest living embodiment of the Liberal principle that talent was not hereditary'.[7] Hereditary peers were elevated on the 'principle of the first of the litter – you would not choose a spaniel on those principles'. The House of Lords was dismissed as 'five hundred ordinary men, chosen at random from amongst the unemployed'.[8] He could also be hugely effective in turning defence into attack, notably in the Maurice Debate of May 1918 when he destroyed the motion of censure timidly moved by Asquith. He could also be uniquely sensitive in winning over the House. During the debate on the Marconi case in 1912, when he was accused of corruption by making money through investing in a company contracted to the British government, he delivered an extraordinary passionate plea of his innocence and honesty. Mrs Lucy Masterman, the wife of his colleague Charles Masterman, wrote in her diary of this debate, 'The whole House was soon crying. Winston had two large tears rolling down his face. Rufus [Isaacs] was sitting with his head bent so that no one could see his face. Charlie [Masterman] was crying. The PM [Asquith] was crying.' A Liberal backbencher 'boo-hooed in a very vocal manner.[9] Another important parliamentary quality of his on occasion was generosity. Thus when he was fiercely attacked by the young Nye Bevan over the Coal Mines Bill in 1930 – 'better dearer coal than cheaper colliers' – Lloyd George responded with much grace, perhaps mindful of his own onslaughts on the great Joe Chamberlain. An observer wrote that he was 'confronted with the ghost of his own angry youth'.[10]

Compared with Winston Churchill, Lloyd George was far more spontaneous a speaker. Churchill prepared his speeches with intense care, and largely read from them (he broke down in 1904 as a young MP when he departed from the script). Lloyd George spoke to his listeners; Churchill spoke to, and for, history. Lloyd George's major speeches usually had two kinds of material. He carefully had typed out the main themes, including key phrases (e.g. 'cowardly surrender').[11] Then he would use pencil notes as well, which gave him the maximum of flexibility in debate. His People's Budget speech in April 1909 was backed up by a jumble of scarcely coherent or legible pencilled statistics to illustrate the details of land taxation and valuation.[12] His spontaneity could be immensely effective (as in the 1940 Norway debate speech, which helped to bring down Neville Chamberlain) but it could also be dangerous (as with Michael Foot) if he departed from his text without due care. One such instance was his speech at Bristol in the 'coupon' general election in December 1918, when he responded to the encouragement of his audience with references to Germany 'paying to the very last penny', and rashly mentioned a specific sum of damages (£24 million).[13] If Lloyd George's spontaneity could give hostages to fortune, the care which Churchill took in his speeches could be immensely powerful and indeed moving. Thus, in late March 1945, when Churchill was almost overwhelmed with critical political issues after the Yalta conference as the war came to an end, he took a remarkable amount of time in composing a personal tribute to his old comrade in arms over forty years – 'the greatest Welshman produced by that unconquerable race since the days of the Tudors'.[14]

Another prime minister has given us the greatest insight into the impact of Lloyd George's speeches on the House. Harold Macmillan was a huge admirer. 'The wonderful head, the great mane of white hair ... the expressive features, changing rapidly from fierce anger to that enchanting smile, not confined to the mouth but spreading to his cheeks and eyes: above all, the beautiful hands, an actor's or an artist's hands, by the smallest movement of which he would make you see the picture he was trying to paint.' Lloyd George gave Macmillan, as a young backbencher, advice in his private office on how to speak in the House, how to vary his pace and his pitch. He taught him to 'use his arms, not wrists, not hands, not ineffective posturing but the whole of the arms and shoulders, even the back, in a total integration of body into words.' Macmillan once sat next to me at lunch in Oxford and told me that Lloyd George advised him always to let the gesture follow the words, as in 'There is the man who has betrayed his country' – pointing at the victim immediately after, rather than during, these comments. He once criticised one of Macmillan's early speeches. It was not, said Lloyd George a speech at all but a contribution to an economic journal: 'You made 25 points all leading on to one another. That's not the way to speak. You want to make one point, if you are a backbencher, two if you are a Minister, possibly three, but better still two . . . The art of speaking is to leave on the audience a clear picture of what it is you want.'[15] Lloyd George was almost always true to his word.

The supreme communicator in politics of his day, only one form of communication defeated him, and that in old age. He was never at home with radio broadcasting. With no human audience visible in front of him, he could not blossom. His daughter, Megan, tried to get him to be at ease in BBC studios – but 'there was nothing'. The giant of platform, pulpit and parliament was suddenly anonymous, almost tongue-tied.

At every stage of his fifty-four years in the Commons, he was a powerful influence in the House. As a backbencher between 1890 and 1905, he often focused on the local affairs of Wales, frequently in speeches that were satirical and somewhat lightweight. He made a national impact for the first time with his passionate attacks on his old hero, Joseph Chamberlain, during the South African War – 'this electro-plated Rome and its tin Caesar'. He accused Chamberlain, with powerful effect, of profiteering personally from war contracts with the army.[16] But he could also strike a higher note, as when he passed on to his leader, Campbell-Bannerman, Emily Hobhouse's first-hand verdict on the atrocities inflicted on Boer women and children in the British concentration camps on the Veldt – 'methods of barbarism', three words that changed the culture of Edwardian politics. During the debates after the 1902 Education Act, he could move on from nonconformist 'revolt' against an Act which aided Anglican schools to an appeal to transcend religious sectarianism where education was concerned.[17]

As a government minister between 1905 and 1916, he would be brilliantly effective in presenting highly complex proposals. As it happened, perhaps his most important statement was just about his worst. His People's Budget speech on 29 April 1909 saw him almost break down through sheer strain and fatigue. The House took a break to let him recover his stamina.[18] But he did recover and ended with a powerful peroration about the government's plans to make poverty in Britain as removed as the wolves which once infested its forests. That summer, he handled the difficult committee stage with courtesy, charm and humour. He was also excellent in conducting the committee stage of the National Insurance Bill in 1911. Some jaundiced critics wondered whether he had really understood the arcane minutiae of his own bill. In debate in the House Lloyd George showed emphatically that he had.

A quite different kind of speech was an astonishing polemic in the second reading debate on the Welsh Disestablishment Bill in April 1912. The Duke of Devonshire had claimed that the disendowment of the Welsh Church was robbery of God. Lloyd George (perhaps helped in his researches by a strong Liberal, A. F. Pollard, a distinguished historian of the Tudors and grandfather of the celebrated psephologist, David Butler) responded that the fortunes of the Duke, like those of many other land-owners such as the Cecils, were 'laid deep in sacrilege' during the era of the Reformation which saw the dissolution of the monasteries.

'They robbed the Church. They robbed the monasteries. They robbed the altars. They robbed the almshouses. They robbed the poor. They robbed the dead. Then they come here when we are trying . . . to recover some of this pillaged property for the poor to whom it was originally given, with hands dripping with the fat of sacrilege, to accuse us of robbery of God.'[19] He was strongly backed up by G. K. Chesterton who countered F. E. Smith's claim that the bill would offend the souls of Christian people everywhere with the satirical poem 'Anti-Christ', and its memorable finale, 'Chuck it, Smith!'

As Prime Minister between 1916 and 1922, Lloyd George's survival in the House depended on his rhetorical skills. He was a prime minister without a party, and, unlike Churchill in 1940–5, had no assured majority in the House. In the peacetime coalition of 1918–22, he depended solely on the goodwill of the dominant Conservative (or Unionist) Party. Much depended on the Prime Minister's oratorical command, his ability to play on the emotions and at times to strike a tone of high patriotic ideal-ism. Thus in the Maurice Debate, on 9 May 1918, he destroyed Asquith's feeble case, and the under-cover manoeuvring of the military high com-mand with a devastating performance.[20] General Maurice had claimed that the government had not been telling the truth about the comparative number of British troops at the front in 1917 and 1918, and the reasons for the extension of the British line on the western front. Lloyd George showed that in fact his figures came from Maurice's department, the DMO, at the War Office, and that he had never challenged them there or at Cabinet meetings. He also underlined the inconsistency of Maurice acting with such disloyalty and insubordination while claiming to try to be reassuring morale in the armed forces. He ended on a high patriotic note. He appealed 'on behalf of our common country' that 'there should be an end of this sniping'.[21] While historians have debated the statistical evidence on these matters at length subsequently, at the time Lloyd George enjoyed a complete triumph. His enemies, political and military, were annihilated.

Lloyd George exerted his unique personal authority again in April 1919 when he confronted newspaper and other critics who claimed he was being too soft on the defeated Germans in the Paris peace conference. He delivered a slashing attack on Lord Northcliffe, owner of *The Times*.[22] He referred to his 'disease of vanity', tapping his head significantly as he did so. Northcliffe was sowing dissension among the Allies at Paris. 'Not even that kind of disease is a justification for so black a crime against humanity.' Northcliffe was derided and ridiculed. Later on in 1922, when Northcliffe was dead from a mysterious blood infection, Lloyd George could have achieved a kind of posthumous revenge by perhaps becoming owner or even editor of *The Times* himself.[23]

Finally, as elder statesman, from his downfall as prime minister in October 1922, he remained a powerful force in debate. He was very much a front-line player whose return to government was widely canvassed, down to the general election of 1935, when he was seventy-two. In the 1920s he spoke a good deal on economic policy and measures to combat economic depression and mass unemployment. In the 1930s, he lent his matchless prestige to debates on international affairs. He often struck an ambiguous note, perhaps a dangerous one, notably with his remarkable enthusiasm for Hitler after his visit to Berchtesgaden in August 1936. This was by far the most appalling misjudgement of his career.

Conversely, his abiding power as a senior politician was shown in the remarkable impact of his speech of 18 June 1936, attacking the government for its failure to impose sanctions on Italy after the invasion of Abyssinia. He launched a ferocious assault on the government, in what Baldwin called 'an extraordinarily brilliant speech'. He made merciless use of quotations from government ministers. Baldwin had spoken of Britain 'standing like a rock in the waves'. Lloyd George observed that 'the rock has turned out to be driftwood'. The government he compared to an aeroplane popularly known as 'the flying flea'. Neville Chamberlain had spoken of avoiding 'a cowardly surrender'. 'Tonight', declared Lloyd George, 'we have had the cowardly surrender and there [pointing at the government front bench] are the cowards.'[24]

Frances Stevenson, his private secretary, wrote that the government Front Bench 'was literally cowed before his onslaught'. A young Tory MP told Churchill that he had never heard anything like it in the House. 'Young man', replied Churchill with rare generosity of spirit, 'you have been listening to one of the greatest Parliamentary performances of all time.'[25]

There was an even later oratorical triumph, in the Norway debate on 8 May 1940, Lloyd George's last great speech in the House. This was very different, almost unplanned. He had not thought of speaking but was persuaded to do so by Clement Davies, Robert Boothby and others. He spoke largely off the cuff from rough notes only, which added to the powerful effect on his Commons audience. He ended with a tremendous finale. The prime minister had asked for sacrifice. He should set an example himself because he could make no greater contribution to victory in the war than to sacrifice the seals of office.[26] Chamberlain resigned following a major Conservative backbench revolt. Thus the colossus of the First World War helped pave the way for the elevation of the colossus of the Second.

Beyond Lloyd George's personal career, his wider impact on his country and his world was immense – Churchill, for instance, was identified with a dying world, that of the later Victorian empire and a fading class system; Lloyd George more emphatically looked to the future.

As regards the *constitution*, Lloyd George and Asquith, that great partnership, between them transformed relations between the Commons and the Lords for ever. The 1911 Parliament Act tilted power decisively to the elected house. If the statesman's craft of getting the Act through came from Asquith, it was Lloyd George's 1909 Budget which brought matters to the proof. It was the powers of the Lords that always concerned Lloyd George, not its composition. He demonstrated this as prime minister with his mass creation of so many peers, many of them capitalists of dubious origin. He told J. C. C. Davidson that it was better to sell titles than to sell policies, as happened in politics in America. 'It keeps politics far cleaner than any other method of raising funds'.[27]

Constitutionally, his premiership of 1916–22 was a massive landmark. It was the first clear instance of a move towards a presidential type of premiership. Richard Crossman and John Mackintosh were later to see his regime as the first indication of prime ministerial government replacing classical Cabinet government. He set up the Cabinet Office to enable the Prime Minister to control government business and ensure, through his powerful secretaries, Maurice Hankey and Thomas Jones, that decisions were taken and followed up. He also had his own cadre of unelected special advisers, notably the 'garden suburb', his own personal secretariat headed by Philip Kerr who worked in huts set up in the garden of 10 Downing Street. He absented himself from parliament for long periods at a time, and was satirised for it by Bernard Partridge in *Punch* cartoons. The Cabinet met erratically and was often by-passed by carefully chosen 'conferences of ministers'. On one occasion in 1921, the British Cabinet met, not in London, not even in England, but in Inverness town hall, to accommodate the prime minister who was having a holiday in the Highlands.[28] His maverick style was strictly personal, heterodox, unpredictable. He negotiated industrial relations with trade unionists like Jimmy Thomas over a Welsh nonconformist's equivalent of beer and sandwiches at No. 10. He held private conclave with wealthy capitalists about party political funding. He gave confidential briefings to press editors and journalists from home and overseas, and was freely on view for the paparazzi: with his Inverness cloak, his long mane and his delicate feet, he was the most media-conscious politician of his day. He largely conducted foreign policy himself via summit diplomacy: he barely concealed his contempt for the official Foreign Secretary, Lord Curzon. Lloyd George, in short, was first exponent of sofa government, Tony Blair *avant la lettre*.

Two other constitutional changes stand out. First, Lloyd George's government transformed the political status of women. In his 1918 Reform Act, women of thirty and over got the vote. In 1919, Lady Astor became the first female MP. This was appropriate. Lloyd George, unlike

Asquith and Churchill, was always a supporter of women's suffrage, even if his pre-war efforts, like those of most men, proved disappointing to the suffragettes.

Second, Lloyd George ensured that Ireland was removed from centre stage in British politics after the Free State Act of January 1922. After a terribly dark period of bloody retaliation in the era of 'Black and Tans', Lloyd George made the great diplomatic breakthrough with the Sinn Féin leaders with the creation of a self-governed, if partitioned, Ireland. It owed everything to the prime minister's Celtic guile – he pointed out to de Valera that neither the Welsh nor the Irish languages had a word for 'republic', which he felt to be significant.[29] He created a settlement that endures, for good or ill, to the present day. No longer would there be an Irish Nationalist party which might control the balance of power in the House. He had succeeded where Pitt, Peel and Gladstone all failed in finding a solution to the Irish impasse that, if highly controversial, nevertheless stood the test of time. A different vision of the union of the United Kingdom would henceforth emerge. This was appropriate since Lloyd George in his Cymru Fydd days in the 1890s had been an early proponent of devolution. What took place in 1999 in Scotland and Wales was partly his legacy.

He also had a massive impact on the *party system*. Here was a highly paradoxical figure – a vehement partisan who aroused strong emotions amongst friends and foes, yet was also the great champion of coalitions. Through his career, he showed a disposition to work with political opponents in search of higher objectives – as he did back in Wales as early as 1895 over possible Welsh home rule.[30] In 1910, he astonished the political world at a time of high political emotions over the Budget and the Parliament Bill by proposing to Balfour and some Conservative leaders that there should be a coalition to by-pass what he called 'uncontroversial' issues like free trade and Welsh disestablishment in pursuit of the higher objectives of national defence and social reform.

As prime minister, of course, he headed a coalition himself. After the successful outcome of his alliance with the Conservatives during the war, he put forward in 1919–20 the idea of a kind of government of national unity on the lines of the 'unity of command' achieved during the war. His heroes were men who broke with their own parties – Joseph Chamberlain over Irish home rule, Theodore Roosevelt who formed his breakaway Progressive Party under the banner of the New Nationalism in 1912.

In fact, the outcome of his coalitions with the Conservatives in wartime and in peace was a very mixed one. His coalition of 1918 (based on the 'notorious coupon' of electoral co-operation) destroyed the Liberals as a party of government when they split into two. If anything, it also created the Labour Party as the clear voice of progressive opinion: in 1918, the party wisely followed Bernard Shaw's advice – 'Go back to Lloyd George and say nothing doing.' Arguably, he had laid the basis for the Labour Party becoming some day a party of government with his Treasury Agreement with the trade unions in 1915, as earlier with his use of unions as agencies for national health insurance in 1911. The later Lib-Con coalition of 1931 (which Lloyd George vehemently opposed) destroyed the Liberals not just as a party of government, but as a party of opposition as well when they split into three, the National Liberals under Sir John Simon in effect becoming indistinguishable from the Tories. What rewards or calamities the coalition of 2010 will visit upon the heirs of the old Liberal Party remains to be seen. After the university tuition fees imbroglio, the omens do not look too promising.

For *domestic British politics*, Lloyd George's impact was truly remarkable. He was indeed the 'dynamic force' of which Baldwin spoke apprehensively at the Carlton Club meeting of 1922. He was always concerned with ideas and long-term policy objectives. His associates were not just shady people who traded titles or armaments, but distinguished intellectuals like Charles Masterman, Seebohm Rowntree, William Beveridge, the great historian H. A. L. Fisher, the economists of the Liberal Summer School in the 1920s and, of course, Maynard Keynes, who famously declared, 'I oppose Mr Lloyd George when he is wrong, and support him when he is right.'[31] Much of the time, the road that Lloyd George trod was the high road.

Lloyd George was thus a foremost architect of the welfare state. His National Insurance Act of 1911, following his Old Age Pensions of 1908, created the base for future social policy down to the Beveridge report and the National Health Service. It created a new vision of the enabling state and of social citizenship. It is surely Britain's great progressive contribution to modern civilisation, and Lloyd George was its founding father.

His budget of 1909 and (lesser regarded) that of 1914 laid down new principles of progressive, redistributive, graduated taxation which shaped the policy of all political parties down to the 1980s. With higher estate duties, a new super-tax and social novelties such as child allowances, it provided a powerful free trade solution for financing social welfare. The tariff reformers had argued that 'the foreigner will pay'; Lloyd George's riposte was 'the rich will pay'. Ironically the least successful part of his taxes were the controversial land duties which yielded almost nothing and were repealed, embarrassingly, in 1920 when Lloyd George was prime minister.

The post-war coalition of 1918–22 was also far from negligible in social policy. It began publicly subsidised housing policies in the Addison Act, it set up a national framework for free state education in the Fisher Act, it revised and extended the system of unemployment insurance, fortunately in view of the mass unemployment to follow, and it created a pioneering Ministry of Health. Until extinguished by economic depression in the latter part of 1920, it was perhaps the last hurrah of the pre-war New Liberalism.

In opposition in the 1920s, he promoted far-sighted new policies for economic revival and pump-priming policies to combat unemployment. In the Yellow Book and the Orange Book, he was a Keynesian before Keynes: after all, the *General Theory* was not published until 1936, whereas Lloyd George's creative mind was at work on these issues a decade earlier. The spectre of the National Debt never terrified him and he condemned the dismal deflation of the National government. Today, many economists like Lord Skidelsky seem to believe after the credit crunch that the programmes of public investment to sustain employment pioneered by Lloyd George eighty years ago still provide the key to long-term, sustainable economic recovery.

Finally, there is his legacy in *international politics*. He was very much a maker of our world. He had great responsibility for the peace settlement of 1919–22. There has been massive criticism of how the Versailles treaty came about, most famously by Keynes: Margaret Macmillan's *Peacemakers* (2001) has cogently argued the opposite case and seen the view that Versailles led inexorably to another war as simplistic. Of course, there were immense problems resulting from the settlement in the Middle East and the colonial restructuring that followed the end of the old Ottoman Empire. But the post-imperial Europe of Versailles and the later treaties, based on the broad principle of nationality, is still our inheritance. It has, it is true, seen the break-up into lesser states of both Yugoslavia and Czechoslovakia, but in fact Lloyd George had grave doubts about both of them as artificial hybrid creations. Benes of Czechoslovakia was a particular *bête noire*. In any case, alone of the post-war peacemakers, he sought to revise the peace treaties in 1920–2, both with regard to territories and reparations payments, and in time Keynes, his bitterest critic, came to endorse his views.

Our world, therefore, bears Lloyd George's imprint. Every day the newspapers and television bulletins remind us of his legacy. *Si monumentum requiris, circumspice*. Much of it is benign. But far from all. Since the 1960s, British governments have been plagued by three great problem territories – Northern Ireland, Palestine and Iraq. Mr Speaker – they have one thing in common. Like all things wise and wonderful, Lloyd George made them all.

Notes

1. Diary entry of 12 November 1880, quoted in W. R. P. George, *The Making of Lloyd George* (London, 1976), p. 101.
2. See Kenneth O. Morgan, 'The Goat and the Tiger', *Ages of Reform* (London, 2010), pp. 93ff.
3. J. Hugh Edwards and Spencer Leigh Hughes, *From Village Green to Downing Street: Life of the Rt.Hon. D. Lloyd George MP* (London, 1908).
4. David Lloyd George to Margaret Lloyd George, 14 and 19 June 1890, in Kenneth O. Morgan (ed.), *Lloyd George, Family Letters* (Oxford, 1973), pp. 29–30. These papers are in NLW.
5. *Lord Riddell's War Diary* (London, 1933), p. 67 (7 March 1915); *Lord Riddell's Intimate Diary of the Peace Conference and After, 1918–1923* (London, 1933), p. 158 (1 January 1920)

6 For Gladstone's 'terrible eye', see A. J. P. Taylor (ed.), *Lloyd George: A Diary by Frances Stevenson* (London, 1971), p. 306 (17 April 1935).

7 *The Times*, 15 October 1922. Speech at Manchester.

8 *The Times*, 10 October 1909. Speech at Newcastle.

9 Richard Toye, *Lloyd George and Churchill* (London, 2007), p. 97 (quoting Lucy Masterman's diary).

10 Michael Foot, *Aneurin Bevan*, vol. 1 (London, 1962), p. 117.

11 Notes of speeches in Lloyd-George of Dwyfor Papers (Parliamentary Archives, House of Lords), e.g. notes on Abyssinia speech, 18 June 1936 (G 186/5).

12 Lloyd George Papers, C/26/folder 1.

13 *The Times*, 12 December 1918.

14 House of Commons, 28 March 1945.

15 Alistair Horne, *Macmillan*, vol. 1 (Macmillan, 1988), pp. 77–8. Conversation between the present author and the Earl of Stockton, *c*.1970.

16 House of Commons, 8 August 1900.

17 Kenneth O. Morgan, *Wales in British Politics 1868–1922* (Cardiff, 1963), pp. 188ff.

18 House of Commons, 16 May 1912.

19 House of Commons, 9 May 1918.

20 Notes of speech in Lloyd-George Papers, F/235.

21 House of Commons, 16 April 1919.

22 *History of the Times*, part 2, 1921–48 (The Times publishing house, 1952), pp. 685ff.

23 House of Commons, 18 June 1936: notes of speech, Lloyd-George Papers, G/186/5.

24 Taylor, *Lloyd George: A Diary by Frances Stevenson*, p. 324 (20 June 1936).

25 House of Commons, 8 May 1940

26 Memorandum by J. C. C. Davidson, 1927, printed in Robert Rhodes James, *Memoirs of a Conservative* (London, 1969), p. 279.

27 On 7 September 1921, to consider de Valera's latest proposals for Ireland.

28 Keith Middlemas (ed.), *Thomas Jones: Whitehall Diary, III Ireland 1918–1925* (Oxford, 1971), p. 89.

29 See the memorandum on the proposed coalition in 1910, printed in Kenneth O. Morgan, *The Age of Lloyd George* (London, 1971), pp. 150–6.

30 For Lloyd George's views on Theodore Roosevelt, see Lloyd George, *The Truth about the Peace Treaties*, vol. 1 (London, 1938), pp. 231–2. Lloyd George thought Roosevelt was far superior to his great rival Woodrow Wilson in every way.

31 Robert Skidelsky, *John Maynard Keynes*, vol. 2 (London, 1992), p. 249.

6

Liberalism's Flintshire Loyalist: The Political Achievement of John Herbert Lewis

'He had no friends and did not deserve any.' Thus A. J. P. Taylor's dismissive judgement on David Lloyd George.[1] Like several of that historian's famous aphorisms, the effect is more arresting than accurate. The comment echoes a common view, memorably reinforced by J. M. Keynes in his account of the major participants at the Treaty of Versailles, in 1919, that the Welsh premier was but an unprincipled maverick, 'rooted in nothing', using people ruthlessly and callously, then throwing them away in pursuit of his career and his ambitions.[2] Novelists from Arnold Bennett to Joyce Cary have nurtured this view.[3] To adopt the musical tribute to the late Princess Diana, Lloyd George appears at best as simply a candle in the wind. So far as he had close associates, they tended to be hangers-on rather than personal friends, on the pattern of the press lords, 'hard-faced' capitalists and adventurers like 'Bronco Bill' Sutherland, Basil Zaharoff or Maundy Gregory in the darker phases of his peacetime premiership of 1918–22. That people like these did flit in and out of his career at regular intervals cannot be disputed; nor can his casualness with money, principles and loyalties. His career, too, was littered with decent-minded colleagues, Charles Masterman, Christopher Addison, Llewelyn Williams, with whom he quarrelled fatally, breaking off relations with a resounding crash. The picture is all too easily drawn of the casual Welsh freebooter, aggressive, arriviste, contrasted with the assured Balliol values of the Asquithians on the other side.

But there is also a massive element left out in this crude pastiche – the long sequence of honourable, high-principled, intellectually respectable figures who found in Lloyd George a lifelong inspiration and icon – C. P. Scott of the *Manchester Guardian*, the historian H. A. L. Fisher, the pioneering Quaker sociologist, Seebohm Rowntree. And in Wales, there were a whole generation of decent, honest, moralistic Liberals for whom Lloyd George was always a hero throughout all vicissitudes, men like the preacher-poet Elfed, the very embodiment of the folk values of *y werin*. In the political realm, Sir Herbert Lewis, member for first Flint Boroughs and then Flintshire, and finally the University of Wales from 1892 to 1922, junior minister under Asquith and Lloyd George for the last seventeen of those years, devoted servant of Welsh intermediate and higher education, the National Museum and especially the National Library at Aberystwyth, was foremost amongst these. His unbroken attachment to the younger Caernarfonshire Liberal whom he served with total loyalty makes him pre-eminent among the Welsh Lloyd Georgians. With all deference to the late Eirene White, Lewis's creative relationship with his leader makes him probably the most influential Flintshire politician in modern times.[4] He is, therefore, a most suitably eminent Flintshire figure for reassessment.

Herbert Lewis's background was significantly different from that of David Lloyd George's. Born in December 1858 at Mostyn Quay, the Flintshire man was brought up not in a shoemaker's cottage but in an affluent commercial family with strong connections with shipping, including the new steamships. From childhood, his life was punctuated by frequent expensive travels to the sunny climes of the Mediterranean or the Middle East during the winter months. Dr Erasmus correctly remarks that 'there can have been few members of parliament that have travelled more widely'.[5] In 1884–5 he spent a year on a world tour, travelling across the United States, and moving on to Japan, China and India. He also had a far more extensive and privileged education than Lloyd George – Denbigh Grammar School, a period at the University of Montreal in his teenage years, and finally Exeter College, Oxford, where he studied law, though without great distinction. He began training as a solicitor in 1881, first in Chester, then moving on to a more glamorous life in London.

Unlike Lloyd George, his public and private life spoke of sober respectability, as did the dapper suits, wing collars, shiny pointed shoes and trim beard which newspaper cartoons of him featured.[6] He was an earnest Calvinist Methodist, teetotaller and public moralist. His married life was beyond the most puritanical reproach. His first wife, Adelaide ('Ada') Hughes, the daughter of a prominent Wrexham Liberal publisher, was upright and honourable – and also a vigorous Liberal feminist and advocate of women's suffrage, more forcibly so than Lewis himself. When she died, much to Lewis's distress, just before the 1895 general election, he then married in 1897 Ruth, the daughter of the temperance leader W. S. Caine. Compared with Lloyd George, his private life was a model of sobriety and restraint. Nor was he flamboyant as an orator. On the contrary, he himself lamented his lack of rhetorical flair in election meetings,[7] especially in comparison with the meteor from Llanystumdwy already beginning to dominate the Welsh scene. His quiet personality, too, might not have been expected to endear him to Lloyd George on their various jaunts overseas. No-one could accuse him of a sense of humour. In addition, Lewis's diaries reveal him as a persistent hypochondriac, constantly staying indoors to recover from 'chills' and other maladies, great or (usually) small. As late as 1932, Lloyd George spoke to Sylvester and other associates of how Lewis was a lifelong valetudinarian. Years earlier, when speaking at Liverpool, Lloyd George had been told of how the Flintshire man was in bed in Plas Penucha dying of tuberculosis: 'there he was, coddled and muffled up by his wife'.[8] But the wife it was who died, not Herbert. Lewis later survived a serious fall in a quarry in 1925 which broke his spine, but he remained mentally active, even though bedridden. He wrote a letter of farewell to Lloyd George, the latter told Frances Stevenson, but then wrote for the papers and 'received medals of recognition for his work for Wales'.[9] Sylvester observed, 'L.G. always said that Herbert would live to see all his contemporaries die, and write a letter of condolence to their relatives.'[10]

Even so, over thirty years and more, they were good friends and good travelling companions. Lloyd George lived for a time in 1895 in Lewis's flat in Palace Mansions in Addison Road in London. When he needed comfort and companionship in Cannes after the tragic death of his young daughter, Mair, it was his faithful Herbert who travelled there, leaving his own family behind in Flintshire. The transformation of Welsh social and political life in the years following the Reform Act of 1884 and the advent of democratic politics in Wales during Gladstone's heyday, soon drew him and Lloyd George together in the pursuit of the nonconformist and Liberal objectives of the day.[11] Soon he became treasurer of the North Wales Liberal Federation. It is significant, too, that an early private tutor of his was the Revd E. Pan Jones of Cysegr chapel, Rhewl, radical-socialist Independent minister, proto-nationalist and land nationaliser, and the influence stuck. This radical outlook also made him close to that other youthful Welsh leader, Tom Ellis, a man whose Fabian creed of social and national improvement might have made him a more naturally appropriate colleague of Lewis's. Ellis gave Lewis powerful advice on the drafting of his forthcoming election address in October 1891: 'Nationality and Labour are our two main principles, are they not? . . . I think we ought to make clear that, when Disestablishment is settled, Wales will throw itself heart and soul in the Labour movement', not in fact advice to which Lewis's later career showed much response.[12]

For all of them, the advent of local government reform and the political revolution of the county council elections of 1889 was an immense breakthrough. Ellis, an enthusiast for the cantons of Switzerland and the Tyrol, was the advocate of civic populism in parliament, and from platform and pulpit.[13] Lloyd George was too, in a more openly class-conscious fashion, and served on the first Caernarfonshire County Council as 'the boy alderman'. But Lewis was more directly involved than any of them. Elected unopposed as Liberal councillor in the Llanasa district, he became chairman of the first Flintshire County Council, at a meeting in Mold in January 1889 barely at the age of thirty, a testimony to his already powerful local standing. He went on to become chairman of the county Intermediate Education Committee and rapidly built up the new system of 'county schools' in his native county. Intermediate schools at Mold, Rhyl, Holywell, St Asaph and Hawarden resulted. He also worked hard to promote technical education in the county. His achievement here showed both the careful attention to detail on committees that distinguished his later career as a government minister, and also a notable dynamism and capacity for leadership that made Flintshire foremost in getting its new network of secondary education established. He remained Flintshire County Council's chairman until 1893, by which time he was a member of parliament.

It was through his pioneering efforts in local government that he became close to national politicians. He was in close contact with Tom Ellis throughout the parliamentary passage of the Intermediate Education Act in 1889, already being considered as a mature and serious politician whose judgement was valued.[14] He also championed the wider 'nationalist' cause of using the county councils as the basis of a putative Welsh National Council which would propel Welsh Liberalism into a more nationally conscious direction and promote the idea of some kind of devolution or home rule. In this connection, he urged Ellis in 1891, with characteristic insight, 'not to offend the South Wales people. They are touchy in the extreme . . .'.[15] It was this nationalist initiative that particularly chimed in with the Cymru Fydd sentiment of the early 1890s, of which the most vocal champion was David Lloyd George, elected in a dramatic by-election for Caernarfon Boroughs. By 1892, it was clear that Lewis was among the closest allies of the radical group of young Welsh Liberals who emerged as the new political élite of the late years of the century – Lloyd George and Ellis, of course, D. A. Thomas, Sam Evans, Llewelyn Williams, Ellis Griffith, William Jones, the most inspired generation of Welsh political leaders until the rise of Bevan, Griffiths and the products of the Central Labour College after 1918. Herbert Lewis, always correct, modest, uncharismatic, was their enthusiastic and courageous lieutenant. Indeed, of all the younger Welsh Liberal MPs, he was perhaps the most consistent nationalist and devolutionist of them all.

His links with Lloyd George assumed a wholly new dimension when he was elected to parliament for the marginal constituency of Flint Boroughs. It consisted of eight small towns with a combined population of 23,251, of which Flint, Mold, Holywell and St Asaph were the most significant, but which also included Lewis's own Caerwys. The constituency's electorate in 1892 was a mere 3,710, a thousand fewer even than

Caernarfon Boroughs. Anglicised and with some landlord and Church influence, balanced to a degree by nonconformist strength in rural areas and some miners and quarrymen at Holywell and Mold, it was not a wholly secure seat for Lewis and his eventual move to the county seat from 1906 was a distinct improvement. At the same time, his remarkably rebellious career in parliament over disestablishment and other Welsh causes in the early 1890s, during the South African War and later the Welsh 'revolt' on education in 1902–5, is testimony to an uncomplicated attachment to principle whatever the possible electoral impact for himself. Like other rural Liberal solicitors, he had long visualised a parliamentary career. He had worked hard for Lord Richard Grosvenor in the 1885 election, and was only narrowly beaten for the Flintshire Liberal nomination in 1886 by the Englishman Samuel Smith, with whom he always had an awkward relationship.[16] When the Flint District Liberal nomination came up in 1891 Lewis was strongly placed to win it and in the 1892 general election he defeated the squirearchical Unionist , P. P. Pennant, by 359 votes.

At an early stage, the new Flint Boroughs member was part of the awkward squad. He was distinctly cool in his comments on Tom Ellis's agreeing to become a junior whip in Gladstone's final government in 1892, 'grasping the Saxon gold' in the view of more extreme patriots.[17] Lewis was among those who put pressure on the Welsh parliamentary chairman, Stuart Rendel, with whom he had a good relationship, for a Royal Commission to be appointed to investigate the Welsh land question. This was a fairly standard view amongst the Welsh Liberals at this time, and Gladstone was compelled to acquiesce.[18] Far more challenging was the episode when Lewis (joint secretary of the Welsh Parliamentary Party by now) joined Lloyd George, D. A. Thomas and Frank Edwards in a rebellion against the new Liberal Prime Minister in April 1894. They threatened to withhold their support from the Rosebery government (whose small and diminishing majority was wholly dependent on the Irish) on the issue of Welsh disestablishment, and urged their Liberal colleagues to do the same. He told Tom Ellis, 'It is with the greatest regret that I have taken a step which means independence of the Liberal Party. My recent talks with Ministers and members have convinced me that Wales is simply being led on from step to step without any definite goal in actual view, that we have nothing to gain by sub-servience to the Liberal party, and that we shall never get the English to do us justice until we show our independence of them.' He asked Ellis rhetorically 'Will you come out and lead us?' – a pretty forlorn hope when writing to one who was now the government's chief whip. In this episode, Lloyd George appears to have regarded Lewis as a particularly valued ally. Whereas D. A. Thomas was a maverick coal tycoon and Frank Edwards a relative lightweight (who was to lose his seat in the 1895 general election), 'Herbert's presence amongst us will in itself be a source of great strength', he wrote to his brother William.[19]

Lewis was also foremost among those who backed Lloyd George's new attempt to turn the 'revolt' on Welsh disestablishment into a wider campaign for Welsh home rule. Lewis was not a natural zealot for Cymru Fydd. For one thing, he was not anywhere as gifted in Welsh as were men like Lloyd George or Llewelyn Williams. T. Marchant Williams (with much exaggeration, admittedly) was to ridicule Lewis's attempts to give a Welsh speech during the Montgomeryshire by-election of April 1894. He speculated that Lewis's audience in Llanbrynmair might have im-agined they were listening to ancient Hebrew or modern Greek.[20] Lewis did improve his command of Welsh considerably as his career pro-gressed, though it is notable that his lengthy diary, which he kept from 1888 until his death in 1933, was almost always written up in English. Even so, Lewis appears to have had no problem with Lloyd George's undoubtedly divisive tactics in trying to turn the Liberal Federations of North and South Wales into a framework for his quasi-separatist Cymru Fydd League. Lewis's influence was important in winning over the North Wales Liberal Federation. Meanwhile Lloyd George reassured him over opinion within the South Wales Liberal Federation. 'I do not see any reason for discouragement in the fact that South Wales has not yet 'risen' to the Cymru Fydd movement. It is only a question of getting a thoroughly good organizer.'[21]

The sudden death of his beloved wife Ada on 7 June 1895, which left Lewis grief-stricken, removed him from the political forefront for a short time. It is significant that Lloyd George was with him in the Gwalia hotel in Llandrindod Wells when he heard the news, and was the first to comfort him. Indeed, it is testimony to his close relationship with Lewis at this time that he spent much time and trouble interrogating the hapless doctor whom he correctly suspected of giving a wrong diagnosis of Mrs Lewis's medical condition, and arranging for a post-mortem. He described the scene poignantly to his wife: 'His grief was appalling. The poor boy was trying to pack. He was distracted. I couldn't leave him in that state, so I took charge of him. By degrees I quieted him down.' It was he who took Herbert to grieve alone in the large empty house in Caerwys.[22] The whole episode casts light on a tender, gentler side of Lloyd George which his critics often miss.

Despite this bereavement, there is no doubt that Lewis was totally supportive when, a few days later, Lloyd George tried to tack on a Welsh National Council to administer the secularised Church endowments, within the framework of Clause Nine of the Welsh Disestablishment Bill. Many severely criticised Lloyd George for his role at this time. On 20 June, the tottering government's majority fell to only seven on the Welsh bill. The next day, the Rosebery government was defeated by seven votes in the Commons on the trivial 'cordite vote'. It resigned almost in a sense of relief, amidst much criticism of Ellis's competence as party whip, while Liberals like J. Bryn Roberts and, more notably, Asquith, the former Home Secretary, condemned Lloyd George for disloyal tactics that weakened Rosebery's government at a critical time.[23]

Herbert Lewis never did. On the contrary, he argued that Lloyd George was absolutely right in trying to push Welsh Liberalism in a more openly nationalist direction. After he narrowly retained his Flint District seat in the general election, he watched with consistent approval Lloyd George's autumn campaign in the south Wales valleys to win support for Cymru Fydd. Lewis himself gave him frequent oratorical and tactical assistance.[24] He also showed a good deal of tactical shrewdness, using personal contacts and links with journalists with a skill not far behind that of Lloyd George himself. When, in the famous meeting of the South Wales Liberal Federation at Newport on 16 January 1896, Lloyd George was shouted down by the 'Newport Englishmen' and Cymru Fydd was rejected, Lewis took this as merely one battle in an unending campaign.

'This will be the end of the negotiations with them (the SWLF) and the WNF (Welsh National Federation) will go ahead.'[25] Throughout 1896 and 1897 Lewis acted as though Cymru Fydd was very far from defeated. He drafted a scheme for a Welsh national organisation, based on the premise that they should not be provoking the South Wales Liberals and encouraging national sentiment in Glamorgan and Monmouthshire. This proposal for 'a Welsh National Liberal Federation' aroused all the old animosities of the Cymru Fydd episode and it finally collapsed in February 1898 in the face of further attacks from the Cardiff Liberal Association.[26]

Lewis had been its main proponent. He showed, indeed, rather more persistence in promoting the idea of a Welsh National Federation at this period than did Lloyd George himself. In his diary in February 1899, he noted his surprise that Lloyd George was reluctant to give his backing to a Welsh amendment to the Address: 'it was curious that I should have had to argue the subject in such a quarter'.[27] Two months later, he turned down an offer from the new Liberal leader, Campbell-Bannerman, that he should take up a junior whipship. In Lewis's view this would compromise his role as an independent voice for Welsh Liberalism.[28] The fires of rebellion still surged within him. Lewis flatly refused to fall into the trap as his recently dead colleague Tom Ellis had done when he took office under Gladstone in August 1892.

In the years of opposition after the 1895 general election, Lewis was Lloyd George's man, though not exclusively so. He remained friendly with Ellis to the extent that they travelled in South Africa in the autumn of 1895; they met Cecil Rhodes, a momentous encounter for both, though Lewis, a 'little Englander' in his view of the world, appears to have been more guarded than Ellis in his enthusiasm for so aggressive a voice for empire.[29] At the end of 1898 he again went on holiday with Ellis, this time to Egypt and Palestine; this was a more sombre trip in view of Ellis's delicate health and indeed he was to die shortly after his return to Britain, at the age of only forty.[30] But on the great contemporary issues, Lewis was always in Lloyd George's camp and manifestly regarded his younger colleague as having unique gifts of leadership. He went on holiday with him also, to Patagonia in the autumn of 1896. Their correspondence and diaries do not shed much light on the details of their visit, though Lloyd George does comment on Lewis's enthusiasm for the deck game of shovelboard.[31] At any rate, Lewis does not show any great qualms for Lloyd George's involvement in the bizarre Patagonia gold scheme, with which he himself had an indirect financial connection.[32]

On a more serious personal issue, Lewis gave Lloyd George the strongest backing during the Edwards paternity and divorce case when Lloyd George was accused in late 1896 of adultery and fathering an illegitimate child. Lewis's response was tough and to the point. He told Lloyd George: 'The line you are taking is right and necessary. I am confident you will come out of the business stronger than ever'.[33] Lewis's position was far more straightforward than, say, the Liberal member for Anglesey, the barrister Ellis Griffith, who actually represented Dr Edwards to Lloyd George's intense fury. Politically, Lewis was with Lloyd George at every turn. Following a jaunt to Boulogne together, they were both suspended in a parliamentary protest against the 1896 Education Bill. The Bishop, the Brewer and the Squire were constant targets of Lewis's measured oratory.

His association with Lloyd George's brand of radicalism reached a dramatic new level when the South African War broke out in September 1899. Like Lloyd George (who was in Canada at the time), Lewis was an immediate and vehement opponent of the war. No-one was a more consistent 'Pro-Boer'. Not for a moment does he seem to have flinched from vehement attacks on the government, on Chamberlain and on imperialism. On 20 April 1900, he deplored how leading Liberals in Holywell were 'all more or less jingo. Militarism has got hold of my people in the most extraordinary way. The light of Gladstone, Bright and Cobden is quenched in darkness'.[34] The precariousness of his election majority had no effect in moderating Lewis's passionate anti-war crusade. Like Lloyd George he faced danger and violence from jingo ruffians at election meetings. He spoke with Lloyd George and Bryn Roberts at a great anti-war rally in Caernarfon, which in fact proved to be distinctly more orderly than one of Lloyd George's at Bangor.[35] Lewis was one of four 'pro-Boer' Welsh members (Lloyd George, Humphreys-Owen and Bryn Roberts being the others) in the vote on Sir Wilfrid Lawson's anti-war motion in the Commons on 25 July 1900, when the Liberal Party divided three ways.[36] Lewis's sense of moral outrage was such that he even considered resigning his seat rather than trim to the jingo views of some in his local constituency Association.[37] It was perhaps the noblest and most selfless phase of his career, as much so as that of Lloyd George which has been so fully recorded in relation to Birmingham Town Hall and elsewhere.

Virtue was rewarded when Lewis got home, with an increased majority of 347 (11 per cent) in the 'khaki election' for Flint Boroughs that October. But he pursued his crusade against the war to the bitter end, with all the more passion when Emily Hobhouse's account of the deaths of thousands of Boer mothers and little children in Kitchener's concentration camps in the Rand was published.[38] Since the effect of the war was to strengthen radicalism in the party under Campbell-Bannerman's leadership and to give the 'pro-Boer' minority a new stature, the outcome was politically advantageous to Lewis. But there is no doubt that his approach was based solely on principle, an old Liberal's adherence to the historic imperatives of peace, retrenchment and reform.

Equally principled, though perhaps intellectually more tortuous for a member of the legal profession, was Lewis's 'prominent role as Lloyd George's lieutenant in the 'Welsh revolt' against Balfour's Education Act of 1902, which nonconformists bitterly condemned for favouring and subsidising the schools of the established Church. Lewis, unlike Lloyd George, had professional expertise in the organisation of education and much technical experience in the development of intermediate schools. But he had no qualms in endorsing Lloyd George's strategy that the Welsh county councils should collectively act to thwart the operation of the Act in Wales. Indeed, he often gave his friend useful tips on the legal loopholes that could be identified to their political advantage. For Lloyd George's oratory and tactics, his admiration knew no bounds. When they both took part in meetings at Cardiff in May 1902, Lewis observed: 'I have heard Lloyd George make many brilliant speeches but the four speeches he delivered at Cardiff were a perfect tour de force. He did not repeat himself by a single sentence and every part of the speech was on the same high level.'[39] He was equally enthusiastic over Lloyd George's using the Educational Revolt to promote Welsh national objectives as over disestablishment in 1895. When the Welsh members, influenced by cautious figures like Bryn Roberts and Humphreys-Owen, were divided over tactics on 12 November 1902, Lloyd George 'swept everything before him in the most peremptory fashion and carried them in favour of the English plan'. Lloyd George's and Lewis's ultimate aim at this point appears to have been to create a Central Board for Wales for elementary schools, in addition to that already set up for secondary schools in 1896, on 'a red letter day for Welsh nationality'. 'L.G. showed tremendous determination and driving force in carrying the thing through'.[40]

During the tortuous negotiations of the next three years, revolt against the government and default over operating the Act combined with attempts at negotiations variously with Sir William Anson and Robert Morant at the Education Board and even with A. G. Edwards, the controversial Bishop of St Asaph, Lewis was constantly at Lloyd George's side. He was a shoulder to lean on when his hero was nearly roughed up by hostile crowds – admiringly, he noted how Lloyd George kept a mob at bay on St Albans station platform by the expedient of very deliberately lighting his pipe.[41] Nothing, it seemed, should come between a man and his right to smoke. When Lloyd George impatiently inquired of Lewis whether he needed a court suit when meeting the King at a social engagement at Lord Tweedmouth's, Lewis lent him his own, since they were roughly the same size.[42] They were also frequent partners on the golf course, notably at Lewes in matches arranged by Timothy Lewis, Liberal Welsh MP and the husband of one of Lloyd George's alleged mistresses.

The years of Liberal hegemony begun by the election landslide of January 1906 brought a golden period for Lewis no less than for Lloyd George. He observed his friend's rapid ascent to power with unbridled admiration and affection. He endorsed his attempts to sort out the Welsh clauses of Birrell's abortive Education Bill of 1906 even though this resulted in a phantom Welsh minister of state who was soon wiped out from the bill. Lloyd George's triumphs at the Board of Trade appeared endless. Over the 1906 Merchant Shipping Act, 'L.G. has succeeded where Chamberlain failed. To have brought about an entente between capital and labour and to have promoted a measure which is to the interest of shipowners and sailors alike has meant a display extending over several months of tact, astuteness and a power of managing men which has put L.G. in the front rank of constructive statesmanship'.[43] The President's rattling through most of the 1907 Patents Bill in three hours in committee only brought the comment: 'that wonderful man, by tact, suavity, concession, adroit manoeuvring and skilful handling very nearly got the Bill through'.[44] In February 1908, Lloyd George, emerging from the trauma of the death of his beloved youngest daughter, Mair, triumphed in the very different sphere of labour relations. He achieved his 'third great triumph' in conciliation by settling the engineers' strike, appealing to the more humane instincts of the president of the engineering employers' leader, Sir Andrew Noble of the munitions manufacturers, Armstrongs.[45] This followed close on Lloyd George's remarkable success in settling a threatened national railway strike the previous October.

Lloyd George's further advance to become Chancellor of the Exchequer in April 1908, after Asquith became prime minister, propelled Lewis's idol to new heights of constructive statesmanship. The 'People's Budget' speech on 30 April 1909 was badly delivered, Lloyd George rattling through his lengthy text and almost losing his voice: Lewis was at hand to provide a restorative glass of egg and milk. But it was 'the most daring budget we have ever seen . . . one of the most remarkable triumphs of L.G.'s career', especially in the way he managed to arouse enthusiasm on behalf of the taxes to be levied to finance social reform.[46] Like Gordon Brown in 2002, Lloyd George had made 'tax and spend' policies popular. Throughout the prolonged crises of the Budget, the conflict with the Lords and the final passage of the 1911 Parliament Act, Lewis was an unflinching and vocal supporter at every turn. The National Insurance Act of 1911 was a further triumph – 'probably the greatest social scheme ever put forward in this or any other country'. Lloyd George had raised the idea in colourful fashion when discussing policy with Lewis at Criccieth in April 1908, immediately after he became Chancellor.[47] Lewis also sympathised with Lloyd George's troubles at the hands of the suffragettes, and was severely critical of the militant tactics being adopted by them at Lloyd George's meetings. The latter confided to Lewis his fear of being murdered.[48] Lewis, like Lloyd George, was a women's suffragist, especially when his first wife was alive, but a distinctly gradualist one. On balance, his enthusiasm for womens' suffrage seemed to wane over the years: the disruption of Lloyd George's day at the Wrexham Eisteddfod in September 1912 provoked the comment, 'the usual insane suffragette demonstration'.[49] But here again Lewis was totally convinced that Lloyd George was on the right lines and would triumph in the end.

Apart from this hero-worship, his own career was also progressing, even if only as a minister of the second rank. In December 1905, he did take a whipship, as Junior Lord of the Treasury, and retained that post for four years. Lewis worked well with J. A. Pease, the Liberal Chief Whip, in trying to impose discipline on 'a great mob of new members, most of them absolutely ignorant of the ways of parliament', and with much effect. Lord Althorp told him that he was the 'the popular whip ... it is because you are a Celt', whatever that meant.[50] In 1909 Lewis moved to the Local Government Board under the unpredictable leadership of John Burns, whose egotism alternatively amused and dismayed him. It is clear that Lewis, a most capable administrator, undertook a good deal of the more difficult and detailed business in handling committees and deputations in place of his wayward President. Lewis stayed here until after the outbreak of war in 1914, on the whole a congenial role for one long versed in the minutiae of local government, and one that considerably broadened his political horizon. Thus when war broke out, he was immersed in the complexities of a committee on poor relief in London.

Many of his endeavours as a minister, inevitably, were concerned with Welsh issues, with many positive results. Lewis was heavily involved with patronage matters: for instance he persuaded Lloyd George to support the Oxford history don, Owen M. Edwards, for the post of Chief Inspector of Schools, when the Chancellor himself had his doubts. Lewis was inevitably prepared to accept Lloyd George's assurance over the prospects for a Welsh Disestablishment bill in 1907 when many Welsh Liberals and nonconformist leaders were critical of Campbell-Bannerman. A strongly pro-disestablishment speech by Lloyd George in a convention at Cardiff restored equilibrium. There was further doubt when the Welsh Church Bill of 1909 fell by the wayside. Lewis could in the end point to the introduction of a conclusive Disestablishment Bill in 1912, on which he spoke several times, and to its potential enactment under the terms of the Parliament Act in 1914. Lewis was very apprehensive at the apparent lack of enthusiasm amongst English Liberals for the Welsh Bill: 'Many Liberal members are apathetic and even hostile to the passage of the Bill. They say it will do them a great deal of harm in their constituencies.' However, Lloyd George's 'magnificent' speech on 25 April (he accused the Cecil family of seizing Church endowments and pillaging monastic estates in the time of Henry VIII, leaving them with 'hands dripping with the fat of sacrilege') 'gave the Bill a lift which it greatly needed'.[51]

More constructively, perhaps, Lewis lobbied Lloyd George with much effect on behalf of his cherished cause of the National Library, along with the Museum and the funding of the University Colleges. This was a lifelong crusade of his: since his first entry into parliament he had pursued the question of museum and library grants being applied to Wales. As champion of the new copyright National Library in Aberystwyth, Lewis was extraordinarily effective. He used his friendship with Lloyd George to excellent purpose in February–March 1909, at a time when the Chancellor was heavily engaged in dealing with the financial troubles of the naval estimates and preparing the People's Budget. Lewis noted privately that, apart from Lloyd George, there was no-one to speak for Wales throughout the entire ranks of government, but he used his powers of man-to-man diplomacy extremely well. In early March 1909, after private meetings with Lloyd George, Lewis was able to announce grants of £4,500 to the Library, £2,000 to the Museum, and £16,000 of grants to the Welsh colleges. 'L.G. has behaved with great courage and determination'.[52] A year later, there was even better news, with the Chancellor agreeing to £4,000 a year to the library and a further grant of £500 per annum for two years towards cataloguing the manuscript collections. 'A courageous action on L.G.'s part', given the depleted state of the nation's finances.[53] Lewis was able to persuade such local prima donnas as Dr John Williams, the Library's president, and John

Ballinger, its imperious librarian, that there was a secure financial basis for this national treasure-house at last.

Lewis was therefore a pivotal and characteristic figure at this high noon of Welsh Edwardian Liberalism. He was involved in most of the political, social and cultural achievements of the period. He was also a voice for that style of progressive, reformist liberalism which captured the public mind before the First World War, a constructive phase in our politics to which Tony Blair amongst others has looked back nostalgically. Lewis was a perfect symbol of how the Old Liberalism gradually yielded to the New. The older issues of disestablishment, Church schools, temperance and land reform remained unfinished business. But, increasingly, social welfare was dominating the public agenda. Lewis viewed all Lloyd George's new enthusiasms with equanimity. At the same time, it is clear that for him the reforms served in some measure as a bulwark against socialism. The national strikes of 1911–14 disturbed him as they did other traditional liberals, with their violence and apparent threat to the constitution and economic fabric. He worried at the impact of the 1912 miners' strike, not least on the Flintshire miners in the small pits around Buckley in his own constituency. He thought an ILP socialist like Fred Jowett was callously unaware of the attachment of Welsh miners to 'home and people and language' and the importance to them of the rents they paid on their cottages.[54] Tom Ellis's old advice to him back in 1891, to focus in the longer term on labour issues, did not appear to bear much fruit in Lewis's case. Other Flintshire Liberals, like Fred Llewellyn Jones, the solicitor and coroner of Isfryn, Mold, were to gravitate in time towards the Labour Party. For Lewis that could never be an option.[55] But a combination of measured social reform (Lewis became friendly with Lloyd George's reforming doctor associate, Dr Christopher Addison) and beguiling Lloyd Georgian labour conciliation would steady the ship and keep the Tories at bay. To read Lewis's diaries and letters down to August 1914 is in no sense to gain an indication of what Dangerfield so misleadingly described as the 'strange death' of Liberal England – or Wales. Lewis enjoyed power. He felt that the Liberals had control of it, deserved it, and had the greatest Welshman in history in place to ensure that they retained it. The Tories – wrong-footed on National Insurance, yoked with difficult allies like the Diehard peers, the Welsh bishops and the Ulster Covenanters, unsure in their philosophy about either the state or social cohesion[56] – were not in Lewis's view close to returning to power at all, and certainly did not deserve to.

His confidence was fortified by his strength in his new county constituency. He had been elected for Flintshire in January: his dour predecessor, Samuel Smith, had announced his reluctant resignation in 1904 as a consequence of some tortuous local manoeuvres.[57] Apart from significant pockets of nonconformists, there was a good industrial vote for the Liberals in Connah's Quay and Shotton, and Lib-Lab miners around Buckley. Hence both the 1910 elections were won with some comfort even though 'territorial persecution was rife in some parts of the county, particularly in Maelor and the Bodfari district' and the Trade 'being very keen and active'. This was remarkable, since the Ballot Act of 1872 decades earlier was supposed to have ended this kind of intimidation.[58] Lewis, now into his middle fifties, was still full of zest for the fight, despite littering his diary with accounts of endless colds and 'chills', and days spent almost incomprehensibly in bed. In June 1914, when Lloyd George was shortly to tell the London Mansion House audience that 'the sky was relatively blue' in the international field, Lewis himself had a cheerful tour of Germany, going on from Hamburg and Bremen as far as Berlin.[59] His diary notes show no sign of detecting an imminent international catastrophe. For Herbert Lewis of Plas Penucha, it seemed, smiling and serene blue skies also lay ahead.

Then came the Great War. Of course, it brought a seismic transform-ation in the role of Lloyd George, coalition with the Tory enemy and an eventual almost six years in 10 Downing Street, followed by his abrupt ejection from office for ever. Herbert Lewis followed him faithfully at every turn. Like his colleague, he accepted the necessity and indeed morality of the war. It was being fought, he believed, on behalf of liberal principles of self-determination and natural justice. He was fortified in this view by having to handle the reception of immigrant Belgian refugees who migrated to Britain in the autumn of 1914, which he did with characteristic efficiency. Lloyd George's growing role in war strategy as well as war finance in early 1915 evoked only further admiration. His friend 'has taken a greater part in the world's affairs than any Welshman that ever lived', Lewis reflected.[60]

He felt apprehension at Asquith's Liberal government giving way to a coalition in May 1915, and reluctantly accepted the new post of Under-Secretary at the Board of Education on 28 May. He would have preferred a complete break from office, he confided to his diary, giving vent to his usual concern at his delicate health. But, in fact, he continued as an active, even robust minister, and was to serve in his new department for almost seven and a half years. He struck up a good relationship with his initial President of the Education Board, Labour's Arthur Henderson. This period saw Lewis launch with a grant of £25,000 the supremely import-ant initiative of the Department of Scientific and Industrial Research, which he saw as bringing the universities and the business world closer together. He worked even better with Henderson's successor from December 1916, H. A. L. Fisher, the distinguished Liberal historian and future Warden of New College, Oxford.[61] Lewis certainly showed plenty of intellectual energy in this important new post, especially in piloting the historic 1918 Education Act through the Commons with much aplomb. It was the Lewis Act quite as much as the Fisher Act. Like Mark Twain's death, Lewis's decline was distinctly exaggerated. After the 'coupon election' of December 1918, he continued at Education for almost four more years, his energies apparently undiminished.

Lewis followed closely the twists and turns of Lloyd George's political career during the war. As his oldest living friend, he saw the prime minister quite frequently: his diary records a series of lunches, breakfasts or political conversations with Lloyd George through the war years, often at Downing Street. Lloyd George saw in Lewis a reliable, totally discreet observer of the political world in general. Lewis's expertise on the shipping industry was especially useful to him during the war years. He also introduced the premier to the progressive young naval officer and critic of the Admiralty, Commander J. M. Kenworthy.[62] Nearer home, Lloyd George used Lewis skilfully in March 1915 in persuading Welsh Liberals that the government intended to persevere with the dis-establishment of the Welsh Church, until it came into operational effect after the war, despite the government's temporary tactical confusions.

Prophetically, Lloyd George was recorded as saying that 'he believes that the great question of reconstruction which will arise after the war will peremptorily push aside sectarian controversy.' Lewis concluded: 'After all, but for him there would have been no Parliament Act and no Disestablishment Act'.[63]

Throughout the tortuous political manoeuvres of 1916, Lewis (like Ellis Griffith but unlike Llewelyn Williams) backed Lloyd George solidly over military conscription (despite his own Gladstonian, anti-military background). He was among the hundred-odd who signed up secretly when Addison, David Davies and others canvassed Liberal MPs that spring about the prospects of a Lloyd George premiership in succession to Asquith. He was a wholly committed supporter of the new Prime Minister from December 1916 and stayed on at Education: if he was disappointed at failing to gain further promotion, Lewis does not show it. He backs Lloyd George at every turn, including the crisis of the Maurice Debate in May 1918, when the prime minister was accused of falsely representing the strength of the military reserves at the western front. Lloyd George's speech of self-defence, said Lewis, was 'a triumphant vindication' while he dismissed Maurice scornfully as a disappointed general not worth an undue amount of bother.[64] The ferocity of Lloyd George's rhetoric (e.g. 'cocoa slop') does not seem to have disturbed him.

In 1918 he loyally accepted Coalition Liberal nomination for the new University of Wales seat: he himself had been active in alliance with Lord Kenyon in securing a parliamentary seat for the Welsh university in the Representation of the People Act, after an initial defeat on amendment.[65] With his election address rightly emphasizing his long service to Welsh education, he trounced a female Labour candidate, winning 80.8 per cent of the vote. After the election, indeed, for a time his career rose to new heights of activity. After receiving many accolades (including from Fisher himself) for his role in carrying through the new Education Act, he was also variously preoccupied with Teachers' Superannuation, a Libraries Act, educational grants for ex-servicemen and the Royal Commission on the University of Wales. In 1921, he told E. W. Evans, editor of the weekly *Cymro*, that his experience at the Education Board showed how far more could be achieved for Wales within a British government rather than in independent sorties on the political fringe. Fisher's educational policies had brought tangible and measurable benefits to Wales: the 'Fisher formula' would give Wales an additional £100,000, while the Education Act of 1918 would give new educational opportunities to 20,000 boys and girls.[66] By comparison, the office of Secretary of State for Wales proposed in some Liberal circles, by men like the shipowner MP Sir Robert J. Thomas, was a trivial matter. Manifestly, the youthful nationalist rebel of 1894 had long since vanished.

For his part, H. A. L. Fisher clearly regarded Lewis, rather than the local worthies on the Central Welsh Board, as his most reliable sounding-board on Welsh education. It was a constructive time of change. Education, after all, was a foremost element in the government's proclaimed intention of a brave new world of social reform after the election. Things became far more difficult from 1920 with the rigours of economy and 'anti-waste' being applied to the government's educational programmes. Lewis joined Fisher in strong defence of the day continuation schools. They threatened a joint resignation against Cabinet proposals which 'would automatically have the effect of scrapping the Education Act'. He wrote to thank the Prime Minister for backing them in Cabinet in the face of economy proposals from the Chancellor, Austen Chamberlain.[67] They got their way but had an even tougher fight in resisting the Geddes Axe which loomed over education in 1921. In fact, the ministers had somewhat more success in fending off educational cuts than is frequently represented, notably over the school entry age, the size of classes, and maintaining the Burnham awards on schoolteachers' salaries. Lewis felt able to claim afterwards that the bulk of Fisher's achievement for public education remained undisturbed.[68]

Politically, Lewis appeared to have no problem with the coalition government. He saw in the coalition a government of national unity, 'the embodiment of the spirit of accommodation'. 'Party,' declared Lewis, 'would rather have no bread than half a loaf.'[69] Ever loyal to his master, he was one of the Liberal ministers who attended the Leamington meeting of the National Liberal Federation at Leamington Spa in May 1920, a famous brawl occurring when government ministers were heckled by Asquithian partisans and walked out in collective defiance.[70] Lewis was also prepared to take part in the turbulent Cardiganshire by-election in February 1921 when two Liberals, one Lloyd Georgian, one Asquithian, contested the seat in a passionate atmosphere. He told his wife, Ruth, 'This election is dividing up families in the most peculiar way.' The outcome was a narrow, but decisive defeat for the Asquithian Liberal candidate, Lewis's old ally of Cymru Fydd days, W. Llewelyn Williams, now a bitter opponent of Lloyd George who had broken with his old friend over conscription and then Ireland.[71] No doubt some of his bitterness spilled over in the direction of Herbert Lewis as well.

However there were limits to the political compromises that even Lewis might make. At the curious meeting of Coalition Liberal ministers on 16 March 1920, when Lloyd George and Churchill tried to persuade them to endorse a 'fusion' with the Coalition Unionists, Lewis was one of many who dissented – perhaps the only time in his career when he and Lloyd George were at odds. 'In Wales it would be practically impossible to get anything in the shape of fusion between the local Associations.'[72] Even in the very changed politics of post-war, with the old aspiration of Church disestablishment now accomplished amid a sense of anti-climax, Lewis remained the traditional Liberal of Gladstonian days. He would not give up the old faith, the old principles, certainly not the old party name. In the end, he and Lloyd George's followers were forced into a political cul-de-sac. The Liberal supporters of Lloyd George had nowhere else to turn when the rank-and-file Tories broke with them in October 1922 over Lloyd George's handling of the Chanak crisis which threatened war with Turkey. The Unionist revolt at the Carlton Club on 19 October 1922 abruptly turfed Lloyd George out of office and out of power. His political career, in the event, was far from over. But that of Herbert Lewis, who had announced his resignation from parliament long before and planned an extensive series of overseas tours to tropical climes to celebrate freedom at last, undoubtedly was. At least he ended up with a knighthood, one of Lloyd George's far from dreadful knights.

Herbert Lewis's last phase was conducted largely away from the limelight and on the margins of politics. His major public concerns now were his continuing campaign to get proper funding for the National

Library of Wales, and his work for Bangor and the University of Wales.[73] He continued to campaign for improved grants for the National Library, he bought major collections of manuscripts from his own funds to present to its archives, and he was to serve as its president. His imposing bust casts its gaze on visitors to the library today. His tragic accident when he fell down a quarry at J. H. Davies's home in north Cardiganshire in 1925, and broke his spine, effectively ended his career. Lloyd George ignored him from now on. Lewis had nothing more to offer. As has been noted, Lloyd George regarded him somewhat quizzically as a long-term surviving hypochondriac who was somehow miraculously still alive despite decades of alleged ill-health. Prior to his accident, Lewis toured India. He received Welsh and other honours by the score. He had become, as he approached his seventies, the classic embodiment of late Victorian and Edwardian 'official liberalism' and a conformist nonconformity, a public-service professional, a symbolic remnant of a disappearing past in a new society dominated by the polarity of capital and labour.

Many politicians kept in close touch with him, especially Fisher who developed a warm admiration for his sterling qualities, and used Lewis as a sounding-board for his concerns for the various crises of Liberalism in the 1920s.[74] But Lloyd George, his intimate friend for nearly forty years, the focus of so much of his energies and his admiration, simply dropped him. In the great campaign against unemployment and industrial stagnation, the crusades for the Green, Yellow and Orange Books in 1925–9, even as a name to be used in election propaganda, Herbert Lewis need never have been. He died in November 1933, almost a forgotten man.

But his achievement transcends the ages. Indeed, so many of the badges of modern Welsh nationality – Museum and Library and University; county councils, county schools and administrative devolution along with Welsh legislation from Intermediate Education in 1889 to Church Disestablishment in 1919 – are an essential part of his legacy. The Liberalism of pre-1914 remains the source of so much of the institutional and cultural distinctiveness of modern Wales, and Herbert Lewis was not the least of its architects. Indeed, his supreme objective, that devolution for which he campaigned in vain in the 1890s, has indeed now come into vigorous fruition, a hundred years later. In accounts of the career of Lloyd George, the devoted friendship of Herbert Lewis is hugely underestimated. He sustained his tempestuous colleague in numerous crises – the 1894 disestablishment rebellion, the Cymru Fydd crusade, the South African War, the Education Revolt – when they were young colleagues and rough political equals. But as a source of disinterested advice and reassuring judgement, Lewis was always there, whenever Lloyd George felt he needed him – and he frequently did. No doubt he had to turn a frequent blind eye as he pursued higher political causes. Neither Lloyd George's peccadilloes with money or philandering with women get a mention in his diaries. He backed up his friend to the hilt when he was accused of corruption during the Marconi case in 1912, while his observations on Dame Margaret (whom he greatly admired) never suggest that the Lloyd George family home was anything other than a nest of domestic bliss. But in the broader context, Herbert Lewis was one of those who kept Lloyd George politically and perhaps personally honest – not at all a straightforward task. He helped to ensure that, throughout all the vicissitudes of party and coalition, of industrial turmoil and economic decline, in war and in post-war reconstruction, his charismatic Welsh colleague remained at bottom the same populist democrat and committed progressive that he had always been. Men such as Lewis, like C. P. Scott, ensured that Lloyd George stayed a man of the centre-left, part of that fount of reformist energy which men like Beveridge, Keynes and Michael Young later replenished. If Lloyd George never lapsed into the fate of Joseph Chamberlain, still less of Ramsay MacDonald, if he retained his radical impulses even during the later years of Hitler-worship and the final descent into an earldom, it was decent, honest free spirits like Plas Penucha's guardian of the faith, who kept him so.

Notes

[1] A. J. P. Taylor, *English History, 1914–1945* (Oxford, 1965), p. 73. In a foreword to a book by the present author, Taylor also advanced the view that Lloyd

George 'was the greatest ruler of England [sic] since Oliver Cromwell', in Kenneth O. Morgan, *Lloyd George* (London, 1974), p. 8.

2 J. M. Keynes, *Essays in Biography* (London, 1961 edn), p. 36.

3 Arnold Bennett's *Lord Raingo* (1926) depicts Lloyd George as the Scotsman Andy Clyth (Raingo himself is based on D. A. Thomas, Lord Rhondda), while Joyce Cary's *Prisoner of Grace* (1952) depicts him as the Englishman (? Devonian), Chester Nimmo.

4 The most helpful study of Lewis is the Welsh-language collective book edited by his daughter, Kitty Idwal Jones (ed.), *Syr Herbert Lewis 1858–1933* (Cardiff, 1961). Two of the authors wrote centenary tributes in *Flintshire Historical Society Publications*, vol. 18 (1960), Sir Ben Bowen Thomas, 131–41, and W. Hugh Jones, 142–55, the latter dealing with Lewis's work in local government. A useful thesis is Timothy P. Erasmus, 'Herbert Lewis and Welsh Radicalism: a study of the political career of John Herbert Lewis (1858–1933) with special reference to the period 1892–1906' (University of Wales, Bangor, unpublished Ph.D. thesis, 1988). The author summarised his conclusions in Timothy P. Erasmus, 'In his Earnest Way: a brief outline of the life and political career of Herbert Lewis (1858–1933)', a lecture to the Flintshire Historical Society, 31 October 1992. I should like to pay my personal tribute to the late Mrs Kitty Idwal Jones, a delightful lady who gave me generous hospitality and guidance when I first worked on the Lewis papers in Plas Penucha in 1960.

5 Erasmus, 'In his Earnest Way', p. 4.

6 E.g. cartoon by Will Morgan in T. Marchant Williams, *The Welsh Members of Parliament* (Cardiff, 1894), p. 20.

7 Lewis's Diary, 22 January 1906 (NLW, Lewis Papers B20).

8 Colin Cross (ed.), *A. J. Sylvester: Life with Lloyd George* (London, 1975), p. 63.

9 A. J. P. Taylor (ed.), *Lloyd George: A Diary by Frances Stevenson* (London, 1971), p. 245.

10 Cross, *A. J. Sylvester*, p. 63.

11 For these matters, see Kenneth O. Morgan, *Wales in British Politics 1868–1922* (Cardiff, 1963), pp. 76ff.

12 Ellis to Lewis, 31 October 1891 (NLW, D. R. Daniel Papers, A19k).

13 See especially Tom Ellis, *Addresses and Speeches* (Wrexham, 1912); Neville Masterman, *The Forerunner* (Llandybie, 1972); and Kenneth O. Morgan, 'Tom Ellis versus Lloyd George: the Fractured Consciousness of *Fin-de-Siècle* Wales', in *Modern Wales: Politics, Places and People* (Cardiff, 1995), pp. 62ff.

14 Cf. Ellis to Lewis, 24 July 1889 (NLW, Daniel Papers, A19k).

15 Lewis to Ellis, 15 August 1891 (NLW, Ellis Papers). See also J. Graham Jones, 'Alfred Thomas's National Institutions (Wales) Bills of 1891–2', *Welsh History Review*, 15/2 (December 1990), 230–1.

16 Cf. Samuel Smith to Lewis, 12 September 1904 (NLW, Lewis Papers, A1/173).

[17] J. Arthur Price to J. E. Lloyd, 14 October 1892 (University of Wales, Bangor Library, Lloyd Papers, MSS 314, no. 449); Lewis to Ellis, 19 May 1892 (NLW, Ellis Papers).

[18] Ellis to Herbert Lewis, 7 and 18 November 1892 (NLW, Ellis Papers, 2896, 2899); Lewis to Ellis, 17 and 22 November 1892 (NLW, ibid., 1403–4); Rendel to Lewis, 14 and 15 November 1892 (NLW, Lewis Papers). More generally, see Morgan, *Wales in British Politics*, pp. 123–6.

[19] Lewis to Ellis, ? May 1894 (NLW, Ellis papers); David Lloyd George to William George, ? April 1894 (NLW, William George Papers, 252).

[20] Lloyd George to Herbert Lewis, 22 June 1894 (Lewis Papers). The Lewis Papers are a rich source of information on the Cymru Fydd movement, 1894–6.

[21] Williams, *The Welsh Members of Parliament*, p. 22.

[22] W. R. P. George, *Lloyd George: Backbencher* (Llandysul, 1983), pp. 168–70; David Lloyd George to his wife, 7 June 1895, in Kenneth O. Morgan (ed.), *Lloyd George Family Letters, c.1885–1936* (Oxford and Cardiff, 1973), p. 85.

[23] J. Bryn Roberts to H. H. Fowler, 5 October 1895 (NLW, Bryn Roberts Papers, 236); Asquith to Ellis, 30 November 1895 (NLW, Ellis Papers); Morgan, *Wales in British Politics*, pp. 156–8.

[24] Lewis's Diary, 1895 (NLW, Lewis Papers, B7); D. Lloyd George to Lewis, 5, 11 and 31 December 1895, 4 and 16 January 1896 (ibid., D/30/36–43).

[25] Lewis's Diary, 16 January 1896 (ibid., B8).

[26] Memorandum, Lewis to Lloyd George, 1897 (NLW, William George Papers, 4271).

[27] Lewis's Diary, 6 February 1899 (NLW, Lewis Papers, B12).

[28] Lewis's Diary, 27 April 1899 (ibid.).

[29] Lewis's Diary 1895 (ibid., B7); cf. T. I. Ellis, *Cofiant Thomas Edward Ellis*, cyf. 2 (Liverpool, 1948), pp. 122–3, for Ellis's earlier enthusiasm for Rhodes.

[30] Lewis's Diary (Lewis Papers, B11).

[31] Lewis's Diary, 1896 (ibid., B8) refers to his enthusiasm for this (to my mind) incomprehensible game.

[32] Lewis's Diary, 1896 (ibid., B8).

[33] Herbert Lewis to Lloyd George, 2 November 1896 (NLW, William George Papers, 4219).

[34] Lewis's Diary, 20 April 1900 (NLW, Lewis Papers, B13).

[35] Lewis's Diary, 24 April 1900 (ibid.).

[36] *The Times*, 31 July 1900.

[37] Lewis to P. Harding Roberts, 23 July 1900 (NLW, Lewis Papers).

[38] Lewis's Diary, 1901 (ibid., B14).

[39] Lewis's Diary, 21 May 1902 (ibid., B15).

[40] Lewis's Diary, 12 November 1902 (ibid.).

[41] Lewis's Diary, 6 February 1904 (ibid., B18).

[42] Lewis's Diary, 6 March 1904 (ibid.).

[43] Lewis's Diary, 16 November 1906 (ibid., B20).

[44] Lewis's Diary, 9 August 1907 (ibid., B21).

[45] Lewis's Diary, 25 February 1908 (ibid., B22).

[46] Lewis's Diary, 29 April 1909 (ibid., B23).

[47] Lewis's Diary, 4 May 1911 (ibid., B25); Bentley B. Gilbert, *David Lloyd George*, vol. 1 (London, 1987), p. 339.

[48] Lewis's Diary, 24 November 1911 and 5 September 1912 (ibid., B25, B26).

[49] Lewis's Diary, 5 September 1912 (ibid., B26).

[50] Lewis's Diary, 22 March 1906 and 24 April 1907 (ibid., B20. B21); Cameron Hazlehurst and Christine Woodland (eds), *A Liberal Chronicle: Journals and Papers of J. A. Pease, 1908 to 1910* (London, 1994), p. 14.

[51] Lewis's Diary, 25 April and 22 May 1912 (NLW, Lewis Papers, B26); Lewis to his wife, 24 April 1912 (Lewis Papers). For Lord Hugh Cecil and Lloyd George's speeches, see *Parl. Deb.*, 5th ser., XXXVIII, 1294ff.

[52] Lewis's Diary, 26 February and 11 March 1909 (NLW, Lewis Papers, B23).

[53] Lewis's Diary, 23 February 1910 (ibid., B26).

[54] Lewis's Diary, 1 March 912 (ibid., B26).

[55] Fred Llewellyn Jones, later Sir Frederick Llewellyn-Jones (1866–1941), one of the last of the Liberal grandees of the Ellis–Lloyd George era, joined the Labour Party in March 1918. However, he later rejoined the Liberals and became Liberal (later National Liberal) MP for Flintshire, 1929–35.

[56] On this general theme, see Ewen Green, *The Crisis of Conservatism* (London, 1995).

[57] See John Owen to Lewis, 23 June 1903; R. Llew Jones to Lewis, 22 August 1903; P. Harding Roberts to Lewis, 31 August 1903 (NLW, Lewis Papers, A/143, 150, 151) for aspects of these manoeuvres.

[58] Lewis's Diary, 24 January 1910 (ibid., B24).

[59] Lewis's Diary, 3–6 June 1914 (ibid., B28).

[60] Lewis's Diary, 8 February 1915 (ibid., B29).

[61] See H. A. L. Fisher, *An Unfinished Autobiography* (London, 1940), and the chapter by Ben Bowen Thomas in Kitty Idwal Jones (ed.), *Syr Herbert Lewis*, pp. 84, 95.

[62] D. Lloyd George, *War Memoirs*, vol. 1 (London, 1938), p. 698.

[63] Lewis's Diary, 24 March and 15 March 1915 (NLW, Lewis Papers, B29).

[64] Lewis's Diary, 9 May 1918 (ibid., B32).

[65] Lewis to Beriah Gwynfe Evans, 30 January 1918 (NLW, Lewis Papers).

[66] Lewis to E. W. Evans, 7 January 1921 (ibid.).

[67] Herbert Lewis to Lloyd George, 13 and 20 December and 'Nadolig' 1920 (House of Lords Records Office, Lloyd-George of Dwyfor Papers, F/32/22–4).

[68] Kenneth O. Morgan, *Consensus and Disunity: the Lloyd George Coalition Government, 1918–1922* (Oxford, 1979), pp. 288–94. For Fisher's comparatively successful resistance to the economies proposed by the Geddes committee

and the Chancellor, Robert Horne, see 'Report, Proceedings and Memoranda of the Cabinet Committee appointed to examine Parts II and III of the First Interim Report of the Committee on National Expenditure', meetings between 10 January and 17 February 1922 (TNA, CAB 27/165), and Austen Chamberlain to Fisher, 13 January 1922 (Bodleian Library, Oxford, Fisher Papers, box 1). To a degree, Fisher was using statistical and other material supplied him by Herbert Lewis.

[69] Lewis, 'Notes on the Coalition Government, 1920' (NLW, Lewis Papers).

[70] Morgan, *Consensus and Disunity*, p. 202.

[71] Lewis to his wife, 17 February 1921 (Lewis Papers) and Lewis's Diary, 18 February 1921 (ibid., B35). See also Kenneth O. Morgan, 'Cardiganshire Politics: the Liberal Ascendancy, 1885–1923', in *Modern Wales: Politics, Places and People* (Cardiff, 1995), pp. 242–7.

[72] Lewis's Diary, 16 March 1920 (Lewis Papers, B34).

[73] For important material on Lewis's work for the University College, Bangor, of which he became Vice-President in 1906, see J. Gwynn Williams, *The University College of North Wales: Foundations 1884–1927* (Cardiff, 1975), pp. 125–7, and Thomas, in Jones (ed.), *Syr Herbert Lewis.*

[74] There are several reflective letters from Fisher to Lewis in the later 1920s in the Lewis Papers in NLW, Class A.

7

Wales and the First World War

The British government decided that from 2014 the country would embark upon a four-year commemoration of the centenary of the First World War. Precisely what the British government intended to commemorate, and how, was not fully clear. David Cameron at first drew a comparison with the celebration of The Queen's Diamond Jubilee, an extraordinary approach to a grotesque tragedy which cost the lives of 745,000 young British men, and 2,500,000 injured, many of them seriously disabled. Fears were expressed in the Lords that it might turn out to be a celebration of militarism anywhere, from Belgium in 1914 to Afghanistan in 2014, somewhat on the model of Remembrance Sunday in recent years. Since then, the government rowed back from triumphalism, with even £95,000 given to the Peace Pledge Union to commemorate the experiences of conscientious objectors, so viciously attacked at the time of the Great War. Subsequently, we heard a different interpretation, that of not being beastly to the Germans, by making the war an opportunity to foster good feelings with our former enemy, whose assistance is so urgently needed as Britain grapples with the political problems of the European Union. Instead of a national celebration, what may transpire is a prolonged exercise in political correctness, against which knowledgeable historians like Max Hastings, arguing that aggressive German policy was the fundamental cause of the war, are rightly anxious to warn us.[1]

The French historian, Pierre Nora, has shown in his *Lieux de Mémoire* how ambiguity and contradiction can surround retrospective treatment of a nation's past, whether it be an event like the 1789 Revolution, an institution like the Panthéon, or individuals from Joan of Arc to General de Gaulle. But there can be no doubt that the British centenary commemoration will greatly enlighten the public about military and naval aspects of the Great War. The exhibitions and educational packs planned by the Imperial War Museum alone will surely be of immense educational and scholarly value. The war, however, was not only a central episode in our military history. It was also a huge divide in our social, economic, cultural and imperial history. It brought about at home not only the trauma of the so-called 'missing generation' but a positive new status for women, granted the vote at long last (at least those over the age of thirty). It also variously witnessed a new centrality for the trade unions in our industrial life, the brutal rupture of the Easter Rising in Ireland, and the impact of the brutality of war upon the sensibilities of an extraordinary generation of war poets. In India, war meant not only the loyal support of gurkhas and other regiments in combat, but also a powerful stimulus to the young Gandhi and the 'swaraj' movement for self-government. It was during the war that Gandhi developed his non-violent strategies of protest. Within Britain, the war meant greater social equality, more occupational mobility, a new impact of central government on people's lives, an erosion of pre-war moral values. At all levels in our society, to quote R. D. Blumenfeld, 'that horrible ogre, tradition, lies in the dust'. Several central features of these changes are illustrated by the impact of the Great War on Wales, quite apart from the distinctive transformations wrought upon Welsh culture and the sense of nationhood. No part of the United Kingdom, indeed, showed more dramatically than Wales the revolutionary impact of the events of 1914–18. Liberal Wales, the basis of later Victorian society in our nation, its status and its values, were a casualty of total war. In the British commemoration of the First World War, therefore, Wales merits its important place.

In the Edwardian years, right down to August 1914, Wales experienced an unprecedented period of optimism, a golden glow of hope. The present writer, in a literary conceit, once pronounced it to be, in Gibbon-like terms, 'Wales's Antonine Age'. This came out strongly in August 1911 with the investiture of the future Edward VIII as Prince of Wales. It was a distinctly artificial ceremony, with no historical connection to the events of Edward I's reign. It was devised partly for political reasons, by two serpentine operators, David Lloyd George, Chancellor of the Exchequer and a future Prime Minister, and Alfred George Edwards, Bishop of St Asaph and a future Archbishop of Wales. But the excitement and national pride that it aroused are unmistakable. In the monthly periodical *Wales* in August 1911, that often acerbic Celtic scholar, W. J. Gruffydd, used the ceremony to sing the praises of the various heroes of Liberal Wales, in particular Lloyd George himself and the *littérateur* Sir Owen M. Edwards. 'The spirit of modern Wales is as fertile in songs of action as in plans of social reform', wrote Gruffydd with much euphoria.[2] It was the mid-Victorians' 'forgotten Wales' no longer. The Investiture was an opportunity to project this self-confident country and its vibrant culture upon the national and world stage.

There was much to justify this mood of celebration. First of all, Wales of the years before 1914 was a land of unprecedented prosperity. The Welsh coalfield continued to boom down to the advent of war. It was humming with the industrial activity of its mines, its iron and tinplate works, its railways and its docks, and with the growth of towns from Wrexham to Newport. It was the largest coalfield in Britain, with over a quarter of a million miners employed from the anthracite fields of the Gwendraeth and Amman valleys in the west, to the steam coal of the Gwent valleys close to the English border. It was also the world's greatest exporting coalfield, with coal exports reaching £37m in value in 1913. Cardiff was the greatest coal exporting port in the world, though in 1913 it was actually outstripped by its up-and-coming rival Barry, a few miles down the coast. Elsewhere in the Welsh economy, the tinplate industry of east Carmarthenshire was also prospering again, having survived the American tariffs which came to be known as 'the curse of McKinley'. A growing and ever more sophisticated urban society grew up with it. In the rural areas of the north, west and mid-Wales, there was still much insecurity among tenant farmers, as a committee under Sir Alfred Mond reported in the spring of 1914.[3] But even here the worst features of the agricultural depression of the 1880s and 1890s seemed to have passed. Nothing more vividly displayed this great self-confidence of rural Wales than Llandrindod Wales in thinly-populated Radnorshire. Its 'seasons' had never known such buoyancy, and its nine hotels, such as the Gwalia and the Highland Moors, had never done such good business, especially in the summer months when young people came not only to sample the spa waters but also to survey possible partners in marriage. For Llandrindod, the pre-war years were truly its *belle époque*. It was Wales's answer to Vichy or Marienbad.

Second, Welsh and more specifically Welsh-language literature was never more thriving. The grammarian and linguist John Morris-Jones and the popular writer and historian Owen M. Edwards, supplied the culture in a contemporary view with 'a body and a soul'. While Morris-Jones's *Y Beirniad* appealed primarily to specialist scholars, Edwards, as editor of the red-jacketed children's magazine *Cymru'r Plant*, ensured that the culture appealed to the very young, as well as to adult custodians of *Cymru Fydd*. A new generation of younger poets had emerged, their presence heralded by the youthful socialist T. Gwynn Jones, whose *awdl*, 'Ymadawiad Arthur' (The Passing of Arthur) created a sensation at the National Eisteddfod in 1902, and roused the festival from a phase of literary torpor.[4] There were brilliant, even younger bards, like R. Williams Parry and T. H. Parry-Williams, the latter in his early twenties, who actually won both Chair and Crown at the 1912 National Eisteddfod. Another cultural landmark came with the publication of a major history in 1913, the two-volume study of Wales down to the Edwardian conquest in 1283, written by J. E. Lloyd of Bangor, who applied scholarly rigour to the history of Wales as no-one had previously done.[5] At the same time, coming from an active Liberal who was the close friend of the late Tom Ellis, Lloyd's history is suffused with national emotion: the Edwardian conquest is portrayed as a massive cultural and political tragedy. Since Lloyd's time, Wales has manifestly had a usable past, and a sense of its historical continuity as a nation. His masterpiece, which still dominates the field, is a profound work of cultural renewal. Musical culture also flourished, with the male voice choirs and ladies' choirs of Wales achieving new levels of fame, from Dowlais in the south to Rhosllanerchrugog in the north Wales coalfield. Conductors like Dan Davies ('Terrible Dan') and Harry Evans of the Dowlais choir became celebrities, if sometimes controversial ones. Furthermore, the manifestly democratic ethos and message of the Welsh choirs was widely praised. Defeats in competitions by English choirs, largely from the north of England, were greeted with consternation and a sense of national crisis.

Third, Wales was a land of political stability. This was provided by the overwhelming ascendancy of the Liberal Party. This reached its climax in 1906, when Wales became a Tory-free zone, with the Liberals capturing every seat in the land, save for the socialist Keir Hardie in the two-member constituency of Merthyr Tydfil (and even he lagged below the Liberal in his vote). The years of Liberal government since December 1905 had focused attention on Wales in a new way. The main focus of national pride was naturally David Lloyd George, by 1914 an enormously influential and charismatic Chancellor of the Exchequer, but there were other Welsh Liberals in government like Herbert Lewis, Samuel Evans and Ellis Griffith, apart from English interlopers like Reginald McKenna. Under this Liberal hegemony, at a time of much bitterness in English politics, a good deal of the passion of Welsh political life appeared to be diminishing. The Welsh land question no longer aroused the class passion of two decades earlier, while Welsh landowners made long overdue efforts to integrate themselves more fully into the life of the community, for instance by helping to launch local historical societies. The Education 'revolt' directed against the 1902 Education Act was by now dying out, as Church schools were peacefully transferred to the hands of the local authorities. Disestablishment of the Church showed signs of becoming a dated issue: Lloyd George was keen that it should be settled on a compromise basis so that Wales could move on to deal with more pressing issues of social reform. In any case, by July 1914 the Disestablishment Bill looked certain to become law shortly under the terms of the Parliament Act since it had passed three times through the House of Commons. For almost fifty years since 1868, the nonconformist middle class had fought for social equality. By the

Edwardian years, especially with the advent of the new 'county schools' and the county councils, the democratic revolution in Wales had ensured that that cherished objective had indeed been won.

Fourth, the fact of Welsh national identity was being increasingly recognised at the highest level. The Investiture was an example of this in terms of sentiment and showmanship. More solidly, there was the federal University of Wales, comprising Bangor, Aberystwyth and Cardiff, and founded in 1893. There was also the National Library at Aberystwyth, based on the remarkable collection of manuscripts and antiquities accumulated by Sir John Williams, who had once been Queen Victoria's doctor. Most striking of all, perhaps, was the neo-Baroque National Museum established on the south side of Cathays Park in Cardiff, one of a range of national monuments created as indicators of the vitality of the newly-crowned capital city of Wales, and as testimony to Welsh pride in its history and pre-history. National identity was evident everywhere, in the vitality of the chapels following the 1904 Revival, and in the range of publications in Welsh as well as English, weeklies and monthlies, to cater for popular and other culture. Magazines like *Y Geninen* and *Y Traethodydd* kept up a remarkably high level of intellectual discourse. For many ordinary people, the national greatness of Wales was most apparent in the field of sport. Boxing produced new working-class heroes like 'peerless' Jim Driscoll of Cardiff and two world champions, Freddie Welsh of Pontypridd at lightweight and Jimmy Wilde of Tylorstown at flyweight. Rugby triumphs were even more legendary, as the national team entered upon a golden age of almost unending victory from 1905, culminating in the historic triumph over the all-conquering All Blacks of New Zealand in December 1905, a match that went down in history and legend for ever. Commentators reflected on the precise Celtic qualities illustrated by a rugby champion like the centre three-quarter Gwyn Nicholls.[6] This was Welsh patriotism on full display – but not Welsh nationalism. The Welsh focused on their growing fame in Britain and within the mighty Empire. Cymru Fydd was forgotten. The Welsh home rule bills of E. T. John brought before the House of Commons attracted little attention. For Wales was neither separatist nor anglophobe at this great period of its history. Wales, in short, was not Ireland.

In one area, this pattern of prosperity and tranquillity was emphatically not on display. This was in the history of the Labour movement. From 1909 to 1913, south Wales was engulfed in passionate, and sometimes violent, revolt against capitalist employers, invariably on issues of wages and coal prices. At Tonypandy, after a wage dispute at the Ely Colliery, fierce battles took place between miners and the local police, the dreaded 'Glamorgans' directed by their right-wing chief constable, Lionel Lindsay. One miner was killed. Winston Churchill, who had been a reforming home secretary, nevertheless authorised the sending of two squadrons of hussars and two infantry companies with fixed bayonets to mid-Rhondda. They stayed there to intimidate the local population until October 1911. As Dai Smith has brilliantly explained, an enduring legend was to be created, and Churchill's name would be vilified in mining areas for the rest of time. In 1911, six men were shot down by troops at Llanelli during a railway strike. In 1912, Welsh miners stopped work for a month on behalf of a national minimum wage. There were mighty confrontations between the Miners' Federation and the coal-owners, even when they were Liberals, like D. A. Thomas who owned the pits at Tonypandy. More alarming to some, there were revolts also not just against the employers but even against the miners' own leaders. This was the burden of the Unofficial Reform Committee, led by young Marxist militants like Noah Ablett and Noah Rees, who produced the famous document *The Miners' Next Step* at Tonypandy in 1912, a call to arms on behalf of workers' control and industrial democracy at the pithead instead of state nationalisation.[7] Some appeared to jettison the whole idea of constitutional parliamentary politics in place of the direct action of workers at the point of production, including the general strike. This appeared to be at least part of the message of another publication, *The Rhondda Socialist*, launched in August 1911, which was popularly (and ominously) known as 'The Bomb' of the Rhondda workers.

Even so, this mood of conflict in industrial relations can be exaggerated. Quasi-syndicalist militancy focused on the Rhondda and the Aberdare valleys; it was not so evident elsewhere. The Lib-Lab tradition was still powerful. 'Mabon', with his Welsh hymns to quieten unrest, was still the miners' president and in parliament; his colleague, William Brace, was re-elected to the SWMF executive in 1914. A new generation of miners' agents and leaders, including George Barker and Vernon Hartshorn, cleaved firmly to the constitutional, non-violent path. Even the militants behind the Unofficial Reform Committee, men like Noah Ablett, S. O. Davies and Arthur Horner, even younger radicals like Ness Edwards, owed much to the older culture and values of nonconformist Liberalism. Davies had trained to become an Independent minister; Horner and Edwards sought a similar role among the Baptists; Edwards was profoundly influenced by a left-wing minister, the Revd Towy Evans of Abertillery's Blaenau Gwent Baptist chapel. Noah Ablett preached in local pulpits from the age of twelve. For them the religious revival of 1904–5 had been an inspiration which kindled their socialist faith – and in the end drove them out of the chapels. The Central Labour College and the Plebs League owed much to the populist democracy of the Sunday Schools. Keir Hardie in the *Labour Leader* spoke less of the world-wide unity of the working class and more of the harmony of 'the red dragon and the red flag'. He understood the socialising force of community. The ILP's *Merthyr Pioneer* denounced the parochialism of 'the little Bethel stage of Wales for the Welsh'.[8] To a degree often underestimated, the Welsh labour movement was still firmly tied to that stage when world war broke out in August 1914.

* * *

This thriving, buoyant society was suddenly cast asunder by the outbreak of war. At the very start, Wales displayed much the same jingoism and war frenzy as did the rest of Britain. Chapel opinion was stung when the Bishop of St Asaph alleged that recruitment amongst Welsh nonconformists was falling that behind that of the Anglicans. Several leading Welsh nonconformist ministers, therefore, issued a manifesto on 9 October 1914 calling for the mass enlistment of Welsh recruits since this was a war on behalf of small nations, as the German invasion of Belgium had demonstrated. Whatever the cause, eventual figures, later strongly contested, were to show that Wales had actually a higher rate of recruitment, proportionate to its population, than either England or

Scotland, a proportion of 13.82 per cent. Recruitment was assisted at the
end of 1914 by allowing the minimum height required of recruits to fall
to five foot three inches, which better catered for the average stature of
Welsh men. In all, a total of 280,000 Welshmen served in the armed
forces.[9] Some 40,000 of them never returned.

The war was alleged to be on behalf of Liberal values. In belligerent
speeches at the Queen's Hall, London, on 19 September 1914, and later
in his constituency in Bangor on 26 February 1915, Lloyd George hailed
the courage of 'the little five-foot-five nations', 'gallant little Serbia and
Montenegro', 'gallant little Belgium' – and, by extension, gallant little
Wales.[10] There was much historical effort devoted to extolling the historic
glories of the Welsh at Crécy and Agincourt. Much was done to identify
the Welsh nation with the causes and objectives of the war. A total of
4,500 Belgian refugees came to Wales, some of them staying in the comfortable hotels of Llandrindod Wells, others in pleasant seaside resorts
like Aberystwyth and Barmouth. Lloyd George fought hard to create
first a Welsh Army Corps, running to over 40,000 men. Then, in late 1915,
there emerged from it the Welsh Division, the 38th Division, 'one of the
most magnificent little armies ever turned out', declared Lloyd George,
which first saw action, of a horrific kind, at the battle of the Somme.[11] It
was initially commanded by General Sir Ivor Philipps from a famous
Liberal dynasty, though also a man with very limited experience of
military command, and that mainly in India. Still, Lloyd George could
claim to have created a version of his 'Welsh Army', despite the stubborn
hostility of the mighty Kitchener, Secretary of State for War. Recruits also
flooded separately into the Royal Welsh Fusiliers, the Welch Regiment
and the Welsh Guards. They were heavily involved in titanic battles on
the western front in France and Belgium. The 53rd Welsh, a Territorial
Army division, experienced fierce fighting at Gallipoli, in Suvla Bay,
and then in Palestine in a series of desperate battles for Gaza. My own
father, serving in the Cardiganshire battery of the Royal Engineers, was
among those who fought in Palestine under General Allenby and ended
up in Damascus. Another combatant in that theatre was E. H. Jones
whose post-war memoir, *The Road to Endor*, provided an exciting account
of his escape from a Turkish prisoner of war camp, while adding to

popular prejudice against 'the unspeakable Turk'. Welsh patriotic fervour was especially aroused up by the bloody successes of the 38th Welsh Division at Mametz Wood during the battle of the Somme in 1916, and the capture of Pilckheim Ridge in 1917. In all, sixteen Welshmen were awarded the Victoria Cross during the First World War, thirteen of them posthumously, fifteen in the army and one at sea.

Conscientious objectors were relatively few in Wales, although they had a hard time, as in the case of the celebrated poet Gwenallt who went to gaol. Welsh organisations like the Honourable Society of Cymmrodorion and the London Welsh Committee became recruitment agencies. The Welsh university colleges built up their various Officer Training Corps. No less than 82 per cent of Bangor's male students joined; one of them, Arthur Lascelles, an Englishman, was to win the Victoria Cross for his bravery at Masnières in 1917, finally losing his life four days before the Armistice. Meanwhile, women students in the Welsh university colleges were no less jingoistic, busy in handing out the 'white feather' to those they believed were 'conchies'.[12] Women in the college at Aberystwyth were said to undertake the traditional 'quadding' parade around the main hall for precisely this purpose. Anti-war male students complained, and compared the knitting of their needles while making socks for serving soldiers to that of the *tricoteuses* in France in 1793.

The atmosphere could turn very ugly at times. In Aberystwyth, the eminent scholar Hermann Ethé was driven out of the town by a xenophobic mob for no reason other than his German birth. The principal of the college, T. F. Roberts, son of an Aberdyfi policeman and one of two Aberdyfi principals of that institution, showed some moral courage in standing up against mass prejudice in that instance.[13] Later, the college authorities were to demonstrate less nobility of spirit, notably in trying to damage the career of the distinguished poet T. H. Parry-Williams, a declared pacifist. Eminent Welsh scholars and writers like John Morris-Jones, Henry Jones and Owen M. Edwards devoted their academic talents to denouncing the primordial cruelty and racialism of 'the Huns' down the centuries. Morris-Jones, seldom before moved to political pronouncement, denounced in the unlikely pages of the scholarly *Beirniad* the 'New Religion' of the German people, the nationalist philosophy of Nietzsche,

Treitschke and Bernhardi. He issued in late 1914 a belligerent address to the Welsh people, *At y Cymry* (To the Welsh People), appealing for mass enlistment in the armed services; he wrote eight pamphlets in all in this vein.[14] This attitude was especially remarkable for Owen M. Edwards who had written poignantly in *Tro yn yr Almaen* (A Visit to Germany) of Goethe and Schiller, and of the peaceful culture of the universities of Heidelberg and Göttingen before the war, when the apparently centuries-old tradition of German folk nationalism was not evident to him at all. Another fervent critic of German philosophy and culture was Sir Harry Reichel, the principal of the university college of Bangor, a man of German extraction which he was anxious to disavow.

The National Eisteddfod was especially caught up in the war fever. Lloyd George's speech to the Aberystwyth Eisteddfod in August 1916 had powerful emotional effect when he compared the singing of the Welsh choirs to the nightingales that sang in the darkest hour of the night. An even more moving event came at the *eisteddfod* held in Birkenhead in August 1917. It was announced that the winner of the chair, a young shepherd boy named E. H. Evans of Trawsfynydd in Merioneth, who had written his poem 'Yr Arwr' (The Hero) under the bardic name of 'Hedd Wyn', had fallen at Pilckheim Ridge a few weeks earlier. In response, the bardic chair at Birkenhead was draped in black. It was sadly ironic that Hedd Wyn became a kind of talisman of war, rather like Rupert Brooke in England, since he was a gentle pacific man whose earlier poem 'Rhyfel' (War) had passionately condemned the cruelty and human waste of war. It spoke of 'The anguish of the young, whose blood is mingled with the rain'.[15] So it was at Pilckheim Ridge when he was shot down. Hedd Wyn became for ever after a symbol of patriotic sacrifice. He was celebrated as such in 2013 in the powerful verse of 'Hedd Wyn's War' by the major Welsh poet, Gillian Clarke. A statue was erected at Trawsfynydd after the war. It bore an inappropriately jingoistic inscription, since it talked of the gentle Hedd Wyn 'leaving a bloodstain on Germany's fist of pain'. His simple home was turned into a museum. A fine Welsh-language film of his life in the 1990s, nominated for an award, correctly portrayed him as a tragic hero with a deep dislike of nationalist extremism.

Wales and its media during the First World War evoked a Welsh hero of a quite different kind – the Christian warrior, a man like Brigadier-General Owen Thomas, later to be elected, improbably, as the first Labour MP for Anglesey. To this end, nonconformist ministers took a vigorous part in recruiting and in preaching a warlike nationalist message. One remarkable phenomenon was the Revd John Williams of Brynsiencyn, an exhibitionist who chose to preach in the pulpit in full military uniform. It was a curious advertisement for the Prince of Peace. He informed the readers of the literary periodical *Y Beirniad* that the outstanding char-acteristic of the German people was their love of war.[16] For his services as an army chaplain, he was promoted to the honorary rank of Colonel, while he enjoyed breakfasts at 10 Downing Street. His lengthy and remarkably immodest entry in *Who's Who in Wales* in 1921 declared him to be 'a lifelong friend of the Rt. Hon. D. Lloyd George'. But no-one was more passionate in appealing to the most belligerent qualities of the Welsh than their political leader, Lloyd George himself. In the first weeks of the war, he seemed becalmed, almost silent in indecision in knowing how to respond to the conflict.[17] After all, he had made his name as anti-war politician during the South African War after 1899. But the German invasion of Belgium gave his decision a certainty which his earlier membership of the Committee of Imperial Defence and his belligerent anti-German speech during the 1911 Agadir crisis in Morocco had long ago anticipated. He was pushing at an open door. A marked change of tone and of role came with his speech to a massed audience of London Welshmen at the Queen's Hall in London on 14 September. Thereafter, his rhetoric was replete with belligerent imagery, often of a racist kind. He thus poured scorn on 'the Hun', 'the road hog of Europe'. At Bangor in February 1915, he went further still. 'Germany would quench every spark of freedom either in its own land or any other in rivers of blood. I make no apology . . . for waging a holy war against that'.[18] A kind of post-Christian religiosity coloured his subsequent speeches, notably in his volume of wartime speeches *From Terror to Triumph*, published in September 1915. In the political crisis that beset the Asquith Coalition in the winter of 1915–16, he joined with the Unionists to become the leading advocate of military conscription, so passionately opposed by many of his old Liberal comrades as a fundamental attack on civil liberties.

As prime minister from December 1916, he became the uncompromising advocate of 'the knock-out blow', 'the fight to a finish' and 'unconditional surrender'. He equalled the French premier, Georges Clemenceau, in nationalist belligerence. When he moved into 10 Downing Street, his centrality for the Welsh commitment to the war effort was underlined. His household was strongly Welsh in tone and language, including his Welsh cook (though significantly not his Welsh wife, Margaret). His Cabinet Office had as its deputy secretary the Welsh-speaking Thomas Jones;[19] his office secretariat featured Welsh assistants such as John Rowland, and later Ernest Evans, Evan R. Davies and Clement Jones, some of whom, like Jones, had graduated through the Welsh National Insurance Commission before the war. The premier's 'garden suburb' in 10 Downing Street included Welsh figures such as the erratic David Davies and the shipping magnate J. H. Davies. Welshmen served in his government in key posts such as Lord Rhondda who became Food Controller. The erstwhile suffragette Margaret Mackworth, a passionate supporter of the war effort, was a vigorous director of Women's National Service in Wales, though she did also what she could to advance the career promotion of Welsh women as well.[20] The 1921 volume *Who's Who in Wales* testified to the generation who advanced to high position through working with Lloyd George in his wartime period. The vast majority of his countrymen seemed to flock behind him as a kind of national icon, put crudely 'the man who won the war', alternatively 'the greatest Welshman yet born'.

* * *

This, however, was always a deceptive, incomplete picture. There were always important areas of dissent hidden by the public hysteria of wartime. For instance, Bertrand Russell's anti-war tour of Wales in July 1916, organised by the No Conscription Fellowship, found strong support in all parts of south Wales, especially in such places as the ILP stronghold of Briton Ferry.[21] Its impact led to much anxiety within the Home Office and the domain of the intelligence services and the Special Branch. First, there were important and growing areas of Liberal dissent. At first the critics were few in number. Nearly all the press in both languages was pro-war, while the few organs of criticism were subject to censorship under the Defence of the Realm Act (1914). Scholars like John Morris-Jones, Owen M. Edwards and Sir Henry Jones, as already noted, prostituted their scholarship by turning to crude anti-German propaganda. The celebrated Independent minister, the Revd D. Miall Edwards, in an article on 'German Philosophy in the Present Crisis' in Y Geninen in January 1915, depicted the war as a Christian crusade, directed against the philosophy of such Germans as Nietzsche, whose ill-understood doctrine of the Will to Power stamped him an ideological Antichrist.[22]

But in the course of 1915, humane Liberal dissent was growing. Principal Thomas Rees of Bala–Bangor theological college, in the Independent newspaper Y Tyst, on 30 September 1914, attacked the mindless anti-Germanism coming from Christian bodies in Wales, and evoked the old pacifism of men like Henry Richard, 'the apostle of peace'. He urged his fellow nonconformists not to accept uncritically official accounts of German atrocities at the front. The fury aroused by his views led to his being expelled from Bangor golf club. But he continued his crusade undaunted, even though his preaching invitations were reduced and doubts were expressed as to his moral suitability to serve as principal of his college. Another eminent nonconformist minister vocal in his opposition to the war was the blind Independent preacher, the Revd J. Puleston Jones. This was hard for him, since his home town, the little seaport of Pwllheli on the Llŷn peninsula, was a remarkably strong hotbed of pro-war sentiment.[23] Amongst men and women of letters, Y Wawr, published in Aberystwyth and edited by young students like the future Plaid Cymru leader W. Ambrose Bebb, became the vehicle for pacifist writers like T. Gwynn Jones, Parry-Williams and the future novelist Kate Roberts, but was later suppressed by the college authorities.[24] Parry-Williams was later to face attempts at the end of the war to have his promotion to a professorial chair rescinded: the pain remained with him when he reluctantly discussed the matter with me forty years later. It was pointed out that Hedd Wyn himself had been strongly pacifist, as the poem 'Rhyfel' demonstrated. Indeed his bardic name meant 'pure peace'. Another journal launched in October 1916, *Y Deyrnas*, edited by the redoubtable Principal Thomas Rees, was more openly political than *Y Wawr*. Its treasurer and secretary were both nonconformist ministers, the Revd John Morgan Jones and the Revd Howel Harris Hughes. It took up the cause of civil liberties, notably the harsh treatment of conscientious objectors by appeals tribunals, often dominated by landowners. It attacked not just the war but its social and civil consequences, and worked closely with the pacifist body, the Fellowship of Reconciliation. When the armistice came, it turned its attention to the equally unjust war being waged in Russia against the new revolutionary regime.[25] Other publications also became severely critical of the war, significantly all of them in the Welsh language, such as *Y Brython* and *Y Dysgedydd*. J. H. Jones, the editor of *Y Brython*, was to be prosecuted for sedition under the Defence of the Realm Act.

The attacks on civil liberties brought in new allies like the old Liberal MP, Llewelyn Williams. He was a former associate of Lloyd George in his Cymru Fydd days and had bitterly denounced German atrocities in 1914, especially the destruction of the great library at Louvain,[26] but was now a passionate opponent of military conscription. In the 'khaki election' of 1918, he was an immediate recruit for the Asquithian Liberals. Such Liberals as D. R. Daniel, Tom Ellis's old friend, left public life in disillusion. Others turned to pacifism, like the minister George Maitland Lloyd Davies, imprisoned in Wormwood Scrubs and Winston Green prisons, who became a major figure in the Fellowship of Reconciliation. He was later to be elected Christian Pacifist MP for the University of Wales in 1923, a dramatic portent of changing viewpoints among young graduates. Many more Liberal dissenters switched to the Labour Party, whose values seemed far closer to theirs than a Liberal Party headed by men like Lloyd George. One such was E. Morgan Humphreys, the editor of the hitherto impeccably orthodox Methodist newspaper *Y Goleuad*. There were four Welsh branches of the anti-war Union of Democratic Control (at Bargoed, Cardiff, Merthyr Tydfil and Pontardawe) calling for popular democratic sanction for military intervention and an end to secret wartime treaties. Welsh intellectuals, especially among the young, were no longer instinctively or necessarily Liberal in their political allegiance. Life had become far more complicated. The moral certainty and social conviction of pre-1914 Wales had been undermined.

Beyond that, the society which had nurtured Welsh Liberalism during its great years was being subtly eroded. In the rural areas, tenant farmers, on whom the Welsh Land League of agrarian radicals in the eighties and nineties had focused, were now diminishing as a class: a new 'green revolution' in the years 1918–22 offered them the prospect of buying up their own holdings.[27] Several great estates disappeared and country houses found a new, perhaps more useful, role as hospitals, government offices or university hostels. The immediate control of landlords over tenant farmers was being replaced by the more remote long-range direction of banks and building societies expressed through loans and mortgages. The indebtedness of mortgaged rural owner-occupiers became more and more central to the rural economy. By the 1930s, estate agents and solicitors were in effect becoming alternative landlords, and social relationships in the Welsh countryside becoming far more complex.

In a far broader context, the age-old ascendancy of the bishop and the squire over local society was becoming out of date. Both were being disestablished. Very importantly, the cultural and spiritual influence of the nonconformist chapels was being eroded, especially among the young. The war meant challenges to the old puritan ethic and the institutions of Sabbatarianism. The mere fact of military conscription from 1916 onwards necessarily introduced young serving Welshmen to a distinctly more secular way of life with many, often unsettling, new choices. The prestige of the chapels appeared to many to have been cheapened by the militaristic pulpit bravado of the Revd Colonel John Williams, Brynsiencyn DD. His wartime appeals for blood and sacrifice led to his post-war reputation plummeting rapidly. The chapel ethos was mercilessly satirised in the wartime short stories of Caradoc Evans, who saw it as shallow, hypocritical and drenched in sexual guilt.[28] After the war, the membership of the chapels, all of them, showed a steady decline, year on year, particularly in the more anglicised mining valleys and ports of the south. One important episode was especially revealing.

Shortly after signing the Treaty of Versailles in July 1919, Lloyd George finally achieved the disestablishment of the Church in Wales on the basis of a settlement over the terms of disendowment. To assist with the costs of the commutation of tithe, the Treasury undertook to pay the Welsh Church the sum of £1,000,000.[29] This took effect in the summer of 1920, with Bishop A. G. Edwards being installed as first Archbishop of Wales. Yet, for the chapel congregations, the attainment of their holy grail pursued for so many decades seemed almost a non-event. Ironically, the religious community that most obviously benefited from it was the disestablished Church itself, newly liberated from state control, revitalised, more prosperous and far more obviously the Church of Wales than it had ever been in the past.

Labour dissent during the war was more powerful and aggressive. At first, trade union personalities appeared to subscribe to the conventional 'patriotism' of the time. Several miners' leaders, including many miners' agents, were active in recruitment campaigns. As noted earlier, Dai Watts Morgan, later a Labour MP, was transformed into Major David Watts Morgan CBE, DSO, MP, for which he was popularly christened 'Dai Alphabet'. In the left-wing Rhondda valleys, the miners formed the Rhondda Parliamentary Recruiting Committee, with Mabon as president, to raise troops and equipment. Local Trades and Labour Councils played a supportive role, though they also served as voices of discontent on such social grievances as food prices and pensions.[30] *Llais Llafur*, the famous old ILP newspaper of Ebenezer Rees published at Ystalyfera in the Swansea valley, changed its name, language and politics to become a spokesman for 'patriotic Labour'. Anti-war members of the ILP faced violent hostility in many of the valleys, as did Keir Hardie himself in Merthyr Tydfil. When Hardie died, a memorable by-election contest took place in Merthyr in November 1915.[31] The official Labour candidate, James Winstone, was attacked as a pacifist, even 'pro-German', although he had actually supported the war and his son was serving at the front. He did not help himself by enlisting ILP opponents of the war, like Ramsay MacDonald and Fred Jowett, to speak at his election meetings. He was confronted by Charles Stanton, until then a militant, almost syndicalist, miners' agent in Aberdare, but now the aggressive voice of 'patriotic labour'. This old class warrior stridently attacked 'the brutish butchers of Berlin' and heaped personal abuse on Winstone, even threatening fisticuffs. In the end, Stanton's bellicose campaign saw him capture the old constituency of the pacifist Henry Richard with a majority of 4,206 (25.6 per cent) on a low poll. It was widely seen as an historic turning-point in labour attitudes, and the 'nationalist socialist' Lord Milner shortly afterwards created his 'patriotic labour' British Workers' League, of which Stanton became a noisy member.

Nevertheless, anti-war dissent among workers in the valleys soon built up. There was a portent of crises to come in July 1915, when the South Wales Mines Federation, at the height of wartime, began a week-long strike throughout the coalfield on behalf of a new wage structure for underground workers. Newspapers denounced 'Germany's Allies in Wales'. Lloyd George was called in to help negotiate a settlement, as so often in the past, but the Miners' Federation won its point hands down by gaining a standard wage of 3s 4d. a day plus 50 per cent. After the coming of military conscription in early 1916, so unpopular with many trade unionists, opposition to the war became far more vocal. There was dissent from left-wing bodies like the Workers' Socialist Federation, while the No Conscription Fellowship became ever stronger. Several prominent socialists were imprisoned as conscientious objectors. They included the Marxist poet Gwenallt (D. Gwenallt Jones), who wrote a powerful novel *Plasau'r Brenin* (The King's Mansions) after the war to recapture his bitter experiences as a prisoner. Ness Edwards, as an 'absolutist' conscientious objector, was sent by the local tribunal first to Dartmoor and later to Wormwood Scrubs. Others gaoled included the future Labour MPs Morgan Jones and Emrys Hughes, the latter who would eventually marry Keir Hardie's daughter, Nan. Often, they faced very harsh treatment. The twenty-year-old Ness Edwards, for instance, was beaten in Brecon barracks and chased naked by soldiers with fixed bayonets; later he had to work in local stone quarries in freezing weather. For socialists and radicals protesting against what they saw as an unjust war, doctrines of human rights and the rule of law were contemptuously disregarded in the illiberal, jingo atmosphere of the time.[32]

The new mood of protest was not evident in politics at first. In the 1918 general election, the Labour MPs elected – men like Vernon Harts-horn in Ogmore, Alfred Onions in Caerphilly and Tom Griffiths in Pontypool – were far from being extremists and had supported the war effort. Such 'bolshevist' candidates as the preacher-poet the Revd T. E. Nicholas ('Niclas y Glais') were crushed at the polls. But this concealed a growing surge of industrial and political protest. The revolutions in Russia, first in February and then in October 1917, were a powerful stimulus to militants, adding to the growing numerical strength and industrial power of the miners' union. Soldiers and workers councils sprang up in the coalfield. Maerdy was popularly named 'little Moscow'; the red flag flew at pitheads. A young miners' leader, Arthur Horner, who had gone to Dublin in 1916 to fight for the Easter Rising, was im-prisoned for sedition.[33] When Lloyd George appointed his Commission on Industrial Unrest in 1917, the report on 'No. 7 Division', South Wales, painted an especially alarming picture of deteriorating labour relations and widespread unrest against a background of social deprivation and virtual class war.[34]

By the end of the First World War, the pre-war doctrines of syndicalism and workers' power were again alive and abroad in the valleys. The pre-war Unofficial Reform Committee of Tonypandy fame re-emerged, while the Central Labour College, now based in London, created a new generation of militant young socialists, men like Aneurin Bevan, Morgan Phillips, James Griffiths and Ness Edwards, who were to stamp their influence on the Welsh and British world for a generation to come – just as Tom Ellis, Lloyd George and their colleagues had done in the era of Cymru Fydd thirty years earlier. There was a huge ideological and emotional gulf between the Marxist message of the Central Labour College and the didactic Victorian values of Aberystwyth or Bangor. Unlike its Liberal predecessors, the Labour Party, hitherto sternly male, now gave prominence to women's sections and the Women's Co-operative Guild. Further to the left, the new Communist Party struck roots in South Wales, and formed five branches in the Rhondda alone. These were among a new elite of left-wing miners' leaders who linked industrial protest to opposition to the war – men like Noah Ablett, Noah

Rees, S. O. Davies and Arthur Horner, with the charismatic leadership of an English immigrant, A. J. Cook from Somerset. Despite the pro-war atmosphere of the 'coupon election' of December 1918, which saw Lloyd George and his mainly Conservative allies returned with an overwhelming majority, it was clear that the Welsh working class had changed utterly. The reign of Mabon and the old generation of Lib-Labs was consigned to the labour historians. Welsh miners were now to be in the forefront of every strike and lock-out. They were turning away from the community values of the valleys and the Welsh nation, to the class values of the workers of the world. So it would remain.

* * *

The Wales that emerged after the Armistice was a far more troubled, tormented nation compared with the confident people of the Edwardian years. On a series of levels, there was evidence of an endemic decline. First, and most obviously, this was true of the economy, especially in the south Wales valleys. For a deceptive, brief period, the pre-war economy based on heavy extractive and manufacturing industry held its ground. The coal mines continued to thrive in 1919 and the early months of 1920 as the growth of the wartime years continued. New pits even were opened up, for example Llay main colliery near Wrexham in the north Wales coalfield. At the start of 1920 there was a record number of 272,000 men employed in coal pits of Wales in all grades of work. A terrible rude awakening soon followed. From May 1920 onwards, British trade lapsed into a severe decline of demand and production, and coal was the most obvious victim. By the early 1920s, stagnant trade and rising high unemployment were prevalent in Welsh coal and the associated steel and tinplate industries, and the docks of Cardiff, Barry and Newport. Recovery was effectively blocked by Winston Churchill's decision as Chancellor for Britain to rejoin the gold standard and at the pre-war parity. This meant a 10 per cent appreciation in the external value of sterling, at a time when other countries, notably Poland (and, through its enforced reparations payments, Germany), were dangerous competitors. It seriously increased the comparative price of British coal, a savage blow for an essentially exporting coalfield like South Wales. Mass unemployment inevitably followed. The huge slump in demand after the financial crisis of 1931 made matters even worse. The Industrial Survey of South Wales, directed by Professor Hilary Marquand of Cardiff in 1932, spelt out the grim facts: 30 per cent unemployed amongst the insured population of the Pontypridd-Mountain Ash-Rhondda districts, a similar figure in Rhymney-Tredegar to the East, and 34.7 per cent in Newport with its steel industry in a state of near collapse.[35] There were a few brighter spots. The port of Swansea found new work with the tankers working in the recently-constructed BP oil refinery at Llandarcy. Some of the coastal resorts in north and mid Wales found new business through tourism. But the general picture of south Wales was conveyed by cloth-capped miners having to travel to London, singing to middle-class theatre-goers to earn a few pence. In all, 430,000 people, largely able-bodied younger men, had to leave south Wales in the interwar years, some to work in the new car plants in Dagenham, Coventry and Oxford, and on the Slough trading estate. They took their radicalism with them. In the Cowley car works and the Pressed Steel plant in Oxford, the immigrant Welsh (10 per cent of the total migration into Oxford in 1926–35) were seen as industrial activists with some becoming militant shop stewards in the Transport Workers' Union.[36] Back home in Wales, however, the official designation for the valleys was that of a 'Depressed Area'. The optimism and buoyancy of pre-1914 had almost totally disappeared.

Less visibly, but no less durably, the vigorous Welsh-language culture of the pre-war period also entered a period of decline. The linguistic census of 1921 showed an absolute drop in the total of Welsh-speakers to 929,000 (37.2 per cent), a fall of 50,000 compared with the census of 1911. It was the perhaps inevitable product of many factors, including the pressures of secularisation and anglicisation during the social upheavals of total war, and the declining influence of the nonconformist chapels. Along with this went a diminution of Welsh community sentiment in rural areas and industrial villages alike. This had many consequences for national life. The great male-voice choirs suffered acutely with the migration of robust young singers. Great choral conductors died or moved away, not always to be replaced.[37] The most popular

Welsh song of the wartime period was Ivor Novello's patriotic ballad 'Keep the Home Fires Burning', to the dismay of aficionados of the Welsh choral tradition. Haydn and Handel took a back seat, other than as Christian names. Another, less expected, consequence of the erosion of this communal world came in sport. Welsh rugby fell sharply away from the high standards of the Edwardian 'golden age'. Many more international matches were lost, as sturdy colliers, dockers and steelworkers were less available as props in the front row, and young men from the few Welsh public schools, such as Llandovery College, appeared behind the scrum. In literature, the young titans of pre-war, men like T. H. Parry-Williams and R. Williams Parry, had survived the trauma of war and still wrote distinguished poetry. T. Gwynn Jones was still highly creative. Despite this, it is noticeable, however, that there was nothing in Wales resembling the school of anti-war poets, men like Wilfred Owen and Siegfried Sassoon who made their impact in England. There were some young Welsh poets who condemned the experience of war, like Gwenallt who had been imprisoned for his principles. However, a famous poem like that of Cynan (the Revd A. E. Jones), 'Mab y Bwthyn' (Son of the Cottage) was more a lament at war and violence in general than a public condemnation of the mass slaughter of young lives. Nevertheless, a wider disillusionment with pre-war, and even more of wartime, values soon became evident among Welsh-language poets and prose authors. There was a significant cultural compensation in the 1930s with a brilliant school of the so-called 'Anglo-Welsh' novelists and poets, like Jack Jones, Gwyn Jones or Dylan Thomas. Some of them achieved international fame, extended to Wales itself in print and later on screen in Richard Llewellyn's *How Green was my Valley*.[38] But the consequence of the war was in key respects a loss of cultural, as well as economic energy. Wales was becoming not only less prosperous but also less Welsh.

Political and social change was equally profound. The Old Liberalism of Lloyd George's heyday rapidly evaporated. The temporary ascendancy of the Welsh prime minister in the coalition government of 1918–22 soon disappeared as normal party politics returned. He himself suffered a rapid slump in his postwar reputation, unlike Clemenceau who was honoured ever after in France as *Père La Victoire*. The Liberals in Wales suffered a huge collapse, catastrophically so in south Wales to the advantage of the rising Labour Party. By 1923 Labour held almost every seat in south Wales outside Cardiff, as well as Wrexham in the north, along with less durable gains in Anglesey and Caernarfon. Even the rout of Labour in the 1931 'doctor's mandate' general election proved to be only a temporary setback; even in 1931, Labour maintained its ascendancy. As noted, in 1923 the University of Wales constituency, that citadel of nonconformist Liberalism, was captured by the saintly Christian Pacifist George Maitland Lloyd Davies, who voted in the House with the Labour Party even if not running under its colours. Perhaps appropriately, he was defeated in 1924 by Lloyd George's former private secretary, Ernest Evans. The Liberal Party was now manifestly an ageing, declining force, despite Lloyd George's attempts to revitalise it in 1935 with a 'New Deal' programme for economic revival. Its tally of Welsh seats (including the University of Wales seat) fell from 21 in 1918 to 11 in 1924 and to only 7 in 1935. After the Second World War it fell still further until, in 1966, Emlyn Hooson in Montgomeryshire was the sole survivor, orphan of the storm. The new political titans were Labour men like the centrist James Griffiths in Llanelli, and the socialist firebrand Aneurin Bevan. It was Labour which was the unique voice of social protest against mass unemployment and despair in the beleaguered industrial communities of the south. Several of its key figures, including Griffiths, Bevan, George Hall and Ness Edwards, were to figure prominently in the Attlee government after 1945, with Morgan Phillips, once of the Marxist Central College, as its general secretary. This Labour ascendancy was seen not only in parliament but equally in local government where Labour-led local authorities in the 1930s, backed by the co-ops, fought a valiant rearguard action against cuts, the means test and communal decay.

Fourth, the national ideals of pre-1914 Wales emerged as less vibrant, if not completely tarnished after years of patriotic jingoism. So many of their monuments, notably the university colleges, had been the product of the self-confident, chapel-based, grass-roots national pride of the late-Victorian and Edwardian periods. That movement was now in retreat, even though it retained important influence, seen in the ethos of the BBC in Wales which ensured that Sunday programmes, for instance, consisted of interminable hymn-singing and general puritanical gloom. The national idealism of Welsh Liberalism, many felt, needed to be fundamentally revisited: the *Welsh Outlook*, the progressive journal of national opinion and commentary founded by Thomas Jones, intelligently agonised over the issue. A few responded to this sense of crisis with a wider internationalism. This was seen particularly in the idealistic outlook of David Davies, once a member of Lloyd George's 'garden suburb'. He was a passionate supporter of the League of Nations Union in Wales, and personally financed a new chair of International Politics at the University College of Aberystwyth. Its first holder was the eminent Greek scholar and political philosopher Sir Alfred Zimmern, who at least was committed to idealistic support of the League even if a controversial later successor was not.[39] The Temple of Peace and Health in Cathays Park, Cardiff, opened in 1938 and now used as the Welsh Centre for International Affairs, was Davies's most visible gift to his people. Its most sombre feature is the Welsh Book of Remembrance. The internationalism of David Davies was countered by the new and more intense nationalism of Plaid Genedlaethol Cymru, the National Party of Wales (later Plaid Cymru), founded at Pwllheli in 1925 by two distinguished Welsh-language writers, Saunders Lewis and W. Ambrose Bebb. They poured scorn on pre-1914 'nationalism' which they regarded as hypocritical, pompous and of no moral worth. Their nationalism was to a high degree a direct reaction to the war, since Saunders Lewis had served in the trenches and was wounded at Bourlon Wood: his brother Ludwig was killed in Belgium. W. Ambrose Bebb had edited the anti-war *Y Wawr* at Aberystwyth. Both pointed out repeatedly the way in which the Treaty of Versailles had paid tribute to the force of nationality, as shown in such hybrid inventions as Czecho-Slovakia and Yugo-Slavia (which Lloyd George had resisted), and how smaller peoples such as the Welsh and the Irish had been ignored and betrayed. A heavy emphasis in the publications of the new nationalist party was on international affairs; it was contemptuous towards the League and insisted in the thirties that there was no case for another European war. There, however, Lewis and Bebb diverged. Lewis, along with J. E. Daniel, played down the alleged threat from Germany and Italy as the product of 'poisonous English propaganda'. Bebb, by contrast, a French scholar and strong Francophile, was alarmed at the threat from 'Hitler and his fellow Satans' to the territorial integrity of France and the security of the European continent. Plaid's counsels were divided during the Second World War. Bebb strongly supported the war and resigned from the party. Lewis (in *Y Ddraig Goch*, October 1939) saw it 'as an English war for English aims' and refused to back it in any way, which seriously undermined his authority. It took a later generation of nationalists after 1960 to create a more lasting niche for Plaid Cymru in Welsh life comparable with their predecessors in Cymru Fydd.

The war, then, left a bitter legacy for Wales. After it was all over, the Welsh, like many other people, were uncertain how to commemorate it. Angela Gaffney's fascinating analysis has shown how memorials commemorating the fallen could provoke argument about the competing claims of Wales, Britain and the Empire, for whom the Welshmen who had sacrificed their lives were supposed to have died.[40] There was some emphasis on Welshness, but even the choice of language to be used on war memorials could be the cause of contention. A town like Ammanford, which witnessed a savage strike by its anthracite miners in 1925, with much violence between miners and an aggressive local police, found it hard to work out a consensus, including on whether an appropriate memorial would be a public amenity like a hospital or a public park, or a purely ceremonial landmark. The size, form and (especially) cost of memorials could give rise to constant argument. The noble war memorial on the sea-front in Aberystwyth, the work of the Italian sculptor Mario Rutelli, aroused controversy of a different kind, with local chapel-going nonconformists shocked by the bare-breasted young maiden who confronted the waves of Cardigan Bay. On balance, a striking feature of Welsh war memorials is their anonymity, their identification with the worldwide glories of an empire on which an English sun never set, rather than with the more familiar qualities of the democratic 'little five-foot-five nations' for whose interests Lloyd George in 1914 had declared that the supreme sacrifice was being asked. Memorials after 1945, following a far more acceptable war, seemed to attract and generate warmth and unanimity.

The experience of the First World War in Wales was not wholly negative. There were positive aspects such as the new attention paid to health and housing, which saw the first experiments in public-assisted housing in towns like Swansea and Wrexham in the 1919 Addison Act. There were advances in education, especially higher education after the Haldane report on the University of Wales, which resulted in a new university college being established in Singleton Park in Swansea in 1922. The status of women in some limited areas of professional life in Wales, such as education, also reflected wartime changes and was significantly promoted in the 1920s by idealistic pioneers like Margaret, Lady Rhondda with her Six Points Group for social and political rights for women. But the comparison with the pre-war years remains striking. There was a manifest loss of self-confidence, perhaps of vitality, compared with the Edwardian golden age. So there was, perhaps, in Britain as a whole in the 'locust years' of the twenties and thirties. But it had a special impact in Wales with its distinctive national experience. The legacy of pre-war national Liberalism lived on in the principality for many decades. In the 1960s it was still visible in many great institutions, as noted above with the BBC in Wales (notably when it branched out into television in 1963), in the Court of the University of Wales, in the myriad complex committee world which emerged from the administrative achievement of pre-war bureaucrats like Sir Alfred T. Davies and Sir Percy Watkins, and in civil society more generally. At the end of the twentieth century, this old national consensus was waning fast. The advent of devolution, the product of a new generation and somewhat different secular traditions, sought to give it new life. But the effective demise of the University of Wales after 2010, in the face of hostile criticism from the Welsh government and from anglicised administrators, was symbolic of changing values. Devolution has given Wales a new sense of its creative destiny. But the organic national vitality of its Edwardian heyday a hundred years ago, extending from the Sunday Schools to Cardiff Arms Park, has never quite been replaced. There would be much dignity in Wales in commemoration of the First World War in 2014. Families like mine would reflect on the faith and bravery of their forbears. But perhaps Welsh men and women, including the

Lloyd George Society, for whom these thoughts were originally composed, would reflect too on the tarnished glory of a world we have lost.

Notes

1 Max Hastings, *Catastrophe: Europe goes to War* (London, 2013), and his essay in *BBC History Magazine* (November 2013).
2 W. J. Gruffydd, *Wales* (June 1911), p. 81. See John S. Ellis, *Royal Ceremony and National Identity in Wales 1911–1969* (Cardiff, 2008).
3 Kenneth O. Morgan, *Rebirth of a Nation: Wales 1880–1980* (Oxford and Cardiff, 1981), p. 125.
4 David Jenkins, *Thomas Gwynn Jones* (Dinbych, 1973), pp. 173ff.
5 See Huw Pryce, *J. E. Lloyd and the Creation of Welsh History: Renewing a Nation's Past* (Cardiff, 2011).
6 See David Smith and Gareth Williams, *Fields of Praise* (Cardiff, 1981), for the definitive account of Welsh rugby at this period.
7 See Kenneth O. Morgan, 'Socialism and Syndicalism: the Welsh Miners' Debate, 1912', in *Modern Wales: Politics, Places and People* (Cardiff, 1995). The definitive analysis of Tonypandy and its riots is David Smith's seminal article in *Past and Present* (1980), reprinted in Dai Smith, *In the Frame: Memory in Society. Wales 1910–2010* (Cardigan, 2013), pp. 387ff.
8 *Merthyr Pioneer*, 14 March 1914. Here and elsewhere, I am indebted to my Lords colleague, Baroness Golding, for fascinating information about her father, the Rt. Hon. Ness Edwards MP.
9 These somewhat contentious statistics appear in Ivor Nicholson and Lloyd Williams, *Wales: Its part in the War* (London, 1919), p. 26. See also Robin Barlow, 'Did Wales go willingly to the First World War?', in Huw V. Bowen (ed.), *The New History of Wales: Myths and Realities in Welsh History* (Llandysul, 2011).
10 Speeches printed in David Lloyd George, *From Terror to Triumph* (London, 1915).
11 See Colin Hughes, *Mametz: Lloyd George's 'Welsh Army' at the Battle of the Somme* (Gerrard's Cross, 1982) and Wyn Griffith, *Up to Mametz* (London,1931). Griffith, later a distinguished public servant, served at Mametz as a captain in the Royal Welch Fusiliers.
12 J. Gwynn Williams, *The University of Wales 1893–1939* (Cardiff, 1997), pp. 107–8.
13 E. L. Ellis, *The College by the Sea* (Cardiff, 1972), pp. 171–3, and David Williams, *Thomas Francis Roberts* (Cardiff, 1961).
14 John Morris-Jones, *At y Cymry* (Bangor, [1914]); a particularly virulent publication by Morris-Jones was 'Buddugoliaeth ffydd' (The Triumph of Faith), a fierce attack on pacifists and conscientious objectors, published in *Y Brython*, 12 January 1918.

[15] See Alan Llwyd, *Out of the Fire of Hell: Welsh Experiences of the Great War 1914–1918 in Prose and Verse* (Landysul, 2008).

[16] John Williams, 'Y Rhyfel', *Y Beirniad* (January 1915).

[17] 'I am moving through a nightmare world these days': David Lloyd George to Margaret Lloyd George, 3 August 1914, in Kenneth O. Morgan (ed.), *Lloyd George: Family Letters, c.1985–1936* (Oxford and Cardiff, 1973), p. 167.

[18] See, in this vein of religiosity, Lloyd George's speech 'The Righteousness of our Cause', delivered at the City Temple Congregational Church, 10 November 1914.

[19] See E. L. Ellis, *Thomas Jones* (Cardiff, 1992), and R. K. Middlemas (ed.), *Thomas Jones: Whitehall Diaries*, 3 vols (Oxford, 1969, 1971).

[20] Angela John, *Turning the Tide: The Life of Lady Rhondda* (Cardigan, 2013), pp. 142ff.

[21] Jo Vellacott, *Bertrand Russell and the Pacifists during the First World War* (Brighton, 1980). I am indebted to Professor Vellacott for valuable information on Russell's tour.

[22] D. Miall Edwards, 'German Philosophy in the Present Crisis', *Y Geninen* (January 1915).

[23] See T. Eirug Davies, *Prifathro Thomas Rees, ei Fywyd a'i Waith* (Llandysul 1939), pp. 138ff.; R. W. Jones, *John Puleston Jones M.A. D.D.* (Caernarfon, n.d.), pp. 186ff., and their writings in *Y Tyst* and other newspapers.

[24] A complete run of *Y Wawr* is held in the National Library of Wales, Aberystwyth. It urgently requires its historian.

[25] *Y Deyrnas*, November 1918.

[26] W. Llywelyn Williams, 'Rhyfel', *Y Beirniad* (October 1914). It was, pronounced Williams, 'a holy war'.

[27] John Davies, 'The end of the Great Estates and the rise of Freehold Farming in Wales', *Welsh History Review*, 7/2 (December 1974), 186–212.

[28] See especially Caradoc Evans, *My People* (1915) and *Capel Sion* (1916).

[29] Kenneth O. Morgan, 'The Campaign for Welsh Disestablishment', in *idem*, *Modern Wales: Politics, Places and People* (Cardiff, 1995), for the disendowment settlement in 1919.

[30] Chris Williams, *Democratic Rhondda* (Cardiff, 1996), pp. 101ff.

[31] Kenneth O. Morgan, *Keir Hardie: Radical and Socialist* (London, 1975), pp. 273–4.

[32] Wayne David, *Remaining True: A Biography of Ness Edwards* (Caerphilly Local History Society, 2006), pp. 4–5; conversations between the present author and Baroness Golding.

[33] See the autobiography, Arthur Horner, *Incorrigible Rebel* (London, 1960), and Nina Fishman, *Arthur Horner: a Political Biography* (London, 2010). I have benefited from conversations on Horner with the late Nina Fishman.

[34] *Commission on Inquiry on Industrial Unrest, 1917–18*. Report No. 7 Division. South Wales (Cd. 8668).

[35] Hilary Marquand, *Industrial Survey of South Wales* (Cardiff, 1932), chapter 1.

[36] R. C. Whiting, 'The Working Class in the "New Industry" towns between the war: the case of Oxford' (unpublished D.Phil. thesis, University of Oxford, 1978), especially pp. 186ff. and 274ff. I have benefited from conversations with Dr Whiting.

[37] See Gareth Williams, *Valleys of Song. Music and Society in Wales 1840–1914* (Cardiff, 1998), which provides the definitive account.

[38] See David Berry, *Wales and Cinema: The First Hundred Years* (Cardiff, 1994), p. 268.

[39] See below, pp. 175ff.

[40] Angela Gaffney, *Aftermath: Remembering the Great War in Wales* (Cardiff, 1998); also see J. M. Winter, *The Great War and the British People* (London, 1986). For events in Ammanford, see Lester Mason, '"Is it nothing to you, all ye who pass by?" Commemorating the Great War in Ammanford 1920–1937', *Llafur*, 11/1 (2012), 49–62; and Hywel Francis, 'The Anthracite Strike and the Disturbances of 1925', *Llafur*, 1/2 (May 1973).

8

Alfred Zimmern's Brave New World: Liberalism and the League in 1919 and after

'The tents have been struck and the great caravan of humanity is once more on the move.' 'We are making the world safe for democracy.' Thus General Smuts and President Woodrow Wilson on the new post-war outlook in 1919.[1] There was an apocalyptic mood, symbolised by the creation of the Woodrow Wilson chair of International Politics in the University College of Wales, Aberystwyth, in 1919, the first such university chair anywhere in the world. It shows vividly how the optimism and brave new world idealism of the immediate post-war period focused on the creation of the new League of Nations at the Paris Peace conference in 1919. The naming of the chair after Wilson reflected the fact that the idea of a League of Nations was in practice very much an Anglo-American one. Wilson had developed the idea during the war – the League provided the climax of his famous Fourteen Points. He regarded it as the pivotal aspect of the Peace Treaty signed at Versailles, and got his close friend and confidant, Colonel House, to work out a detailed scheme.[2] At the peace conference in Paris that spring and summer, it was widely noted that Wilson seemed prepared to make concessions on other matters – the composition of Czechoslovakia and Poland, even German reparations – in order that his cherished idea of the League could come into being.

But Wilson's ideas were very sketchy and imprecise. Hence there was a strong practical input from Britain to flesh out the details. This came initially through the Phillimore Committee in 1918, which proposed an international concert of powers that could impose economic and even military sanctions to enforce its wishes. Important also was the key role of individuals like Lord Robert Cecil and especially General Smuts of South Africa, 'that fine blend of intellect and human sympathy which constitutes the understanding man', a powerful influence on the British prime minister Lloyd George at the time.[3] The League of Nations department within the Foreign Office in many ways supplied the architecture for a League. In particular, key proposals for the structure and mechanics of such a body were worked out by a relatively obscure cloistered Oxford scholar, hitherto best known for a learned work on the Greek Commonwealth, Dr Alfred Zimmern, of whom much more presently.

The Covenant of the League only came about after fierce battles in many countries. The League was simultaneously seen as both too strong and too weak. In the United States, isolationists were hostile to what appeared to be a damaging intrusion into US hemispheric independence, while liberal writers for the political weekly *New Republic*, such as Walter Lippman, Walter Weyl and Herbert Croly, rejected the Versailles Treaty, of which the League was a key part, *in toto*. It 'merely substituted the perverted nationalism of the victors for the rabid nationalism of the vanquished'.[4] In Britain, radicals on the Union of Democratic Control saw the League as a replay of the Holy Alliance after 1815, a crude attempt to enshrine the national interests of the victorious great powers. Conversely, the French largely condemned it for being toothless, and not having the force to give effect to its decisions. Clemenceau and Marshal Foch thought the League illustrated the philosophical vagueness of the Anglo-Saxons in general. This negative view, broadly speaking, was also that of the British premier, Lloyd George, despite the impression given in his subsequent *Truth about the Peace Treaties*, in which he visualises the League as 'the effective guardian of international right and international liberty throughout the world'.[5] In any case, the League was given an almost impossible range of new responsibilities – world disarmament, administering the new mandate territories such as Palestine, even internal ethnic disputes in the new post-war states. So, from the start, it was much contested in Europe, quite apart from arousing isolationism in the United

States. And yet, the very idea of a League aroused huge enthusiasm worldwide. The League of Nations Union in Britain attracted hundreds of thousands of members.[6] It symbolised hope of a new dawn for world peace and order in international relations. It commanded the eloquent enthusiasm of Liberal intellectuals such as General Smuts, Salvador de Madariaga and Professor Gilbert Murray. They hailed what was seen as a new 'Parliament for Mankind'. This was broadly the view of Alfred Zimmern.

In this wave of brave new world euphoria, was there much of it evident in Aberystwyth?[7] Only to a limited degree. The mood in the University College during the war had broadly been one of grim support for the war effort, and for the policy of a Welsh prime minister who preached the 'knock out blow' and 'unconditional surrender'. Anti-war dissenters were severely dealt with. The eminent German scholar, Professor Hermann Ethé, was expelled from the town.

However, post-war idealism found one powerful voice in Aberystwyth. This was David Davies, the college vice-president, later Lord Davies of Llandinam, who was to be president in 1926 and a major benefactor of the college through the Llandinam foundation.[8] He was also Liberal MP for Montgomeryshire. A highly individualist figure in the Welsh Liberal party, his is an instance of a prominent figure drawing on the values of pre-war liberalism to provide a realistic critique of international affairs. After the war, he had set up the League of Free Nations Association, using his own funds to get it going. In May 1922 this evolved into the Welsh Council of the League of Nations Union, the body set up two years earlier in England by a group of idealists including Lord Robert Cecil and Professor Gilbert Murray. In Wales, Davies substantially financed the new Council, which had the Baptist minister the Revd Gwilym Davies as its honorary director, and kept close links to the nonconformist churches. Davies, a pacifist, had previously been chairman and president of the Welsh School of Social Service. He focused on such initiatives as a radio message of peace from Welsh children to the world. Major Wynn Wheldon, Calvinist Methodist and university registrar of Bangor, was another prominent Liberal in its ranks.

In setting up the new Council, Davies worked closely with another of Lloyd George's advisers, Thomas Jones, deputy-secretary to the Cabinet under Sir Maurice Hankey. He had backed Jones, without success, to be appointed the new principal of Aberystwyth. It was Jones who now persuaded Davies to set up his new chair of international politics, not in Oxford or in Strasbourg (to be named after Sir Edward Grey) as Davies originally visualised, but in the 'college by the sea' on the seafront in Aberystwyth. Davies and his two sisters, Gwendoline and Margaret, put up the considerable sum of £20,000, over half the cost, themselves.[9] It was the first such chair anywhere in the world. Its purpose was clear: it was to study 'the best means of promoting peace between nations', in other words to promote the League of Nations. Davies spelt out two central themes that would guide it – the 'will to create a new World State' with its own laws, and the emergence of 'democratic nationalities'. A new chair would enable a small nation like Wales to conduct scientific research into the supreme problems of the post-war world. It should aim 'to cultivate an international intelligence in the mind of the Welsh Democracy in view of the ultimate Democratic control of Foreign Policy', as Davies grandiloquently phrased it.[10] The College Senate accepted the proposals for the chair on 14 May. As if that were not enough excitement for one day, it was also agreed that men and women could play mixed golf together on the local golf links.

Through the subtle agency of Thomas Jones, the first new professor was acquired. He was Alfred Zimmern, one of the authors of the idea of the League. No other candidate was considered, let alone interviewed. Zimmern had sparkling references of approval from various eminences – Graham Wallas; the historian and President of the Board of Education, H. A. L. Fisher (whose pupil Zimmern had once been); the former Lord Chancellor, Lord Haldane; and A. L. Smith, Master of Balliol. Zimmern was able to negotiate his own terms – a research programme to attract foreign students to Aberystwyth; the appointment of a brilliant young idealist, Sidney Herbert, as his lecturer in the new department; additional funds of £200 to start up a specialist library; the provision that the new Woodrow Wilson professor could spend one term in three on overseas travel; and the not inconsiderable starting salary of £750 for Zimmern.

The entire appointment was felt to be an enormous coup for Aber-ystwyth.[11]

The new professor had a complicated intellectual background.[12] There were three main influences upon him. There was first the civic ideals of the Hellenic Greeks – of that Greek Commonwealth on which Zimmern had written a famous scholarly monograph, embodying Aristotelian ideas of citizenship, civic morality and responsibility. Second, there was Idealist philosophy drawn from Hegel, a major influence upon the New Liberalism and Fabian Socialism of the day, which led to Zimmern's interest in social questions at home and overseas, and his wish to create a worldwide moral community. Neo-Hegelianism impelled many into socialism. This was not true of Zimmern, although he stated that he had been 'as close to socialism as Agrippa had been to Christianity' (presumably meaning very close indeed). But it gave him an exalted view of the state and its moral dimensions. During his time at the Ministry of Reconstruction in 1916–18, he took a particular interest in the economic structure of a League of Nations, calling for a World Economic Council and a dedicated Labour department. And, third, there was the Round Table ideology, originating from Milner's Kindergarten in South Africa after the Boer War, which led Zimmern to work with men like Philip Kerr and especially Lionel Curtis in fostering the idea of a multi-national British Commonwealth which he believed would form a prototype for the League of Nations, which in turn would nurture it. 'The League,' he told members of Columbia University in 1925, 'is exactly fitted to meet the constitutional and other difficulties of adjustment with which the British Commonwealth is confronted.'[13] Zimmern was very confident on the moral and ideological superiority of British political and civic ideas, but he also took a liberal, pluralist view of the role of the Empire in its new guise.

Zimmern was indeed a public intellectual of much authority. He was in close contact with the liberal intellectuals of the *New Republic* in the United States. He had also had important contacts with French intellectuals such as Élie Halévy, and had built up a powerful inter-national reputation. He saw education as the key to the building up of an international awareness, leading on to a notion of world citizenship, and he would begin in Aberystwyth.

Zimmern's appointment created great enthusiasm. There was some incipient alarm. 'Is he a German?' one lady was moved to ask; she was apparently reassured, however illogically, when told he was a product, indeed a scholar, of Winchester.[14] Zimmern had to explain his parents' original decision separately to move from Germany to England in the mid-nineteenth century, his father migrating from the duchy of Baden, his mother from the city of Frankfurt: he kept quiet on his Jewish blood. Progressives throughout Wales were hugely excited by having him amongst them. Winifred Coombe-Tennant, an activist in the Welsh School of Social Service, wrote to him, 'We have a great man in Wales now. I think it must be many years since any good befell her greater than your coming to share her life.' In the press, excited journalists nominated Zimmern as a kind of dream-team prime minister of the world. He was immediately active as a propagandist for Aberystwyth as well as for the League. He sought to involve himself in Welsh life and even learnt the Welsh language; there is Welsh correspondence in his papers in the Bodleian.[15] His views were always passionately expressed. He urged an idealist vision of international citizenship, shaped and buttressed by the great League itself.

However, things soon went awry. He did not see eye to eye with the imperious David Davies, who pressed the case for an international military force to enforce decisions by the League, an issue on which he agreed with the French. Zimmern also made enemies in other ways, notably criticising the limitations of the teaching methods currently being practised in Aberystwyth, the calibre of the students enrolled, and the restrictions on the social life of women students (on the last he was surely right, since my own family's recollections suggested an atmosphere of repressive moral Puritanism not greatly removed from the world of the Taliban). He tried unsuccessfully to bring in other scholars, such as the celebrated Shakespeare authority, J. Dover Wilson, as professor of English, and the global public intellectual, Salvador de Madariaga, as professor of Spanish.[16] Perhaps surprisingly, he did not put pressure on the Law department to develop international law. He was the candid friend more widely in Wales, on many issues of national concern. His famous pamphlet, *My Impressions of Wales* (1921), originally a lecture to the Oxford University Cambrian Society at Jesus College, was to criticise Wales for the relative poverty of its political life and for not punching above its weight in international debate. Overdoing the candour of the candid friend, he declared that 'Welsh higher education is neither really Welsh, nor really education.' Wales, he pronounced, was a sick country, not giving the world what she could and taking refuge in filling major positions with mediocrities.[17] It is perhaps not surprising that his popularity amongst Liberals in the principality rapidly waned.

It was, therefore, almost inevitable that he should create tensions in Aberystwyth. The college was in something of an introspective mood in 1919. It appointed J. H. Davies, the registrar and a local Cardiganshire man, as principal instead of Lloyd George's deputy-secretary of the Cabinet, Thomas Jones.[18] There was criticism of Zimmern as a brash, tiresome colleague. Worse still, there was criticism of his private life. He entered into a very public affair with the strong-willed Madame Barbier, the music-loving wife of the professor of French, herself a controversial figure who had fallen out with David Davies over the musical programmes offered in Gregynog, Davies's home and a centre for the arts. Zimmern's liaison with her aroused Old Testament passions in the chapel-going Calvinist fastnesses of Aberystwyth and, when he was named as co-respondent in the divorce case, he had to leave his chair in 1921 (Professor Barbier himself stayed on in Aberystwyth and died there in 1944). Zimmern was succeeded by a distinguished international relations historian, Charles Webster, also strongly pro-League, but far less of a propagandist than Zimmern. Although Zimmern left behind in Aberystwyth his colleague and disciple, Sidney Herbert, the Wilson chair now entered a different phase.

After 1919 the idea of the League lost some esteem. It was inevitably caught up in Keynes's savage onslaught on the Versailles Treaty in *The Economic Consequences of the Peace*. Lloyd George was never an enthusiast. He was always anxious that what he saw as essential British national interests should be protected from the operations of the League. He instanced in particular 'freedom of the seas' – it might be noted that

Wilson and the Americans insisted in Paris that the League should exclude the Monroe Doctrine from its remit.[19] The League, of course, suffered a huge blow at the end of 1919 when the US Senate rejected it. The support for the Cabot Lodge reservations, while benignly regarded by some scholars, seems to show a clear wave of enthusiasm for isolationist sentiment, whatever Lodge's own views.[20] Wilson, the victim of a stroke, was now a negligible force. There was always a problem of how the League could impose its authority. The Permanent Court of Justice set up at the Hague, following up pre-war international peace congresses, had little practical authority or ways of imposing its will.

By the time, Lloyd George fell from power in October 1922, the League was losing some of its early glamour. It lost prestige through its apparent ineffectiveness. At the outset, as Lloyd George himself pointed out, it failed to protect Armenia from being invaded and absorbed by revolutionary Russia. 'The League, I am sorry to say, is a failure', he observed as early as August 1919.[21] It could do nothing except pass resolutions. There was scant evidence that it could ever fulfil its central purpose of preventing war or armed annexation. David Davies himself focused on this issue henceforth, and elaborated schemes for a world police force. The League, however, lost credibility in the 1920s with the failure of successive peace conferences, followed by repeated failure in the 1930s to deter aggressors. The Japanese in Manchuria, the Italians in Abyssinia, and finally the Germans in one *démarche* by Hitler after another, all drove nails into the coffin of the League, and left it looking like the ineffective talking-shop that Lloyd George had derided back in 1919. Significantly, the Welsh League of Nations Union saw a rapid fall in membership, down to only 13,570 adult paid members in 1930.[22]

If the League lost prestige, so to a degree did its great evangelist, Alfred Zimmern. His career went through many gyrations after he left Aberystwyth. He became more of an anti-establishment critic. Thus in the 1924 general election, he surprisingly stood as Labour candidate for Caernarfon Boroughs, the seat of none less than David Lloyd George.[23] He fought on a radical programme. He claimed that of the political parties, Labour alone really supported the League, and he hailed Ramsay

MacDonald's plans for peace and disarmament. Labour alone had turned the League 'from an academic idea into the chief instrument of policy'. At home, Labour stood for 'the Democracy versus the classes'; Zimmern now championed the nationalisation of the mines and the railways, and the adoption of scientific programmes to promote national production. It was a surprisingly left-wing programme for one who had rejected socialism during the First World War. But, inevitably, poor Zimmern was routed. He gained only 17 per cent of the vote and Lloyd George breezed home with a majority of over 12,600.

After this, Zimmern rather drifted through the 1920s. He moved away from the Round Table group, partly because of his criticisms of Lloyd George,[24] but could not find a secure niche elsewhere. He worked variously in Cornell, Paris and Geneva. His authority in international relations was deflated by the excessive enthusiasm he showed for the abortive Locarno pacts in the mid-1920s. He lamented to Thomas Jones, somewhat pathetically, that 'it is no good imagining that the other Great Powers are as *good* (socially-minded in a world sense) as we are or that the other Great Powers are as *great* as we are'.[25] However, he found a new haven in Chatham House, and in 1930 became Montagu Burton Professor of International Relations in Oxford. After the Second World War, Zimmern, now an elderly man, moved to the United States, for which he developed a new enthusiasm. He saw the US as inheriting the liberal international values of the British Commonwealth, and US federalism itself as a logical outgrowth from the ideals of Greek democracy. He worked with international relations specialists like Hans Morgenthau, and had important pupils like the future US Secretary of State, Dean Rusk.[26]

Zimmern remained strongly identified with the League. He published a famous book on its structure and purposes in 1936, perhaps the best account of that organisation.[27] But it had a somewhat dated air and was retrospectively propagandist. It embodied the consoling creed of a 'better yesterday'. His general reputation as an academic and public intellectual was still comparatively high. This standing, ironically, was undermined by events in Aberystwyth. His successor in the Woodrow Wilson chair, E. H. Carr, published in the autumn of 1939, shortly after the outbreak of war, his famous monograph, *The Twenty Years' Crisis*, which bade fair to destroy for all time the reputation of Zimmern as a pro-League evangelist, and that of all those who felt like him.

Carr was appointed in 1936.[28] He was in every way a sharp contrast with Zimmern and with the origins of the Woodrow Wilson chair which he held. He was known, at the time of his appointment, to be highly sceptical about the League, strongly sympathetic to Germany even under Hitler, and a fierce critic of the Peace Treaties and the League. He was an unusual choice. He had held no previous academic post. He had latterly worked in Foreign Affairs. He had published books on Dostoievsky and Karl Marx, and was shortly to publish another on the anarchist Mikhail Bakunin. But he had no record of publication in international relations, while David Davies had strongly opposed his appointment on ideological grounds.

There had been a huge row on the seven-man appointing committee. Davies had wanted to appoint Will Arnold-Forster instead.[29] He was an interesting and civilised man who had worked at the League in Geneva with Lord Robert Cecil, and was also on the Labour Party advisory committee on foreign affairs, chaired by Hugh Dalton. Through his wife, Katherine ('Ka') Cox, he had personal links with Bloomsbury – Katherine Arnold-Forster had had a traumatic affair with Rupert Brooke which is thought to have resulted in a still-born child.[30] They were both friendly with the Woolfs. Arnold-Forster himself was a close associate of such leftish commentators on world affairs as Arthur Ponsonby, Philip Noel-Baker and Leonard Woolf. He was a painter and landscape-gardener, and was a most attractive and liberal-minded personality whose support for the League was beyond doubt. But he was really not much of a scholar. His academic output consisted of just two slight works on disarmament, little more than pamphlets, along with discussion papers on international arbitration. He was not even a university graduate. Davies, with his passion for the League, had to argue, somewhat absurdly, that Arnold-Forster had qualities equal or superior to those of the other candidates, a view with which even the pro-League zealot, Professor Gilbert Murray, disagreed.[31] There was fierce contention between Davies and the Aberystwyth principal, Ifor L. Evans, who stuck to his guns. He described Arnold-Forster as 'a nervous, eccentric person with no academic qualifications . . . by occupation a painter and by predilection a propagandist'. At one stage, passions between president and principal ran so high that Davies stamped out, leaving his fishing tackle behind in the council chamber. He resigned in high dudgeon as college Treasurer, though he was later to relent. In the end, Carr's main rival turned out to be someone perhaps less suitable even than Arnold-Forster, the expert on Hungarian history, C. A. McCartney, a right-wing defender of the regime of the neo-fascist Admiral Horthy. McCartney (later fiercely attacked as an extremist by A. J. P. Taylor and his Hungarian wife, Eva),[32] would, one might surmise, not have been a happy choice for the campus at Aberystwyth.

Carr's duties were relaxed. He spent one day a week in the college, in which he delivered just three lectures. He did not bother to buy a property in the town, staying in the Belle Vue hotel. His view of Aberystwyth as a remote provincial town was patronising and contemptuous. Unlike Zimmern he made no effort to get to know Wales or understand its culture and traditions. He has been called 'no friend to small nations' and someone who acknowledged 'the duty to lie'.[33] He used the long railway journey from Paddington to get on with his writing, rather than look out of the window. He now turned for the first time to international relations. He broke totally with the tradition of Zimmern and Webster by removing the League of Nations as a central preoccupation of research and teaching in his department. His book, *Twenty Years' Crisis*, writes his biographer Jonathan Haslam, was a 'brutal and damning attack' on the idealists, on the 'utopians', who believed in a mythical world order, in the harmony of interests, and the importance of the League of Nations. The Welsh League of Nations Union close to hand was a prime target for ridicule. Carr's view was to dominate approaches to international relations theory for many years to come. His views reflected the rise of the dictators in the 1930s. He strongly defended appeasement on the grounds that Hitler was correct in condemning the injustices of the peace treaties, right to take up arms against them, and also justified in arguing for the need for space in the east for a policy of *lebensraum*. He lavished praise on Munich and on Neville Chamberlain's conduct of foreign policy down to March 1939.[34] It is noticeable that in the second edition of the book, long after war had broken out, a good deal of this praise was whittled down.

Carr's writing was marked by a thorough-going contempt for the very idea of a League of Nations. Zimmern was one of his chief *bêtes noires*. He identified him as foremost among contemporary examples of utopian fantasy, and ridiculed him in numerous footnotes, with much effect, as when Zimmern claimed that the League did not function properly because people in general were not intelligent enough.[35] In retaliation, Zimmern himself, a less unworldly figure than Carr suggests, attacked Carr for his 'moral relativism'. Norman Angell, a more pugnacious peacemonger, called it 'moral nihilism'.[36] Carr replied that they both wilfully ignored the simple element of power in world affairs.

Davies vehemently condemned Carr and his activities at this time. Carr worked during the war as leader-writer for *The Times*, where *inter alia* he campaigned strongly for a second front and a post-war alliance with the Soviet Union. Davies strongly disliked *The Times* in any case, and attacked Carr's far-left views. He also objected to Aberystwyth paying part of Carr's salary while he made money as a journalist in far-away London. Davies now became very embittered. He claimed that every Woodrow Wilson professor since Zimmern had worked against his own ideas for the League, and he resigned as President of the college.[37] His creation, the Welsh League of Nations Union, so vigorous in organising the Peace Ballot in 1935, was by the time of Munich a shadow of its former self, much divided over his repeated calls for an international police force. Davies died in 1944: much of the passion of Liberal Wales for a moral redirection of international relations died with him. Carr stayed on controversially in Aberystwyth, until he also left in 1947. Ironically, in one personal respect he emulated Zimmern, since he also embarked on an affair with the wife of a colleague – in this case the distinguished geographer/anthropologist, Daryll Forde. Carr was publicly named as co-respondent amidst much local scandal, the moral climate of Aberystwyth not having changed very much since 1919. Mrs Forde in due course became the second of Carr's three unhappy wives. His biographer, Haslam, seems to depict Carr's invariable role as husband as insensitive and abusive.

By the time of Carr's departure in 1947, the utopianism of the hopes of Zimmern's generation and of the League of Nations Union in Wales seemed self-evident. The United Nations after 1945 built in the preponderant weight of the great powers to avoid being a replay of the ineffective League that preceded it; it sought to blend realism with idealism in a way that had not been attempted in 1919. Sixty and more years on, it was still relatively thriving. It could claim, as its Charter had declared back in 1945, to be the champion of a global legal order 'securing human rights and fundamental freedoms'. The United Nations Association in Wales, founded in 1945 and based in David Davies's handsome Temple of Peace in Cathays Park, Cardiff, proved appropriately to be far more robust in its structure than its predecessor had been. Its president, active in promoting conferences in international education at Gregynog Hall, was the now venerable but irrepressible Revd Gwilym Davies. He was to die in 1955, still holding aloft the banner of pre-1914 pacifism to inspire a new generation. One of the innovations was an annual Henry Richard lecture, to commemorate and celebrate Wales's apostle of peace.

Davies Davies in his later years had become very disillusioned with the holders of the Wilson chair – all of them. 'I wish to God I had never initiated this proposal', he wrote. Every professor since Zimmern had resisted turning the League into an effective international authority.[38] Was this pessimism justified? Clearly, the history of the Woodrow Wilson chair illustrated the fragility of the brave new world idealism of the post-war settlement in 1919 and its eventual eclipse amid the appeasement of the 1930s and the carnage that followed. So is the story of Davies's venture after the First World War just one of the discrediting of international idealism in the face of the cynical, relentless, tough-mindedness of power politics? Were the dreams of the liberal left ninety years ago nothing more than a hopeless illusion? I do not believe that they were. In the early twenty-first century – despite the relative weakness of the World Court (as over the building of a divisive wall in Palestine by the Israeli authorities), despite the International Criminal Court being undermined by the United States and other countries – the idea of order in world affairs and the force of international law has become more coherent and its impact more effective.

As regards the debate between Zimmern and Carr, scholars have rightly pointed out that the contrasts often drawn between them are often overdone.[39] They have both suffered to a degree from being stereo-typed. Zimmern's own critique of the League and the effectiveness of its powers was in many ways strongly realistic. Carr in certain definitions was something of a utopian, notably in the way his Marxist sympathies made him sympathetic to fundamental social change. Nor should the balance of error be tilted too one-sidedly. Both of them shared serious misjudgements about key issues. In particular, both made predictions about the likely disappearance of the force of nationalism that the history of the world since 1945 has fundamentally discredited. Zimmern's view, conveyed to the readers of *Welsh Outlook* in July 1919 that there was 'no future for political nationalism in the modern world', now seems totally bizarre.[40] Both Zimmern and Carr got Munich hopelessly wrong, although from different perspectives.

But of the two, it is the so-called 'realism' of Carr that has worn much less well. His own writings on history did not aid his cause. In part, they read like a worship of the successful and the powerful. As he wrote, whimsically perhaps, in a passage on cricket, he supposed that the history of that game focused on 'those who made centuries rather than those who made ducks and were left out of the side'.[41] His judgements could become discredited for their moral emptiness. He endorsed the appeasement of Hitler and his assault on neighbouring countries, and appeared to justify the Nazis' demand for *lebensraum* in the east. He endorsed Hitler's programme of enforced regime change, much as President Bush, vice-president Cheney and Donald Rumsfeld did during their invasion of Iraq. Carr went on to write an immense, scholarly account of the Soviet Union in which, however, the Stalinist regime is treated almost wholly uncritically. The massacre of the kulaks or the mass murder of Stalin's fellow Georgians are chronicled with the kind of moral indifference that George Orwell was to see as the hallmark of left-wing intellectuals. Carr's magnum opus now reads as a conspicuous casualty of the Cold War.

Carr, then, was resoundingly wrong on both Hitler and Stalin. More generally, the world has moved on from the thought-worlds of both the two famous Aberystwyth professors. But of the two, in a multi-polar world, with globalisation imposing a sense of interdependence and shared vulnerability, with a new quest for world order on environmental and other issues, it is Carr's approach that now looks far more debatable.

Zimmern, by contrast, is worth rescuing from the condescension of posterity, in E. P. Thompson's famous phrase, along with the ideals of 1919. In Aberystwyth itself, of course, Zimmern's legacy lies in what was closest to his heart – education. He was in many ways a difficult colleague, dogmatic and tactless. He failed to give Welsh Liberals the kind of moral lead that they craved in dealing with overseas relations. But he wanted to make Aberystwyth a unique dynamo in the teaching and research of international relations, and, for all his immediate despondency at the time of his departure, he may surely be judged to have succeeded. He wanted to extend that work into the spheres of international law and the study of a global economic order. The cult of the League is long past, but his wider analysis of the international community has won renewed academic and legal support. It is the idealists who now dominate the world of international relations within academia. The International Politics department at Aberystwyth has a named E. H. Carr chair and formal public lecture. Perhaps, if it is not mischievous to suggest it, the authorities there might also consider setting up a Zimmern chair and lecture as well.

Beyond the confines of the Aberystwyth campus, the debate over the invasion of Iraq in 2003 may be seen as opening up a new phase in the age-long contest between the approaches of Zimmern and Carr. In fact, over issues such as unilateral 'regime change', the paying of heed to the wishes of the international community and the United Nations in particular, questions of legality in the use of force, the opening up of public information and the right to know, and over parliamentary and civil control over military policy, much of the argument has gone Zimmern's way. The legal tribunal in the Netherlands on the Iraq invasion in 2010, very much a tribunal of lawyers unlike the long-running British Chilcot inquiry, brought all this out very clearly in a verdict of comprehensive condemnation. Lawyers like Philippe Sands and Lord Bingham, the former Master of the Rolls, have endorsed the need for stronger and more respected legal parameters for a lawless world.[42] The whole idea of an emergent international legal order has more support since the trial of ex-President Pinochet of Chile in the 1990s. Lord Bingham has written of how rulers and states are more likely to be 'arraigned at the bar of world opinion'.[43]

Robert Kagan famously wrote that 'Americans come from Mars, Europeans come from Venus'.[44] This is perhaps an odd view since Woodrow Wilson, for eight years president of the United States, was the most dedicated Venusian of them all. But the history of the Aberystwyth Wilson chair offers both these deities in stark form. In their attitude towards power, Carr came from Mars, Zimmern was a camp-follower of Venus. Public debate after the attack on Iraq, even during the enfeebled and unduly prolonged inquiries of the Chilcot tribunal, suggests a posthumous victory for Zimmern and those who took his view. So, indirectly, does the decision, in the US and Britain alike, not to bomb Syria unilaterally in August 2013. That, at any rate, would be the judgement of Bingham in the *Rule of Law*. What seemed to be illusions or utopian fantasies when Zimmern left Aberystwyth have now more intellectual credence. International law is a more robust discipline than in 1919. Our world, at a theoretical level at least, is to that degree less obviously lawless. So we should celebrate Zimmern's brief tenure of the Aberystwyth chair, and the encouragement it gave internationally-minded Welsh progressives. Carr's writings in part suggested that history was for the winners, who re-wrote the record in their own interests. It may now be that, nearly a century on, it is Zimmern's that is the winning side. In the eternal struggle with the giant Mars, it may be poor little Venus who has prevailed.

Notes

1 Ruth Henig, *The League of Nations* (London, 2010), p. 27. This is much the best recent work on the formation of the League. Also helpful is Margaret Macmillan, *Peacemakers* (London, 2001), pp. 92–106.
2 Godfrey Hodgson, *Woodrow Wilson's Right Hand* (New Haven, 2006), pp. 198ff.

3   Mark Mazower, *No Enchanted Palace* (Princeton, 2009), pp. 28ff. The quotation on Smuts comes from David Lloyd George, *War Memoirs* (London, 1938 edn), vol. 1, p. 1032.

4   Charles Forcey, *The Crossroads of Liberalism* (New York, 1961), pp. 289–92.

5   David Lloyd George, *The Truth about the Peace Treaties*, vol. 50 (London, 1938), p. 409.

6   Martin Ceadel, *Pacifism in Britain* (Oxford, 1980), pp. 62–3; Goronwy J. Jones, *Wales and the Quest for Peace* (Cardiff, 1969), pp. 93–6.

7   See E. L. Ellis, *The University College of Wales, Aberystwyth* (Cardiff, 1972), pp.171ff.; Kenneth O. Morgan, *Rebirth of a Nation* (Oxford, 1981), pp. 162ff.

8   See Jones, *Wales and the Quest for Peace, passim*. The present author wrote the entry on Davies in the *Oxford Dictionary of National Biography*. Davies left a decent collection of papers, and it is surprising that no biography of him exists.

9   Trust Deed of the Endowment, Council Minutes, University of Wales, Aberystwyth, archive; Ellis, *The University College of Wales, Aberystwyth*, pp. 187ff. Davies's statement about the new chair was published in *The Times*, 7 December 1918. I am greatly indebted to Dr Gerald Hughes for his kind assistance with materials in Aberystwyth.

10   David Davies, 'Memorandum on the Establishment of a chair of International Politics in the University of Wales, 1919' (NLW, Lord Davies of Llandinam papers, D4/2).

11   Materials in Council and Senate minutes, Aberystwyth University archive.

12   For excellent accounts of his ideas, see Mazower, *No Enchanted Palace*, pp. 66ff.; Paul Rich, 'Alfred Zimmern's cautious idealism: the League of Nations, International Education and the Commonwealth', in David Long and Colin Wilson (eds), *Thinkers of the Twenty Years Crisis: Interwar Idealism reassessed* (Oxford, 1995), pp. 79–99; and Paul Rich, 'Reinventing Peace: David Davies, Alfred Zimmern and Liberal Internationalism in Interwar Britain', *International Relations*, 2002, 16/1, 117–33.

13   For the Round Table, see J. E. Kendle, *The Round Table and Imperial Union* (Toronto, 1975). Zimmern's comments appear in *The Third British Empire* (Oxford, 3rd edn, 1934), p. 75.

14   Unidentified to Zimmern, 8 March 1919 (University of Wales College, Aberystwyth council minutes).

15.   Winifred Coombe-Tennant to Zimmern, 11 November 1920 (Bodleian Library, Oxford, Zimmern Papers, 16ff., 120–8); E. Griffith, Dolgellau, to Zimmern, 21 July 1920 (ibid., f. 108).

16   E. L. Ellis, *T.J.: A Life of Dr Thomas Jones CH* (Cardiff, 1992), pp. 207–8.

17   Alfred Zimmern, *My Impressions of Wales* (London, 1921), pp. 34, 39.

18   Ellis, *T.J.: A Life of Dr Thomas Jones CH*, pp. 208–10.

19   Hodgson, *Woodrow Wilson's Right Hand*, p. 211.

20 The converse is argued in Thomas A. Bailey, *Woodrow Wilson: the Great Betrayal* (Macmillan, 1945), but I do not find the argument convincing.

21 Lord Riddell, *Lord Riddell's Intimate Diary of the Peace Conference and After 1918–1923* (London, 1933), p. 118.

22 This was the result of many members failing to renew their subscriptions. See Goronwy J. Jones, *Wales and the Quest for Peace* (Cardiff, 1970), p. 126, fn. 7. Jones's book is by far the best study of the Welsh League of Nations Union.

23 Material in Zimmern Papers, 18, including Zimmern's election address.

24 Lionel Curtis to Zimmern, 30 December 1922 (Zimmern Papers, 17, 158–69). Curtis notes here that 'The Round Table is not a society or an organization from which anyone can secede. It is just a circle of friends who think for themselves.' Zimmern seceded nevertheless.

25 Zimmern to Thomas Jones, 8 May 1930, in K. Middlemas (ed.), *Thomas Jones, Whitehall Diary*, vol. 2 (Oxford, 1969), p. 256.

26 Mazower, pp. 99–100. Zimmern encouraged Rusk in 1949–50 in trying to turn the UN into a pro-American body that could by-pass the Soviet veto.

27 Alfred Zimmern, *The League of Nations and the Rule of Law* (London, 1936). His previous work, *The Third British Empire*, based on lectures given at Columbia University, underlines the affinities as Zimmern saw them between the British Commonwealth and Empire and the League of Nations (Oxford, 1926; 3rd edn, 1934).

28 See Jonathan Haslam, *The Vices of Integrity: E. H. Carr 1892–1982* (London, 1999); Brian Porter, 'E. H. Carr: the Aberystwyth Years, 1936–1947', in Michael Cox (ed.), *E. H. Carr: A Critical Reappraisal* (London, 2000), pp. 36ff.; and John Mearsheimer, 'E. H. Carr v. Idealism: the Battle Rages on', *International Relations*, 2005, 19/2, 139–52.

29 See Porter, 'E. H. Carr', and Ellis, *University College of Wales, Aberystwyth*, pp. 245–7.

30 For Katharine ('Ka') Cox (1887–1938) and her tumultuous relationship with the bisexual Brooke, see Brooke's entry in the *Oxford Dictionary of National Biography*. She and Arnold-Forster produced a distinguished son, the publicist and Liberal politician, Mark Arnold-Forster. I am indebted to my old friend Paul Levy for information on her life.

31 Arnold-Forster's main works were *The Victory of Reason* (1926) and *The Disarmament Conference* (1931), both slight works. He was Labour candidate for St Ives, Cornwall, in the 1929 general election, and later worked for Transport House on foreign policy.

32 Personal knowledge.

33 Charles Jones, *E. H. Carr and International Relations, The Duty to Lie* (Cambridge, 1998), p. 102.

34 Peter Wilson, 'Carr and his early critics: Responses to the *Twenty Years Crisis* 1939–46', in Cox (ed.), *E. H. Carr*, p. 175.

[35] E. H. Carr, *Twenty Years Crisis* (London, 1951 edn.), p. 39.
[36] Wilson, 'Carr and his early critics'.
[37] Ifor L. Evans, *Lord Davies, the Wilson Chair and the Presidency of the College,* February 1941 (University College of Wales archives, International Politics).
[38] Porter, 'E. H. Carr'.
[39] Cf. Mearsheimer, 'E. H. Carr v. Idealism'.
[40] Alfred Zimmern, 'The Intenational Settlement and Small Nationalities', *Welsh Outlook* (July 1919), 171–5.
[41] E. H. Carr, *What is History?* (London, 1961), p. 121.
[42] Tom Bingham, *The Rule of Law* (London, 2010), pp. 111ff.; Philippe Sands, *Lawless World* (London, 2005).
[43] Bingham, *The Rule of Law*, pp. 111ff.; Sands, *Lawless World*, pp. 46ff.
[44] Robert Kagan, *Of Paradise and Power. America and Europe in the New World Order* (New York, 2003).

9

England, Wales, Britain and the Audit of War

The award of the Booker Prize for 1995 to Pat Barker's *Ghost Road* did more than pay tribute to the latest powerful novel in the author's 'Re-generation Cycle':[1] it also emphasised once again how much the historical and cultural consciousness of twentieth-century Britain is dominated by images of war. With the obvious exception of Northern Ireland, Great Britain has been an unusually peaceful and stable country in a century marked by revolution and upheaval. Yet our national experience has been shaped, almost obsessed, by two world wars in a way true of few, if any, other countries. Memories of 1914 and 1939 tower over us like Lutyens's massive monument at Thiepval. The war leaders, David Lloyd George and Winston Churchill, are commonly thought of as our two greatest prime ministers in modern times (though another, more recent, prime minister, victorious in the Falklands, also has her champions). Armistice Day, Remembrance Sunday and the wearing of poppies retain their potency as all-powerful national symbols of sacrifice. The British Legion remains an influential pressure group. The eightieth anniversary of the battle of the Somme in July 1996 emphasised anew the enduring impact of the tragedies of the First World War. More generally, the fiftieth anniversaries of VE Day and VJ Day the previous year were nationwide ceremonies of remembrance for the sacrifices of the second. Almost every episode in current history, especially where Europe is involved, is commonly linked with memories of earlier conflict. Even the 1996 crisis in Anglo-German relations, such as it was, arising from 'mad cow disease' evoked comparison with 1939. The *Independent* satirically evoked Paul Nash's famous sketch, 'Over the Top'. The *Guardian* pondered whether the rifts over possible European Monetary Union or creeping federalism should be linked with national preservation or national purgation, whether with Neville Chamberlain in 1939 or Rupert Brooke in 1914.[2]

However, the received impression of the two world wars shows fundamental differences. The First World War is, irredeemably it seems, associated with tragedy and disaster, with the mass slaughter of the trenches during the war, and cynical betrayal by the 'hard-faced men' in the aftermath of the peace. It is seen not just as slaughter, but as senseless slaughter, conceived in dishonour. The colossal human sacrifice of the war is generally linked with bitter recollection of the total failure to achieve that 'land fit for heroes' in the years that followed. The First World War, indeed, has generated a good deal of historical literature along these themes, notably in the fascinating divergence between Paul Fussell and Jay Winter as to the most appropriate forms of popular commemoration and mourning, whether traditional artistic techniques were sufficient in themselves or a new 'modernist' language needed to tell the brutal truths about total war.[3] A distinguished range of recent literature has explored the potential of both approaches, most notably perhaps in Sebastian Faulks's remarkable novel *Birdsong*, which deals with the social and cultural impact of the battle of the Somme. Other writers have explored the devaluation of language that occurs when poets, historians or other remembrancers attempt to describe the unspeakable.[4]

The Second World War, by contrast, is almost universally seen as a good war. It has been projected not just as the defeat of the tyrant, Hitler, but as a war for social justice, when a people's war was followed, in Britain at least, by a people's peace. The most celebrated treatment of this theme, perhaps, is the moving finale of Alan Taylor's *English History, 1914–1945*:

Traditional values lost much of their force. Other values took their place. Imperial greatness was on the way out; the welfare state was on the way in. The British empire declined; the condition of the people improved. Few now sang 'Land of Hope and Glory'. Few even sang 'England Arise'. England had risen all the same.[5]

The contrast between the two wars is enshrined, forever it seems, in popular legend and cultural imagery. The martial objectives of 1914 are contrasted with the human civilising rationale of 1939. There is an immense gulf between the bitter satire of Joan Littlewood's *Oh, What a Lovely War!* and the affectionate household knockabout of the long-running television series *Dad's Army*.

It may well be that this kind of contrast is the right one to make. Perhaps the First World War is irredeemably dreadful and the second incontestably beneficial, and nothing more need be said. But historians ought surely to examine these two fundamental experiences, to re-evaluate the evidence, and consider whether the contrast between them is really so stark. Certainly, books that challenge the conventional wisdom are to be welcomed, including particularly Correlli Barnett's *Audit of War*[6] – I reject several of its conclusions but I applaud its capacity to provoke debate. For that reason, therefore, I flagrantly appropriate his title here, and hope that the author will condone my doing so as a contribution to an important ongoing debate.

The heroic appeal of the First World War was already seriously tarnished by the time that Lloyd George, Clemenceau and Woodrow Wilson were putting their signatures to the Treaty of Versailles in July 1919. Anti-war critics like Ramsay MacDonald and the members of the Union of Democratic Control were attaining new respectability. Criticism of the 'system of Versailles' began to mount. War demagogues like Pemberton Billing and Horatio Bottomley were on their way to oblivion; in Bottomley's case, to conviction to seven years of penal servitude. Thereafter, there was a growing reaction against what had happened to the nation, especially its lost generation of slaughtered manhood, between 1914 and 1918. The horror of the trenches became the dominant cultural image. The literature, both poetry and prose, of the post-war years was almost wholly anti-war. It is epitomised by Siegfried Sassoon, whose encounters with the army psychologist W. H. R. Rivers provide the core of Pat Barker's *Regeneration* almost eighty years on.

Even the government itself was hesitant about how to respond to the conflict. From the Armistice onwards, ministers' crises of conscience became public knowledge. There was a significant debate in Lloyd George's Cabinet in 1919 over the design and message of Lutyens's Cenotaph. Ministers agreed that triumphalism of a traditional militaristic kind should be abandoned. The memorial should not be situated in Parliament Square as a flamboyant public statement but rather in White-hall as a working street. The emphasis should be not so much on 'the glorious dead' *en masse* but on the finality and uniqueness of individual suffering. It should offer a personalised message, emphasising the fragility of each individual, not an impersonal statement like the grave of the 'unknown soldier'. This, indeed, was very much the view of Edwin Lutyens himself. He would be designing, he told Lloyd George, an empty tomb, 'a cenotaph not a catafalque'. His eventual, powerful monument was stark and simple with the war imagery stripped away. It was a triumph of understatement.[7]

A somewhat similar process occurred in music. The stirring martial themes of the war years gave way to more gentle compositions. The folk melodies of Vaughan Williams and Delius were much in vogue. Edward Elgar was almost reinvented. He became after the war less the composer of the strident tones of *Pomp and Circumstance,* which somewhat lost popularity. It was a reflective Elgar, the composer of the restrained and autumnal cello concerto (1919), who was now admired, not as the celebrant of imperial conquest but as the voice of the Malvern hills, an eternal England, pastoral and humane. In much the same way in politics, the Midlands ironmaster Stanley Baldwin was to turn himself into the ruminating 'Farmer Stan' of Strube's cartoons, the admirer of the rustic novel, *Precious Bane,* Mary Webb's Shropshire idyll.

Leaders of the forces in the war soon became popular scapegoats. The First World War threw up no military heroes, with the possible exception of General Allenby, whose mobile campaign against the Turks in Palestine had necessarily avoided the static slaughter of the western front. Field

Marshal Haig withdrew to Bemersyde from public life, in contrast to the enduring eminence of Marshals Foch or Pétain in France, or Hindenburg who rose to be president of Germany. The political leaders of the war also suffered eclipse. Lloyd George, for all his record of partial achievement as a peacetime premier in 1919–22, was a casualty of total war, overtaken by anti-war critics like Ramsay MacDonald and destined to remain out of power for the remaining twenty-three years of his life. Winston Churchill was another victim, tarred with the failures of Gallipoli for which he largely received the blame. His political recovery began in 1924 when he re-emerged as a Conservative chancellor whose financial policy focused in some measure on severely cutting back expenditure on armaments. But not until the unexpected advent of a supreme national emergency in 1939 were his career and reputation salvaged. The new political leaders after 1922 represented a reaction against the war ethos and free-wheeling individuals like Lloyd George and Churchill. They were led by Baldwin, the apostle of 'peace in our time' at home and abroad, MacDonald whose brave new world rhetoric symbolised the post-war outlook, and, not least, Neville Chamberlain, sacked in 1917 by Lloyd George after mis-handling national service and who subsequently appeared for most of the 1930s as the new giant of British political life.

On the left, the Great War was identified with capitalism, with profit-eering and betrayal. This mood was captured by J. B. Priestley in his radio broadcasts in July 1940:

> I'll tell you what we did for young men and their young wives at the end of the last war. We did nothing – except let them take their chance in a world in which every gangster and trickster and stupid insensitive fool or rogue was let loose to do his damnedest. After the cheering and the flag-waving were over, and all the medals were given out, somehow the young heroes disappeared, but after a year or two there were a lot of shabby young-oldish men who didn't seem to be lucky in the scramble for easy jobs and quick profits, and so tried to sell us second-hand cars or office supplies we didn't want, or even trailed round the suburbs asking to be allowed to demonstrate the latest vacuum cleaner.[8]

There was a constant repetition of the betrayal of the returning warriors with their dreams of a land fit for heroes. Keynes told the world that the root causes lay in the unwholesome 'coupon' election of December 1918 which, he wrongly claimed, was dominated by jingoism and chauvinism. Soon, the British labour movement and many radicals besides were to link the triumphalism of the war with mass unemployment, with the deception of the miners over the Sankey Report which called for national-isation of the mines, with the undermining of the Triple Alliance at the time of 'Black Friday', and with the reactionary social cuts of the Geddes Axe.

If the left condemned the war for its links with capitalism, the right conversely associated it with socialism, with the controls of a war econ-omy, with undermining the party system and the conventions of the constitutional order in general. Hence the peculiarly reassuring appeal of Baldwin's style of normalcy and 'safety first', as against the adventur-ism of men like Lloyd George, Churchill and Lord Birkenhead. An entire generation of war leadership was ridiculed or reviled. Liddell Hart con-demned the generals and the admirals; John Maynard Keynes attacked the politicians; the Left Book Club denounced the industrialists and their allies, the newspaper proprietors, in a collective mood of Never Again.

Interestingly, one other country also illustrated this degree of revulsion against the war, another victorious power, namely the United States. By the 1930s, anger against the 'merchants of death' who had supposedly dragged Americans into a European war, a feeling at first largely con-fined to German-Americans and left-wing radicals like Fighting Bob La Follette, was widespread.[9] It was fanned by the isolationism of the time, and popular hostility to the supposed 'merchants of death' voiced by the Nye Committee in 1935. For businessmen, the war meant the disruption of markets with war debts left unpaid by perfidious Europeans. For liberals, it brought prohibition, the 'red scare', attacks on immigrants both through restrictive racial quotas and through the attack of the judi-ciary on harmless foreigners like Sacco and Vanzetti. The war, victorious though it was, created no military hero in the United States, no new Grant or Robert E. Lee. Ironically, perhaps the only heroic figure popularly acclaimed after 1918 was a civilian, Herbert Hoover, director of the humanitarian relief programme to feed a starving continent, a rare hero in Keynes's *Economic Consequences*, although his reputation did not long survive.

Now no one can dispute the human tragedy and mass destruction that the First World War brought for Britain and other combatants, their centrality in the sorry catalogue of the crimes and follies of mankind. However it should also be noted that the war years did offer Britain a mood of change and new opportunities for reform which over-simplified later accounts have tended to obscure. The much-reviled Lloyd George coalition government did have several positive achievements, both during and after the war years.[10] The social agenda of the pre-war New Liberalism was given a new impetus. There were Christopher Addison's Housing Act to make housing a social service for the first time, H. A. L. Fisher's comprehensive Education Act, a newly created Ministry of Health under Addison, a minimum wage and relatively generous extension of the system of unemployment insurance. There were random social landmarks as varied as the Whitley Councils, the University Grants Committee, and the Forestry Commission with the first vague beginnings of a public concern with the environment. It was not revolutionary, but the Independent Labour Party were ruefully to acknowledge that four years of war had achieved more for the social objectives of Keir Hardie than had decades of peace. And, of course, women saw in the war the first signs of civil liberation, not only in women over thirty being granted the franchise for the first time but also in new employment opportunities in the teaching and other professions.

There were also some broader national landmarks which should be recorded, in economic, foreign and imperial policy. In all of them, new approaches were at least attempted if not carried through. In economic and industrial affairs, Lloyd George's managerial style in wartime suggested a new way forward. A less adversarial system of industrial relations was proposed, for all the attention rightly focused on the massive nationwide strikes of the years 1919–21. The corporate approach foreshadowed by the Whitley Councils in the public services seemed to reach its climax with the National Industrial Conference convened in the spring of 1919, along with the creation of a national rather than a piecemeal system of wage bargaining.[11]

It led to very little, of course. Most of the gains were wiped out in the turbulent strike-torn summer of 1919, while the government's policy of decontrol and deflationary policies intended as a precursor to the return to the gold standard led to major stoppages in the mines, among railway and other transport workers, and in many other industries. Even the police went on strike in 1919, with much resultant violence and loss of life in Merseyside. The armed forces were freely used to coerce the workers and a nationwide strike-bearing apparatus set up under the Emergency Powers Act. The National Industrial Conference proved to be a total failure: it was noted that, in any case, the Triple Alliance unions had stayed away from it from the outset.

On the other hand, not everything was lost. There was much re-structuring on both sides of industry that resulted. Major employers like Sir Allan Smith built on wartime corporatism to form the National Council of Employers' Organisation, which largely superseded the FBI and claimed to speak for industrial employers as a whole. On the trade union side, the General Council of the TUC came into being in 1921, with new claims for authority shown in its meetings with Lloyd George over the problem of unemployment at Gairloch in October 1921.

The impression of unrelieved industrial chaos between 1918 and 1926 is actually distinctly misleading. It applied mainly in the coalmining industry in 1919–21, then as later truly a special case with its own distinct-ive problems in relation to productivity, costs and overseas markets. After 1922 the TUC looked back to a post-war phase under Lloyd George's aegis which saw, if hardly beer and sandwiches at No. 10, at least more access to government and more effective dialogue with the employers. Stanley Baldwin, to some degree, recreated that mood in the later 1920s. Certainly by then, despite the general strike in 1926, the character of British industrial relations could be seen as more orderly and less con-frontational than before the war.

International policy also saw a potential change of direction. It is often forgotten how commanding Britain's position was in world affairs after the armistice, especially with the USA isolationist and choosing to stay on the sidelines. In this new climate, Lloyd George, the most powerful of the peacemakers to survive beyond Versailles, attempted to forge a new, more vigorous form of European – perhaps world – leadership for Britain, in a fashion unique since the end of the Napoleonic wars. He led the way to restoring both Germany and the Soviet Union, the two pariah states, to the comity of nations. He also adapted British foreign policy (with the reluctant acquiescence of his foreign secretary, Curzon) to the needs of industrial and commercial policy: one important landmark was the Trade Treaty with the Soviet Union in 1921 and its *de facto* recognition. It is worth recalling that Lloyd George, after 1918, was the first British prime minister to have to confront the facts of industrial decline and to remodel policy accordingly.

In terms of international security and stability, a possible moment of breakthrough came in December 1921–January 1922. There was the prospect of the remarkable novelty of a British fifty-year treaty guarantee for the eastern frontier of France against future possible German invasion, alongside a moderate settlement of German post-war reparations. It applied only to western Europe; beyond Germany's eastern boundaries, Lloyd George told France's prime minister Aristide Briand that 'populations in that quarter of Europe were unstable and excitable'. It was, however, a major step for British foreign policy which had since 1812 avoided the 'continental commitment', and was visualised as the precursor to a European economic settlement at Genoa. The meeting of Lloyd George and Briand at Cannes in January 1922 would, it was hoped, lay the groundwork for a treaty, despite disputes on French submarine construction and other details. Briand was warned by Ribot, '*Ah, Briand, vous êtes déjà allé à Canossa. Prenez garde que vous n'alliez pas à Cannes aussi!*'[12] In fact, as is well known, the Lloyd George–Briand partnership was disastrously undermined when a political crisis in Paris resulted from the fateful comic golf match on the links at Cannes. Briand fell from power and was replaced by the intransigent anti-German Lorrainer, Raymond Poincaré. Genoa came to nothing, undermined by the Rapallo treaty between the Soviet Union and the German foreign minister, Walter Rathenau, himself shortly to be assassinated. Nevertheless, there had been a fleeting moment when British foreign policy could just possibly have been given a new direction. What journalists nowadays choose to call a defining moment might have perished on the Cannes golf links in January 1922.

Thereafter, a powerful reaction followed against post-war foreign policy, a conviction that there should be no foreign entanglements. Lloyd George's active foreign policy was popularly associated with threats of war. It is indeed true that he fell from office following a belligerent phase of policy in the eastern Mediterranean in support of Greece and a confrontation with the Turks at Chanak. But his government had been crumbling since Cannes. Chanak was an uncharacteristic, if politically fatal, episode in foreign policy. What resulted, however, was something much broader, a reaction against an active foreign policy in general. Herein lay the roots of appeasement in its various forms. Much of the responsibility, in fact, lies in one powerful, brilliantly written book, J. M. Keynes's *Economic Consequences of the Peace*. A best-seller from the start, it proved to be an immensely damaging book: it was not really a work of economics at all, but a personal polemic reinforced by his private attachment to Germany (and perhaps illustrated by his curious homosexual attachment to the German delegate at Paris, Dr Melchior).[13] Keynes was in large measure responsible for the mood of revulsion against the 'system of Versailles', a treaty whose imperfections he exaggerated.

There followed a phase of greater isolation in British international policy. Bonar Law captured the new mood as early as October 1922, during the Chanak crisis, when he warned of the dangers of Britain's acting as 'policeman of the world'.[14] Appeasement, initially in passive form, then more dynamically under Neville Chamberlain in 1937, drove British policy henceforth. Ironically, the first great appeaser was none other than Lloyd George himself. His Fontainebleau memorandum of March 1919, during the Paris peace conference, in which he, Smuts and others warned of the dangers of a stern treatment of Germany over frontiers and reparations, was an early document in the history of appeasement. He helped to undermine his own policy, unwittingly at first, more culpably with his visit to Hitler in Berchtesgaden in 1936. An ineffective British response to the dictators was the partial outcome.

Finally, in imperial policy, there was again a prospect of a new direction after 1918. During the war, the empire was to reach its greatest extent. An Imperial War Cabinet met in Downing Street and General Smuts joined the British government. After 1919, Churchill, as colonial secretary, massively built up the British domain in the Middle East through the mandate system, like a second Alexander the Great. Yet the war also brought a clear sense of the perceived limits to imperial power. This was shown most graphically in events in Ireland. After a very dark period, the 'troubles' of the war with the IRA, the Free State Treaty was signed by Lloyd George with Arthur Griffith and Michael Collins, acting on behalf of Sinn Féin. On the basis of partition, the least of the possible evils, peace was brought to Ireland for the first time since the Act of Union. The Free State Treaty, in contrast to the Unionist rhetoric over home rule before 1914, was now seen as heralding neither the break-up of the United Kingdom nor the fragmentation of the empire. It was viewed rather as a measured, specific act of decolonisation. The cause of the small rump of southern Unionists was swept aside for the greater good. And, until the civil rights movement fifty years later, it worked.

What the war years showed with extreme clarity was that the empire was not cohesive. In the crisis of Chanak, only distant New Zealand was prepared to support the mother country in its possible fight with the Turks. The Imperial War Cabinet was a very short-term phenomenon. The post-war period was actually a phase of moderation and partial de- volution in imperial policy, even though such a conclusion could hardly be gleaned by late-twentieth century film spectaculars on Mahatma Gandhi and Michael Collins. There was a major extension of self-govern- ment in Egypt, and more strikingly in India. The Montagu-Chelmsford reforms pointed India for the first time in the direction of effective home rule on a provincial basis, comprehending Hindu, Muslim and Sikh. The disgraced General Dyer of Amritsar fame was sent packing, for all the protests of the Diehards. There was indeed a supreme irony that, during the 1920s, Lutyens's and Baker's imperial edifices were rising up on the slopes of Raisina at New Delhi. Georges Clemenceau saw them in the later twenties and observed 'it will be the grandest ruin of them all'.[15] An early visitor who came to tea with the viceroy, Halifax, in his new government house in 1931 was to be the Congress leader, Mahatma Gandhi, already perhaps contemplating his inheritance.

In assessing the consequences of the First World War, and its potential for change, there is another important aspect to consider. It should be noted that there were at least five wars that took place in 1914–18: an English war, a Scottish war, a Welsh war, an Irish war and, quite distinct, an Ulster war. The First World War, like much else in modern British history, was an exercise in pluralism and should be considered as such.

The different experience of Ireland, north and south, is obvious and needs no repetition here. In Scotland, there did appear to be a major transformation at work after 1918, which might differentiate it from England. Its epicentre was Red Clydeside, the twenty-one seats out of twenty-eight in Clydeside won by Labour, almost wholly ILP members, in November 1922. It was symbolised by Davy Kirkwood addressing the crowds at Glasgow station as the Labour members set forth to Westminster, tribunes of proletarian revolt: 'When we come back this station and this railway will belong to the people!' But Red Clydeside was not altogether what it appeared to be. It was the product of some adventitious factors, notably the switch of allegiance of Irish voters in Glasgow following the Irish Treaty. In fact, the socialist upsurge was largely confined to the Glasgow area. It was riven here by sectarian conflict between the ILP and mainstream Labour. The later years of Jimmy Maxton, beloved permanent rebel and marginalised author of the 'Living Wage', illustrated the extent of the failure. John Maclean died young in 1923, a charismatic but essentially parochial rebel, his dream of a Scottish workers' republic a hopeless chimera.[16]

In Wales, by contrast, the war years did suggest that wider changes were in train. The Welsh nation and its Liberal nonconformist champions had seemed central to the winning of the war. There was from December 1916 a Welsh prime minister, surrounded in Downing Street by a Welsh Mafia headed by the famous Welsh-speaking 'microbe' and 'fluid person', Thomas Jones of Rhymney.[17] It was also a war claimed to be fought on behalf of Welsh values: Lloyd George told a massed audience of London Welshmen at the Queen's Hall on 19 September 1914 that the First World War was fought on behalf of 'the little five-foot-five nations', Serbia, Montenegro, Belgium – and no doubt Wales.[18] The aspirations of Liberal Wales now appeared to be fulfilled – in 1920, even the age-old aspiration of the disestablishment of the Church of England in Wales was achieved.

The war appeared to confirm the hegemony in Wales of the middle-class Liberal ascendancy that had dominated the nation since the 'great election' of 1868 first saw the erosion of the rule of the Anglican land-owner.[19] But, in fact, it saw major transformations that were to propel that ascendancy to its early demise. Its legacy was disestablishment – not only of the Welsh church, but of the gentry and much of the whole pan-oply of pre-war society, Liberal as well as Tory. The chapels, triumphalist in blessing the war as a righteous crusade for the good, their ministers preaching from the pulpit in full military uniform, were supreme amongst war casualties. A new socialist upsurge had been anticipated during the pre-war industrial turbulence, the era of Taff Vale and Tonypandy. Now, after 1918, the Central Labour College with its Marxist ideology was to produce a new leadership élite, young workers like Jim Griffiths, Morgan Phillips, Ness Edwards, Lewis Jones and, above all, Aneurin Bevan of Tredegar, who were to challenge and displace the old Liberal élite and the values of *Cymru Fydd*.[20]

More than in Scotland, then, the war was to generate a period of sweeping change in Wales. It produced a new nationalism, with the foundation of Plaid Cymru in 1925 under the presidency of a war vet-eran, the Liverpool Welshman Saunders Lewis. It also saw a new inter-nationalism through David Davies and his enthusiasm for the League of Nations Union, symbolised by his Woodrow Wilson chair of Inter-national Politics at Aberystwyth. At a different remove, the return of a Christian Pacifist as member for the University of Wales in 1924 was a reaction against wartime Liberalism of a more startling kind. It suggested the growing disillusion and radicalising of the liberal intelligentsia.[21] Wales – and perhaps Scotland – was less a prey to the post-war Baldwin-ian mood of 'normalcy'.

It is often claimed that the First World War was essentially integrative in identifying Wales and Scotland more completely than ever before with the United Kingdom. In many ways, the precise reverse is true. It marked a regionalisation of cultures, which led in the interwar years to something of a regionalisation of protest. Much of the turbulence of industrial relations from 1919 onwards focused on Scotland and Wales, in Clydeside and the Welsh coalfield in particular.[22] It was they also who experienced the most savage of responses from the authorities, notably from Captain Lionel Lindsay, a veteran of Sir Garnet Wolseley's regime in Egypt, who became a long-serving chief constable of Glamorgan. The Scots and the Welsh were to infiltrate English political culture too in the 1930s, in such previously quiescent places as Coventry and Oxford. Professor Rees Davies's statement in 1995 on the importance of pluralism in analysing the culture of medieval Britain is capable of application to a far more modern period also.[23]

The Second World War has from the first always been vastly more popular. It evokes an image not of betrayal but of solidarity, of 'pulling through together' as the Ministry of Information posters put it. Artistic representations of the war emphasised the ideal of a classless unity, as in Henry Moore's sketches of citizens huddling together for mutual protection in the London underground during the blitz. There has been an abiding sense of a communal ideal, of social citizenship. The dominant intellectual figure is that of William Beveridge, truly another People's William, with the generous comprehensive ideal embodied in his famous 1942 report on Social Insurance. The divided nation of the mass unemployment in 'depressed areas', alongside consumer affluence in the southern suburbs, would be banished. The process of the evacuation of schoolchildren from English cities was commonly (if mistakenly) believed to have eroded the class divide and brought the people to a closer understanding. Unlike 1914–18, the writers and artists and musicians of the time were almost wholly sympathetic, as is shown in the wartime work of Henry Moore, Paul Nash, John Piper or William Walton. Benjamin Britten and Michael Tippett, both conscientious objectors, are distinct exceptions. Tippett, indeed, whose oratorio *A Child of our Time* (1941) had a strongly political thrust, actually went to prison, but he was a very rare phenomenon. Cyril Connolly's *Horizon* was a vehicle for literary criticism, not for political or social protest.[24] Among the population at large, Churchill enjoyed an unambiguous role as the warrior hero. After El Alamein, everyone endorsed his leadership, from the Communists to Colonel Blimp. And the war was won, conclusively, in the last major victory for British arms. Montgomery was for a time hailed as a new Wellington or Marlborough.

Despite Churchill, however, the main impact of the war seemed to be on the British left. This time it truly was a people's war, even though Mass Observation surveys suggested that the people took some time to recognise this fact about themselves. George Orwell united patriotism with social revolution in *The Lion and the Unicorn* – his evocation of Englishness was appropriated by a Conservative prime minister, John Major, fifty years on. Harold Laski went further in *The Revolution of our Time* in suggesting the revolutionary potential of the conflict.[25] A clear left-wing critique of society emerged. There might have been something more, a genuine radical revolutionary moment as indicated in lightning strikes in the Welsh valleys or perhaps the mystique of Nye Bevan in 1942–3.

But mainstream Labour skilfully appropriated the war images for itself. Labour's democratic socialism was constitutional, familiar and reassuring, a paean to neighbourliness, not a threat to private savings or ideas of public morality. Labour ministers like Bevin, Dalton and Morrison impinged just as much on the national consciousness as did Churchill. After 1945, an elderly government, most of whom remembered 1918 with great clarity, concentrated on avoiding the mistakes made after the previous war; they focused on social reform, the mixed economy and 'fair shares'. There was concern in 1946, when Bevan seemed to be building insufficient 'homes for heroes'. The images of the war dominated Labour thinking down perhaps to the leadership of Michael Foot, part-author of *The Guilty Men* in 1940, in the election of 1983. Mrs Thatcher's counter-revolution was directed largely at processes and ideas generated essentially by the war and its 'debilitating consensus' of high taxes and state control.

The war leaders of 1939–45 were almost universally popular, and remained so. Again, there is a parallel with the United States in the abiding popularity of wartime leaders of heroes from Eisenhower and Marshall through to John F. Kennedy and George Bush. In 1952, there was a prospect of Eisenhower being enlisted as presidential candidate by both main parties. It was instructive, though, that another wartime hero, Bob Dole, was reluctant to proclaim his own military achievements in the 1996 presidential election, because it drew attention to his age. An era was ending here, too.

The war evoked above all traditional images – a sense of pastoral Englishness, the peace of the countryside, the non-military and neigh-bourly aspects of British (or, more narrowly, English) life. No one em-bodied them more perfectly than the post-war Labour premier Clement Attlee, with his love of cricket and the *Times* crossword, and his personal devotion to Haileybury school. Small wonder that Anthony Howard has called his regime the most complete restoration of traditional values in British history since the return of Charles II in 1660.[26] Public and civic institutions recovered their old popularity after the depression years – the monarchy (its sheen restored after the mishaps of Edward VIII), 'the mother of parliaments', the armed services, even civil servants with their classical degrees from Oxford, the 'gentlemen in Whitehall' who, the socialist Douglas Jay assured his pre-and post-war readers, genuinely did know better.[27]

The Second World War marked a national climacteric. Down to the 1980s, two generations of British political leaders, from Churchill to Callaghan, were dominated by the memories of the wartime experience. On the right, of course, Churchill himself returned to office in 1951 and, despite failing health, remained premier for four more years. Macmillan, Eden and Heath were all in their own ways heavily influenced by war-time experience (the former, of course, had also been a courageous soldier in the First World War). Conversely, R. A. Butler remained suspect in many Tory circles as a man of Munich in 1957 and in 1963 (even though in 1963 he was defeated by Alec Douglas-Home, once Chamberlain's ministerial aide when he met Hitler in 1938). On the British left, the impress of wartime experiences was even clearer. Their leaders had been intimately involved in service at the highest level, as wartime planners (Gaitskell, Jay, Wilson), as members of the armed services (Callaghan, Healey, Jenkins) or as opinion formers (Foot). A new intellectual aris-tocracy had come into being – Noel Annan's 'donnish dominion' of the liberal-socialist intelligentsia.

Where the First World War aroused a need for change, the Second World War generated a massive nostalgia. There was for decades a cult of Churchill as war hero, and rapt audiences for the biographies of Martin Gilbert and others. Films would replay the old themes – *The*

Wooden Horse, The Dambusters, The Bridge over the River Kwai and countless others down to the mid-1980s. On television, there were huge audiences for the whimsical Home Guard portrayed in *Dad's Army*, the Changi women prisoners in *Tenko* and the grotesque parody of all wartime foreigners in *'Allo 'Allo!* After 1918, the British had turned back to pre-war stereotypes, the cult of 'business as usual', the centrality of the gold standard, even in the cause of reform. After 1945, they turned not to the pre-war years, linked with mass unemployment and the diplomacy of appeasement, but to the heady experience of 1939–45. One notable aspect is that the Second World War produced its own stereotypes of women as did the first. But, in 1939–45, they were all individual women – in fiction, Greer Garson's Mrs Miniver, in real life the Queen Mother, a heroine of the blitz, Myra Hess playing on indefatigably at the National Gallery, or the all-time forces' sweetheart, Vera Lynn. By contrast, 1914–18 produced only Nurse Cavell, the eternal martyred symbol of womanhood in general.[28]

Like the First World War, the second had many wrong lessons attached to it. After 1918, there had been perhaps too indiscriminate a sense of revulsion; after 1945, there was perhaps too much euphoria, with damaging consequences for our national experience.

First it should be noted that, for all the successes of the wartime production drive and the attempts of Cripps and others to promote industrial efficiency after 1945, the economy was not modernised as a result of the wartime experience. In particular, after 1951 the failure to re-equip the economy as other European nations were doing was deeply damaging. In 1950, a quarter of the world trade in manufacturing came from British factories; by 1964, the figure had slumped to 14 per cent. The British growth rate in the 1950s was only 58 per cent of the OECD average.[29] The reason for this did not lie in the frittering away of precious resources in building the New Jerusalem, as has sometimes been alleged. In many ways, the welfare state and post-war regional policies to promote full employment had salutary economic consequences, eventually emulated by other more successful economies overseas. Nor can the limited and moderate programme of nationalisation carried out be seen reasonably as a fundamental cause of industrial failure. Gas, electricity, civil aviation, cable and wireless were all commercial successes. And it would be hard indeed to argue that the progress of the coal mines suffered from the removal of the private coal-owners, many of whom should have been removed for incompetence and a few perhaps prosecuted for criminal negligence in their flagrant ignoring of safety regulations that cost so many lives at Gresford and elsewhere.[30]

Rather, was it a case that inadequate attention was paid to modernisation, to strategies of investment, to the training of managers or the reskilling of labour (here the limited pre-war apprentice system was favoured by both employers and unions). Employers were consistently obstructive towards government initiatives such as Cripps's Development Councils, and of course the bulk of the economy was still in private hands. On all sides there were illusions about the British economy because the war had been won, and because of the export boom between 1948 and 1955 when such potential rivals as West Germany were still in the process of recovery. The emphasis remained on production rather than innovation, on what Dr Tomlinson has called 'present output rather than future competitiveness'.[31] Inadequate advantage was taken of the advent of Marshall Aid, and there was undue attachment to the sterling area. By international standards, rates of domestic productivity were low. They remained low in 1963 when Harold Wilson made his later, perhaps excessively derided, speech to party conference about science and the 'white heat' of a new technology. It was an attempt to break out of a low-growth, low-productivity cycle, but it came too late, and when it came it was inadequately conceived.

The Festival of Britain in 1951 sought to stimulate innovation in industry and technology, and in design. But Gerald Barry's successful attempt to make the Festival a 'national autobiography'[32] led it to become a celebration of traditions, and to a nostalgic view of the national identity. There was little enough evidence of wartime radicalism. More generally, illusions prevailed about industrial relations in Britain, based on war years in which 'we all pulled through together'. In practice, Britain's industrial system was deeply adversarial, and this was not seriously challenged until the abortive Bullock report of 1976, under the Callaghan administration, attempted to introduce something similar to the codetermination of the Germans which Helmut Schmidt tried to promote with his fellow social democrat, the British prime minister. That also failed amid disputes between union leaders and the CBI.[33]

In constitutional matters, also, the Second World War proved disappointing. There had been widespread criticism of the British constitution after the crisis of 1931. Left-wing condemnation of legislative corruption came from Harold Laski and from the Guilty Men school. On the moderate right, Harold Macmillan and others called for an industrial parliament which would be far more appropriate for industrial investment and planning than the Westminster model. But winning the war ended serious constitutional debate for forty years. Margaret Thatcher, in her 1988 Bruges speech, was to hail 'Big Ben chiming out for liberty' and thereby to oppose systemic innovation. The First World War had, in fact, seen much dynamism in both theory and practice. Lloyd George's 'garden suburb' of private advisers included such innovative writers on the constitution as Leo Amery and Professor Adams. There were radical new practices in the War Cabinet and its secretariat.[34] But, after 1945, Attlee suppressed talk of constitutional change whether of the Lords, the civil service or local government. Until 1997, what little reform there has been has mostly come under the Conservatives, including life peers and the remodelling of local government for the first time since 1888.

The war actually reinforced a mood of constitutional conservatism. The ABCA current affairs classes in the army are sometimes represented as cauldrons of political argument, a new version of the Putney Debates.[35] In fact, this is much exaggerated. The ABCA literature hailed 'the mother of parliaments', and referred to John Lilburne and the Levellers as a citizen army of proto-backbenchers in a democratic House of Commons, almost the 1922 Committee under arms. It was the patriotism, not the radicalism, of Freeborn John and his comrades that was emphasised. The effect of the Second World War was to underline the glories of an unwritten constitution and conceptions of national sovereignty rooted Burke-like in history, instinct and prescription. Small wonder that Attlee and his socialist colleagues refused to tamper with it, even in gerrymandered Northern Ireland.

International policy was another area where the Second World War might be thought to have had harmful effects on subsequent British history. Foreign policy might well have been too timid after 1918, or at least after 1922. After 1945 it was surely too ambitious. Britain took pride in its role as one of the 'big three' at Potsdam, and in its intimate relationship to the United States in the Bevin era. The idea of the supposed 'special relationship' reached its high point in the period when Oliver Franks was ambassador to Washington in 1948–52 and when Britain could press its claim, as Franks somewhat curiously put it, to be standing outside and ahead of 'the queue of European powers'.[36] Churchill laid much emphasis on the wartime alliance when pressing for a 'summit conference' with the Russians in 1953, but his old comrade President Eisenhower did not respond warmly.[37]

What the war did for Britain, therefore, was to kindle illusions about its great power role and thereby to indulge in a massive over-extension of its resources around the world – what Correlli Barnett rightly calls 'global overstretch'. Dissenting voices like that of Attlee in 1945 were swept aside by the chiefs of staff.[38] In any case, the strong attachment to the role of Commonwealth leadership felt by Labour and Conservative governments alike encouraged a worldwide outlook. There was also heavy pressure from the United States for Britain, in receipt of massive assistance under the Marshall Aid programme, to retain its strategic presence in the Middle East and South-East Asia. As late as 1966, Harold Wilson was pressed hard in Washington to retain the expensive British naval base in Singapore. For their part, British governments, whether under Attlee or Churchill, viewed a role on the world stage as a posthumous response to Munich, appeasement and pre-war 'pacifism' (of which Labour in particular was deeply conscious). This led to an inflated and unaffordable defence posture from 1945 until the belated withdrawal from bases east of Suez in the later 1960s. National service was expensively maintained to hold on to imperial outposts from Belize to Hong Kong. An unduly ambitious rearmament programme was embarked upon in 1951, relatively more costly than that of the United States, the result of Gaitskell's political attachment to the Americans overcoming the accurate economic criticisms put forward (contrary to many later accounts) by Aneurin Bevan.[39]

More serious still, a long-term independent nuclear weapons programme was begun in 1946, in large measure for prestige reasons and
to retain Britain's symbolic role at the top negotiating table. It continued,
through Polaris and Chevaline, down to the adoption of Trident D5
missiles under Margaret Thatcher. Ernest Bevin had observed in 1946
that, if there was an atomic bomb in the world, '[w]e ought to have a
bloody Union Jack flying on top of it'.[40] It was a major cause of long-term
economic weakness, a failure to recognise the diminution of British
power long before 1939, and a constitutional aberration since – from 1946
onwards – all discussions of nuclear weaponry were carefully concealed
from Cabinet and parliament.

This leads to the final aspect of the damaging consequences of the
war, namely the abiding intense suspicion of 'Europe', however defined.
Wartime memories were repeatedly used to reinforce the British sense
of isolation from the continent. Much was made of memories of Dunkirk
(getting out of foreign entanglements in the most direct way) and 'standing alone' during the Battle of Britain while feeble foreigners capitulated
or collaborated in the face of Hitler's *Wehrmacht*. It bred a patriotism of
an intensely English kind, variously illustrated by Eliot's 'East Coker'
and (especially) 'Little Gidding', John Piper's watercolours of decaying
parish churches, or the war art of Paul Nash – the latter fiercely realistic in
its portrayal of the muddy misery of the trenches in the First World War,
but in the second a hymn to the mystical beauty of the English countryside, which combat aircraft manoeuvring overhead almost seemed to
embellish. On a popular level, this Englishness showed itself in a sentimental attachment to the 'white cliffs of Dover' extolled by Dame Vera
Lynn.

In this climate of opinion, moves towards European integration as
opposed to specific functional co-operation in the Western Union, were
seldom taken seriously by British governments. In 1950, the Labour
government refused to join the Schuman Plan for a coal and steel community; Morrison reported that 'the Durham miners won't wear it'.[41]
Churchill and Eden were no more positive. There were efforts to undermine the Messina conference and almost a kind of contempt for the
Treaty of Rome at its inception amongst British diplomats, as wrong over

215

Europe in 1955–7 as they had been in 1938.[42] The eventual entry into the EEC in 1973 was a reluctant move taken from a defensive posture. The British remained a Euro-sceptic nation. Anti-German prejudice remained widespread on the British right, right down to the outcry over beef exports in 1996 and assaults on the reputation of Beethoven, composer of the EU's *Ode to Joy*. The result was that, with the special relationship with the US increasingly marginal and partly killed off by Nixon and Heath, and the Commonwealth fragmenting with decolonisation, the war helped a process by which British foreign policy was left rudderless for a generation. There remains force in Dean Acheson's much criticised observation in 1962 that Britain had lost an empire and failed to find a role. Governmental and popular attitudes to Europe illustrate his point.

The Second World War, then, helped shape a novel kind of English nationalism. How was this replicated elsewhere in the United Kingdom? Wales, as has been seen, took something of a distinctive course after 1918. This was notably less true after 1945. There was indeed a remarkable lack of attention to the events of war by Welsh poets and other writers. Alun Llywelyn-Williams's volume *Cerddi* (Poems) is a rare exception.[43] The Welsh-language cultural world was embarrassed by the alleged pre-war anti-semitism and neo-fascism of Saunders Lewis, the president of Plaid Cymru, who declared his personal neutrality in 1939. The by-election in the University of Wales constituency in 1943 revealed a power-ful division in the Welsh-speaking community, and especially so in the ranks of the intellectuals identified with the distinguished literary period-ical, *Y Llenor*.[44]

In Scotland, also, many writers largely ignored what they perhaps felt was largely an English war. Edwin Muir's 'Scotland 1941' focuses on the seventeenth century rather than the twentieth.[45] Culturally, the Second World War seems largely to have passed the Welsh and Scots by. The quintessential images of the war, and of what the country felt it was defending, were essentially timeless English concepts. Eliot's later Quartets were one product of them, Orwell's and Priestley's social popu-lism were others. For all that, the war ended with the integrative process much advanced, with the Labour Party's ascendancy in Wales and

Scotland confirmed, and with those nations the more inextricably bound up in the centralist processes of the United Kingdom.

It could be that, as far as Scotland and Wales are concerned, the Second World War might represent a lost opportunity. There was, for instance, the remarkable work of Tom Johnston at the Scottish Office in 1941–5.[46] By all accounts, he used the alleged political threat from the Scottish Nationalists (who actually won a by-election at Motherwell in 1945) to force through the greatest phase of internal change Scotland had known since the Act of Union in 1707. The Council of State and Council of Industry established in Edinburgh implied a dramatic expansion of internal self-government. However, Johnston's premature retirement in 1945 meant that it could not be followed through, and unionism prevailed. In Wales, there was almost nothing by way of devolution. Suggestions to this effect from James Griffiths on the Welsh Council of Reconstruction led nowhere. Ideas of devolution, political as well as industrial, did not emerge seriously until the report of the Kilbrandon Commission in 1973. Probably the sense of national identity was not sharpened by the war in Scotland and Wales as it was after 1918. Only in very recent times, with the idea of a 'Europe of nations' current in Scotland and (to a lesser degree) in Wales in the 1990s, was there some prospect of change in outlook.[47]

The conclusion, then, seems to be that both world wars have been somewhat misrepresented in their effects on British history. There was actually some sense of renewal after 1918. A new kind of middle-class radicalism, powerful in the planning enthusiasms of the 1930s, was released. Conversely, the effect of 1945 was to confirm traditional values and received images. The radical impulse of the war years was in many ways stifled.

Of course, the Second World War also had many far more positive consequences. It helped foster the welfare state, full employment and a more realistic view of empire. The stability of Britain after 1945, and indeed since 1918, has been almost unique in twentieth-century Europe. The threat of foreign invasion and internal economic disaster have both been successfully confronted. We have lapsed neither into Bonapartism nor anarchy.

Yet, in many ways, the wrong conclusions appear to have been drawn from both world conflicts. The reasons for this are diverse and complicated. However, it could be argued that historians themselves have much to answer for. We have had after each war far too much emphasis on 'the lessons of history', and misconceived lessons at that. The history of the First World War was hijacked in the 1920s by the critics, by the Union of Democratic Control, by Keynes and Norman Angell and the critics of the left. They led the search for secret treaties and clandestine diplomacy, and the roots of what Lowes Dickinson called 'the international anarchy'. As Alan Taylor memorably recalled, the dissenters had taken over and proclaimed the conventional post-war wisdom.[48] Conversely, after 1945 there was excessive triumphalism and consensual celebration, epitomised by Trevelyan's praise of the eternal virtues of the yeoman in his wartime *English Social History* and by the writings of Arthur Bryant, his pre-war anti-semitism and support for Franco conveniently set aside.[49] And, of course, no historian had more impact than the wartime titan himself, Winston Churchill.[50] When A. J. P. Taylor tried to present an alternative, if provocative, scenario in his *Origins of the Second World War*, he was (initially) hissed off the stage as an irresponsible gadfly or fellow-traveller.

But, in each case, fortunately, things have improved. Here, too, historians have led the way. The First World War also led to the founding of the Institute of International Affairs, later Chatham House. H. W. V. Temperley's impeccably edited *History of the Peace Conference of Paris* was an early product. Today, we have the seriousness now attached to contemporary history, and the works of historians like Donald Watt and Alastair Parker which have laid down new standards of scholarship for the study of the 1930s.[51] It is possible, therefore, to conclude on a more hopeful note. Historians may now be using their skills to help us fight free from the old stereotypes. Perhaps it may be that, for the British people, the war is finally over. No longer need we designate the second half of the twentieth century as 'post-war Britain'. Perhaps we have at last come to terms with victory as other nations have come to terms with defeat. The British have long prided themselves, and with justice, on a war record of liberating other, less fortunate, peoples. Perhaps they can now turn finally to liberating themselves.

Notes

[1] Pat Barker, *Regeneration* (1991); *The Eye in the Door* (1993); *The Ghost Road* (1995).

[2] *The Independent*, 23 May 1996; Martin Kettle, in *The Guardian*, 23 May 1996.

[3] Paul Fussell, *The Great War and Modern Memory* (London, 1975); Jay Winter, *Sites of Memory, Sites of Mourning: The Great War in European Cultural History* (Cambridge, 1995).

[4] For example, Geoff Dyer, *The Missing of the Somme* (London, 1996 edn).

[5] A. J. P. Taylor, *English History, 1914–1945* (Oxford, 1965), p. 600.

[6] C. Barnett, *The Audit of War: The Illusion and Reality of Britain as a Great Nation* (London, 1996 edn).

[7] Allen Greenberg, 'Lutyens's Cenotaph', *Journal of the Society of Architectural Historians*, 58/1 (March 1989), 5–21; Christopher Hussey, *The Life Sir Edwin Lutyens* (Woodbridge, 1984 edn), pp. 391–5.

[8] J. B. Priestley, *Postscripts* (London, 1940), p. 42; cf. Sian Nicholas, '"Sly Demagogues" and Wartime Radio: J. B. Priestley and the BBC', *Twentieth Century British History*, 6/3 (1995), esp. 254–61.

[9] Cf. John A. Thompson, *Reformers and War* (Cambridge, 1987).

[10] See Kenneth O. Morgan, *Consensus and Disunity: The Lloyd George Coalition Government, 1918–1922* (Oxford, 1979), pp. 80ff.

[11] For the Conference, see Rodney Lowe, 'The Failure of Consensus in Britain: The National Industrial Conference, 1919–21', *Historical Journal*, 21/3 (September 1978), 649ff; or, more generally, see Keith Middlemas, *Politics in Industrial Society* (London, 1979), pp. 137ff.

[12] Conversation between Lloyd George and Briand, London, 21 December 1921. Rohan Butler and J. P. T. Butler (eds), *Documents on British Foreign Policy, 1919–1939*, first series, XV (London, 1967), 786; conversation between Lloyd George and Briand, Cannes, 4 January 1922. W. N. Medlicott, Douglas Dakin and M. E. Lambert (eds), *Documents on British Foreign Policy, 1919–1939*, first series, XIX (London, 1974), 7.

[13] Robert Skidelsky, *John Maynard Keynes: Hopes Betrayed, 1883–1920* (New York, 1983), p. 360. It is unfortunate that Skidelsky's analysis of *The Economic Consequences of the Peace*, particularly its financial arguments, is relatively brief. Keynes added to the impact of his book with his *Essays in Biography* (1933), including a celebrated (and inaccurate) study of Lloyd George, withheld from the *Economic Consequences*.

[14] Bonar Law, letter in *The Times*, 7 October 1922.

[15] Robert Grant Irving, *Indian Summer: Lutyens, Baker and Imperial Delhi* (New Haven and London, 1981), p. 355.

[16] There is a vivid account of the departure from Glasgow station in Emanuel Shinwell, *Conflict without Malice* (1955), pp. 76–7. Shinwell, member for Linlithgow, was not a Glasgow member himself. For Maxton, see Gordon

Brown, *Maxton* (Edinburgh, 1986); and for John Maclean, see David Howell, *A Lost Left* (Manchester, 1986).

[17] See E. L. Ellis, *T.J.: The Life of Dr Thomas Jones CH* (Cardiff, 1992).

[18] This is printed in David Lloyd George, *From Terror to Triumph* (1915), pp. 1–15.

[19] On this, see Kenneth O. Morgan, *Wales in British Politics, 1868–1922* (Cardiff, 1980).

[20] The only book on the College is W. W. Craik, *The Central Labour College* (London, 1964).

[21] Kenneth O. Morgan, *Modern Wales: Politics, Places and People* (Cardiff, 1995), pp. 102ff.

[22] See Jane Morgan, *Conflict and Order: The Police and Labour Disputes in England and Wales 1900–1939* (Oxford, 1987).

[23] Professor Rees Davies's inaugural lecture, delivered 29 February 1995 at the University of Oxford.

[24] Paul Fussell, *Wartime* (Oxford, 1989), pp. 209ff.

[25] Isaac Kramnick and Barry Sheerman, *Harold Laski: A Life on the Left* (1993), pp. 467ff.

[26] Anthony Howard, 'We are the Masters Now', in Michael Sissons and Philip French (eds), *The Age of Austerity* (Oxford, 1986, new edn), p. 19.

[27] Douglas Jay, *The Socialist Case* (1947, 2nd edn), p. 258. To be fair, the author was applying this dicturn specifically to education and health.

[28] On the other hand, Harold L. Smith (ed.), *War and Social Change: British Society in the Second World War* (Manchester, 1988), pp. 208ff, where Smith argues persuasively that the status of women in general was not enhanced by the war years.

[29] Data in Roger Middleton, *Government versus the Market* (1996).

[30] For the neglect of safety regulations, see Barry Supple, *The History of the British Coal Industry*, vol. IV: 1913–46 (Oxford, 1987), pp. 426ff. In the coal disaster of Gresford, Wrexham, in September 1934, two hundred and sixty-five miners (including boys) were killed in an explosion. Despite clear evidence of flagrant negligence by the managers, the outcome was that, in 1937, fines of £15 were imposed on each of four charges, and £20 each on four other charges.

[31] Jim Tomlinson, 'Mr Attlee's Supply-Side Socialism', *Economic History Review*, 46/1 (1993), 122. For a fuller treatment, see Jim Tomlinson, *Democratic Socialism and Economic Policy: The Attlee Years, 1945–1951* (Cambridge. 1996), pp. 68ff.

[32] Fred Leventhal, '"A Tonic to the Nation": The Festival of Britain, 1951', *Albion*, 27/3 (Fall 1995), 449–50.

[33] I cover this episode in some detail in my official biography of Lord Callaghan (Oxford, 1997), pp. 560–2. I am indebted to Lord Callaghan, HE Helmut Schmidt, Lord Murray of Epping Forest and Mr Jack Jones for first-hand information.

[34] See especially John Turner, *Lloyd George's Secretariat* (Cambridge, 1980).

[35] An interesting work is S. P. MacKenzie, *Politics and Military Morale* (Oxford, 1992). For the non-radicalising effect of ABCA classes, see J. A. Crang, 'Politics on Parade: Army Education and the 1945 General Election', *History*, 81/262 (April 1996), esp. 224–6. For some perceptive comments on the Second World War and ideas of 'heritage', see Raphael Samuel, *Theatres of Memory* (1994), p. 208.

[36] This phrase appears in Franks to Attlee, 15 July 1950 (TNA, PREM 8/1405). See also Alex Danchev, *Oliver Franks, Founding Father* (Oxford, 1993), pp. 109ff.

[37] Churchill to Eisenhower, 21 April 1953; Eisenhower to Churchill, 5 May 1953 (TNA, PREM 11/421).

[38] See Correlli Barnett, *The Lost Victory: British Dreams, British Realities, 1945–1950* (1995), pp. 70, 102. Attlee's views appear in TNA, CAB 129/1, 1 September 1945, and CAB 131/2, 13 March 1946.

[39] For a fuller analysis of the dispute between Gaitskell and Bevan, see Kenneth O. Morgan, *Labour in Power, 1945–1951* (Oxford, 1984), pp. 441ff.

[40] Peter Hennessy, *Never Again* (1992), p. 268.

[41] Bernard Donoughue and G. W. Jones, *Herbert Morrison: Portrait of a Politician* (1973), p. 481.

[42] For example, see Sir Roger Makins (British ambassador in Washington) to members of US State Department, 21–2 December 1955 (TNA, FO317/115999), M 1017/14. In the British government, Peter Thorneycroft applied the term 'fool's paradise' to the Messina conference and Macmillan spoke scornfully of 'seismic eruptions' in Sicily.

[43] Elwyn Evans, *Alun Llywelyn-Williams* (Cardiff, 1991), pp. 37ff.

[44] D. Hywel Davies, *The Welsh Nationalist Party, 1922–1945* (Cardiff, 1983), pp. 237ff. Lewis was defeated by Professor W. J. Gruffydd, a former member of Plaid Cymru, standing as a Liberal.

[45] Angus Calder, *The Myth of the Blitz* (London, 1991), pp. 73–4.

[46] Christopher Harvie, 'Labour in Scotland during the Second World War', *Historical Journal*, 26/4 (December 1983), esp. 929–34; and Graham Walker, *Thomas Johnston* (Manchester, 1988), pp. 151ff.

[47] See Christopher Harvie, *The Rise of Regional Europe* (London, 1993).

[48] A. J. P. Taylor, *The Troublemakers* (London, 1957), p. 178, citing works by Bertrand Russell, Lowes Dickinson, G. P. Gooch and H. N. Brailsford, all members of the Union of Democratic Control during the war.

[49] See Andrew Roberts, 'Patriotism: The Last Refuge of Sir Arthur Bryant', in *Eminent Churchillians* (London, 1993), pp. 287ff.

[50] See the excellent collective volume, Robert Blake and William Roger Louis (eds), *Churchill* (Oxford, 1993).

[51] D. C. Watt, *How War Came* (New York, 1989); R. A. C. Parker, *Chamberlain and Appeasement: British Policy and the Coming of the Second World War* (London, 1993).

10

Power and Glory: Labour in War and Reconstruction, 1939–1951

On 2 September 1939 Arthur Greenwood rose in the House of Commons to give Labour's backing for the government's ultimatum to Hitler. As he did so, he was urged, in a famous intervention by Leo Amery on the Tory benches (heard by everybody but not recorded in *Hansard*), to 'speak for England', Greenwood, a social patriot to his core, could equally well have been told, 'Speak for Wales'. For his and his party's uncompromising commitment to going to war was exactly the view of all parts of the labour movement in Wales as it was in Britain as a whole. In the First World War, the party and the unions had been bitterly divided: significant dissenters opposed declaring war on Germany, the imposition of conscription and the policy of fight to a finish. This time, there was virtually no dissent. The Welsh party at all levels and all the major unions were loyalist throughout. They accepted warmly the formation of Churchill's coalition (memories of the troops at Tonypandy set aside) and the policy of unconditional surrender. Indeed, the main line of criticism took the form of urging that the war be fought with greater zeal, notably opening up a second front in 1943 to assist our Russian allies. Whereas in 1917–18 there had been major movements of protest, many inspired notably by the Russian Revolution, in favour of a negotiated peace, this time there were none. Even many of the Welsh Communists were part of the wartime consensus: Arthur Horner was but one who refused to compromise his resistance to Nazi totalitarianism because of the Molotov–Ribbentrop Pact on the eve of Britain's entry into war. There were some cases of individual Labour conscientious objectors, such as the little-known Cardiff school teacher, George Thomas. Some left-wing protesters were mistreated, such as the highly individual minister-bard and unlicensed dentist, the Revd T. E. Nicholas, harassed by the Aberystwyth police and imprisoned without trial in Swansea gaol. There were attacks on civil liberties like the dismissal of the socialist nationalist, Iorwerth C. Peate, from his post in the folk studies department of the National Museum of Wales, which produced a memorable clash between Lord Plymouth and Aneurin Bevan at the meeting of its governors.[1] But, in general, the attitude of the Welsh labour movement throughout these six years was one of solidarity, loyalty and social patriotism.

This was in part because the labour movement itself was now part of the governing process. The Labour Party was fully represented in Churchill's government from May 1940 until after VE Day. Labour local authorities were involved in maintaining wartime services, notably in Cardiff, Barry and especially Swansea which suffered severely from wartime bombing. In ferocious fire-bomb attacks on 19–21 February 1941, the entire town centre was destroyed, with the death of 387 people and 412 others seriously injured.[2] The unions were fully involved in the corporatist industrial policy laid down by Ernest Bevin as Minister of Labour. In return for their role in control of the labour market, they accepted even such disagreeable proposals as Order 1305, which suspended the right to strike. The outcome of the war years in Wales was dramatic. After a decade of industrial stagnation and mass unemployment in the valleys, the economy was transformed. New life was breathed into coal, steel, tinplate and the docks. Full employment returned. The government itself stimulated new growth through a distribution of industries policy operated by the Board of Trade, following the lines of the Barlow Report for the relocation of industry. War contracts led to the opening up of Royal Ordnance factories at Bridgend, Hirwaun, Glascoed and Pembrey in the south, and Marchwiel near Wrexham in the north, a huge new aircraft factory at Broughton in Flintshire, and the massive expansion of the pre-war trading estate at Treforest near Pontypridd. Wales lost its depressed area atmosphere as the economy hummed with new life not known since before 1914. The long march for a somewhat ill-defined New Jerusalem led by pacifists like Keir Hardie over the decades seemed to have reached its appointed end in a time of total war.

Even so, it is obvious that the strains of loyalty and dissent occasioned by wartime circumstances led to inevitable tensions within the Welsh labour movement after 1939, despite the relative quiescence of the South Wales Regional Council of Labour (SWRCL) and the unions. Historians like Stephen Brooke, who have questioned the wartime consensus certainly find some evidence in Wales.[3] There were dissenting Welsh Labour MPs, especially after Russia's entry into the war in June 1941. Aneurin Bevan was a constant and powerful critic of government war strategy, as well as of Ernest Bevin's suppression of union protest, as will be seen. Bevan's onslaught on Bevin's Regulation 1AA (supported, it is often forgotten, by Dai Grenfell, a former Mines Minister) led to his temporary suspension from the party in 1944 and cast an ironic light on his advice to Jennie, his Independent Labour Party wife, to leave her nunnery and the impotence of isolation in the wilderness. S. O. Davies, the sombre-clad Marxist member for Merthyr, was a frequent critic, too, condemning the government for its failure to pursue a second front and its intervention in the civil war in Greece. W. G. Cove, member for Aberavon and the Commons representative of the National Union of Teachers, was another frequent gadfly, especially over the 1944 Education Act, to the annoyance of Labour's Chuter Ede who worked with Butler in pushing through that Act.[4] Perhaps the most dramatic opposition of all, however, came from a solid loyalist, James Griffiths of Llanelli. His powerful motion in February 1943 attacking the government for its failure to endorse the social insurance proposals of the Beveridge Report, attracted over 100 supporters in the House, among them nine Welsh Labour members, and also the veteran David Lloyd George, pioneer of the welfare state before 1914, now casting his last vote in the House of Commons. In time, Griffiths's motion became politically valuable for Labour. They could have it both ways, appearing as the voice of conscience and protest at the same time as being a loyal partner in the Churchill coalition.

In the Welsh constituencies, mostly quiescent and ill-organised during the wartime years, there were motions of protest too, as membership of the wartime coalition produced its strains. The SWRCL protested in 1942 when Labour MPs were asked to speak on behalf of Sir James Grigg, a Tory, in the Cardiff East by-election, in addition to his having a free run under the terms of the wartime election truce.[5] Some Welsh constituency parties also protested at the National Executive Committee's (NEC) decision to suspend the King's Norton constituency party for running a Labour candidate, Elizabeth Pakenham, in a Tory-held constituency in 1941. A more frequent source of protest, however, was not that the government was too consensual, but that it was paying insufficient attention to Wales. The SWRCL, along with individual MPs such as Dai Grenfell, James Griffiths and S. O. Davies, led protests for a fuller recognition of Wales as a distinctive region within the framework of wartime economic planning. They received some apparent encouragement from Harold Laski, a NEC member, when he met them in October 1941.[6] They pressed on with an interim report on post-war planning in April 1942, which took a strongly national line and went on to propose a Secretary of State for Wales. But Transport House was sternly resistant to Welsh separatism in any form, as it was to Scottish. This was very much the view of Morgan Phillips, the Welsh-speaking son of an Aberdare miner, who was strongly opposed to any concessions to nationalism. When he became general secretary of the party in 1944, Transport House's stern centralism and unionism were reinforced.

The main evidence of strain within the Welsh labour movement during the war years, however, lies rather in the domain of industrial and indeed of cultural history. Some historians have spoken of the possibility of a 'radical moment' in wartime Britain, an opportunity for genuine socialist revolution, hinted at by Laski in a famous book of 1943. Marxists like E. P. Thompson linked it with a lack of imagination or plain betrayal by the Attlee government after 1945. There is some evidence that the unions and the workers in Wales shared in a mood of wartime revolt, comparable to the miners of Betteshanger in Kent who caused Ernest Bevin such anguish. The miner-writer B. L. Coombes wrote powerfully in these terms. The miners of 1943–4 in south Wales engaged in a variety of strike or 'go-slow' activities, or in unexplained absenteeism. In February–March 1944, one hundred thousand Welsh miners were at one time on strike following dissatisfaction with the Porter pay awards. It took all the diplomacy of Arthur Horner and other South Wales Miners' Federation (SWMF) officials (many of them Communists) to persuade them to resolve local pay disputes through the usual collective bargaining procedures.[7] The strikes of apprentice boys in 1942–3, initially in the Rhondda and then in the anthracite pits of the western coalfield, testified to a wider mood of industrial protest over wages and working conditions.[8] They served as a reminder that industrial radicalism in the valleys could not be confined in a wartime cocoon of consensus and industrial harmony It was a constant worry for loyalist Labour leaders in the SWMF that Communists were making the pace, taking up local grievances as agents (or as shop stewards in factories) and winning converts in such areas as the Rhondda Valleys. Throughout the war years, this current of rebellion seethed below the surface, and Mass Observation evidence of public opinion frequently detected its presence.

But, in the main, these strikes were limited. Compared with 1914–18, industrial revolts in Wales were relatively sporadic. In general, even in so traditionally radical a community, wartime patriotism prevailed. Far more characteristic were socialist protests conducted within traditional channels. The key figure here is not S. O. Davies, throughout his career too maverick a figure to have much influence outside his constituency, but Aneurin Bevan. His constant crusade for seeing the war as a launchpad for socialist change found its main outlet in his widely reported speeches in the Commons. But his impact can also been seen in *Why Not Trust the Tories?*, a fierce short tract of social criticism published by Victor Gollancz in 1944 under the pseudonym 'Celticus'. In this, Bevan angrily recapitulated the betrayals of the people's hopes after the previous war and the evils of resultant Tory rule at home and abroad. 'Lying is a necessary part of a Tory's political equipment', Bevan told his readers.[9] He poured scorn on the inadequacies of the 1944 white paper on employment, based on taxing the workers through higher social contributions and giving private enterprise another chance. He denounced the refusal of a Tory-led government to commit itself to the Beveridge Report. He condemned the reluctance to build the houses needed post-war: instead, the government offered the people 'half a million steel boxes' in return for their wartime sacrifices. A capitalist government was cynically preparing the way to entrench the old order instead of engaging in the total reconstruction for which the people cried out. In a favourite historical parallel, he recalled Colonel Rainsborough of the Levellers in the Putney debates in 1647 calling for the poor to mobilise democracy to destroy the power of property. It was a theme Bevan picked up again years later in his memorable *In Place of Fear* (1952). This pamphlet showed that constitutional democratic socialism was a powerful force behind the façade of wartime consensus, and that social power was swinging over to the workers after the inequalities of the locust years. It is a sign of the mood of impatient anger in Wales and elsewhere that Bevan's tract sold over 80,000 copies despite its plain appearance and poor wartime paper. It is indicative, too, that later that year he was elected to Labour's NEC for the first time and that the stormy petrel of the war years now became seriously mooted as a possible Cabinet minister.

In the later stages of the war, the broad tendencies of social and economic policy were in a socialist or Labour direction. All the debate and dialogue was in favour of central government planning. This was the thrust of the Welsh Advisory Council, chaired by the distinctly Fabian Professor J. F. Rees, principal of the University College at Cardiff, and whose dominant figure was the Labour MP, James Griffiths. Appointed in 1942, it reported in 1944 in terms that might well have provided the Labour Party with its post-war programme *en bloc*. It emphasised once again the need to avoid the disasters of the interwar years when there was a net loss of 430,000 people migrating from Wales.[10] There was an emphasis on 'pulling through together', on the general will and on common sacrifice. Collectivism and indicative planning were everywhere the agents of change. The Board of Trade, under the Welsh-born Hugh Dalton and his able assistant, the economist Douglas Jay, used the powers of the state purposively to transform the Welsh economy. New light industries were steered to the valleys, such as the watch factory established in Ystradgynlais, an old anthracite mining town at the head of the long-depressed Swansea valley. Douglas Jay, in later life, would

228

recite a litany of the various south Wales mining villages through which he had conducted a kind of progress during the war years.[11] The Factories and Warehouses department of the Board of Trade, under Sir Cecil Weir and Welsh civil servants like Emrys Pride, allocated new industrial space in the older mining areas and set up new regional planning centres for civil servants and businessmen, from Cardiff to Ruthin.[12] The 1945 Distribution of Industry Act embodied the 'development areas' policy of the Board of Trade during the wartime years, with vigorous powers given to government to direct firms to the former depressed areas. The kinds of policies advocated by labour economists like Professor Hilary Marquand of Cardiff in the 1930s now became the conventional wisdom. Industries were taken under state-wide control, such as through the National Coal Board (NCB), though this implied operational direction rather than full nationalisation.

But, in general, it was a Labour agenda and understood as such. It chimed with the strong pro-Labour swing shown in the Gallup polls from the fall of Tobruk in 1942 onwards, even if hardly anyone paid them attention at the time. The mood, too, was one of solidarity and a united movement of workers by hand and by brain. The most dramatic evidence of this came in the mining industry. Early in 1945, the SWMF, the old 'Fed' which had fought the miners' cause from the days of Taff Vale and Tonypandy, agreed by an immense majority of ten to one to become part of a Britain-wide National Union of Mineworkers, with South Wales as one district within it.[13] It was an inevitable consequence of nationwide rather than district wage agreements. But it was also further evidence of the integration and unionisation of Britain, at least at the organisational level. All the Welsh miners' leaders, from Arthur Horner downwards, gave it their blessing.

These forces revealed their full significance in July 1945. Shortly after VE Day, the Labour leaders left Churchill's coalition and a general election soon followed, scheduled for 5 July, with time allowed for organising a forces' vote which would mean the result would be known on 25 July. How well-prepared for the fray Labour was organisationally is open to debate. The SWRCL, with Cliff Prothero as its secretary from 1944 following the death of George Morris, had been increasingly active in south

Wales plugging the gaps. But clearly, as with all political parties, the constituency parties in Wales had allowed their organisation to wind down in the wartime years: Brecon and Radnor, though buoyed up by a by-election victory on the eve of the war in August 1939, was but one party that spoke of local decay.[14] Much depended on the trade unions especially since, in areas like mining seats, individual membership was traditionally low. In 1942, there were accounts of falling membership in several south Wales constituencies, including Swansea, Neath and Newport.[15] In fact, in south Wales from Llanelli to Ebbw Vale the SWMF had kept the local political machinery in being. Elsewhere, the National Union of Railwaymen had been active in places ranging from Carmarthen to Anglesey. In Cardiff South, where the Labour candidate Lieutenant James Callaghan was on naval service in the Far East, his own union, the Inland Revenue Staff Federation, partly through such Welsh figures as Dai Kneath, worked with the agent Bill Headon to keep the local party apparatus in working order.[16] In the end, Labour fought every one of the thirty-six Welsh constituencies save for Montgomeryshire and the University of Wales. It was as well-equipped as the local Tories and Liberals, but it was a mood not machinery that dictated the result.

Of course, the outcome in July 1945 was a massive electoral transformation, a seismic change. It was the last old-fashioned party-political campaign before the television era changed the nature of politics for ever. Candidates spoke at street corners or at factory gates; there were noisy and boisterous public meetings – dozens in Cardiff alone, culminating in a mass rally at the Cory Hall on 4 July, the eve of polling day. There was heckling and face-to-face contact of the most direct kind between candidate and electors. In Cardiff South, Labour hecklers pursued the Tory member, Sir Arthur Evans, and his Penarth mistress with renderings of 'Hello! Hello! Who's your lady friend?'[17] Churchill was heckled with reminders of Tonypandy thirty-five years earlier.

The results were dramatic. Labour made seven gains – the three Cardiff seats, Newport, Swansea West, Llandaff and Barry, and Caernarfon – ending up with twenty-five seats in Wales. In Britain as a whole, it won 48 per cent of the vote. In Wales it was 58 per cent. There were majorities of over 20,000 in Caerphilly, Neath, Ogmore, Pontypridd,

Aberdare, Abertillery, Bedwellty and Ebbw Vale: in Abertillery, local Labour Party workers called for a recount to see if the Tory really had lost his deposit.[18] In Llanelli, James Griffiths won by over 34,000, the largest majority in Britain. There were some interesting new MPs. Llandaff and Barry was won by a prominent Labour lawyer, Sir Lynn Ungoed-Thomas, the son of a Nonconformist minister. In Newport, Peter Freeman, a vegetarian, theosophist, former tobacco manufacturer and tennis champion, defeated a Conservative who had held the seat for only two months. Cardiff produced three talented new members: Professor Hilary Marquand for Cardiff East, professor of industrial relations in the local university college, who went straight into government; George Thomas, a leftish school teacher in Cardiff West, who was to become in due course Speaker of the House; and in Cardiff South, young James Callaghan comfortably straddled a constituency that extended from the villadom of Penarth to Butetown and Tiger Bay. In time he was to rise to the highest office of all.

Labour's strength in the industrial valleys was wholly predictable. But elsewhere, in the more rural areas, there was also Labour progress. Somewhat surprisingly, Moelwyn Hughes lost Carmarthenshire to the Liberal, R. Hopkin Morris, a KC and former regional director of the BBC, who benefited from the absence of a Tory candidate. But the Liberals found themselves under threat in Pembroke, where Gwilym Lloyd George held off Wilfred Fienburgh by only 168 votes, while in Merioneth Huw Morris-Jones failed by a mere 112. Labour's vote also rose substantially in Anglesey, where Cledwyn Hughes, an Aberystwyth-trained solicitor, was the candidate; while in Caernarfon, Goronwy Roberts, a Bangor-trained lecturer, easily defeated the sitting Liberal to show that Welsh national sentiment was alive and well in the modern Labour Party. A victory of a different kind came in Rhondda East, where the veteran one-time syndicalist W. H. Mainwaring very narrowly defeated the Communists' general secretary, Harry Pollitt, by just 972 votes. In fact, it was to prove the Communists' last effective stand in this old left-wing stronghold, indeed their last significant political effort ever in Wales.

The 1945 triumph was as much sociological as political. Of the twenty-five all-male Labour MPs, all save two (Callaghan and Freeman) were

Welsh; nineteen were of working-class background, if one includes the miner's son, George Thomas, a school teacher; James Callaghan, a union official; and the National Union of Teachers' spokesman, W. G. Cove, a former miner at the coalface. Twelve of the MPs were from the mining industry, nearly all former workers underground. In general, they were senior figures, usually former councillors as well, whose presence in parliament reflected their stature in the local community. Dai Grenfell (born 1881), W. H. Mainwaring (born 1884), S. O. Davies (born 1886), Jim Griffiths (born 1890), Ness Edwards (born 1897) and Aneurin Bevan (born 1897) had been socialist activists during the First World War. In a by-election in 1946, they were to be joined by John Evans, another miner, entering parliament for Ogmore at the advanced age of seventy-one. Mainwaring (as a tutor), Edwards, Griffiths and Bevan had been at the famous left-wing Central Labour College, part of its new post-war socialist élite; Davies had led miners' protests against conscription during the First World War and had been prominent in the Minority Movement afterwards; Mainwaring had been a leading author of the famous syndicalist pamphlet *The Miners' Next Step*, published by the Unofficial Reform Committee at Tonypandy in 1912. They symbolised revenge, the conquest of power by a victimised generation. Truly, in Wales they were the masters now.

The Labour hegemony after 1945 did not begin well. The SWRCL had to record sadly that its victory celebration that autumn had to be cancelled because no national speaker could be persuaded to come down.[19] There were frequent complaints at the difficulty in getting Cabinet ministers to visit Wales to listen to local complaints. Cripps, in October 1945, was only just able to squeeze in an early-morning visit to the SWRCL during a trip to see local businessmen as President of the Board of Trade. Far from an immediate unveiling of the New Jerusalem, the first months after Labour's election victory saw a rapid rise in unemployment to over 70,000 (over 10 per cent) by January 1946. There were bitter complaints at Aneurin Bevan's initial slow progress in building new homes, at Ellen Wilkinson for not creating multilateral schools and at Cripps's delays in adapting wartime ordnance factories and bringing in new work to the valleys. Rationing, shortages and general austerity were the pervasive features of what Labour chose to call 'fair shares'. By the end of 1946, however, when the economy was now thriving to meet post-war demand in continental Europe and North America, the response was much more cheerful.

From the outset, Wales was well to the fore in the new Attlee government. In the Cabinet was Aneurin Bevan, the most charismatic socialist of his time, now about to achieve his greatest triumph in the National Health Service. Of only slightly lesser rank was James Griffiths, Minister of National Insurance in 1945 and architect of the 1946 Social Insurance Act, the most notable legislation in this area since the Lloyd George measure of 1911. Others in government were Hilary Marquand at Overseas Trade, Lord (George) Hall at the Admiralty, Ness Edwards at the Board of Trade and, from October 1947, James Callaghan, junior minister at Transport and (from 1950) the Admiralty. The Welsh Labour members were a solid phalanx and the Welsh table at lunchtime well-attended (though seldom by Bevan who, claimed Callaghan, only joined them when he was in trouble).[20] They were rarely critical of the government. Predictable exceptions were S. O. Davies, invariably on the theme of 'a socialist foreign policy' but also on Welsh Home Rule, and W. G. Cove, whose ferocious attacks on Ellen Wilkinson for her failure to promote comprehensive secondary schools alienated several Labour members.[21] Perhaps the more effective Welsh protesters were those who sat for English or Scottish constituencies, representatives of the Welsh diaspora, Rhys Davies (Westhoughton), Harold Davies (Leek) and Emrys Hughes, Keir Hardie's pacifist son-in-law, who sat for South Ayrshire near Hardie's old Cumnock home.

Elsewhere, there were powerful Welsh potentates among the union leaders at a time when the alliance and synergy between the Trades Union Congress and the Labour Party were closer than at any other moment. Among them were steelworkers' leaders like Lincoln Evans and Dai Davies; Arthur Deakin of Merthyr, the right-wing czar of the transport workers, and a range of miners' leaders. Even NUM South Wales Area president and Communist president (later NUM secretary) Arthur Horner was remarkably loyal to the Attlee government, as were other prominent Communists such as Will Paynter, Will Whitehead and

Dai Francis. Horner was even offered a position on the NCB, which would have indeed been the poacher turning gamekeeper, but he declined, although only after careful reflection. Elsewhere, in the central recesses of Transport House, Morgan Phillips directed operations, always sensitive to his Welsh roots and friendships, but also sternly opposed to Welsh national deviations in whatever form.[22] The Welsh presence in the post-war Attlee ascendancy was active and articulate at all levels.

This was even more true in local government. In Glamorgan and Monmouthshire, along with councils like Swansea and the Rhondda, Labour's control was total, dating as it did from the mid-1920s. An overwhelming Labour ethos prevailed, intermeshed with the local worlds of the unions, the Co-operative Society, the world of adult education and a complex network of family and personal relationships. An archetypal figure at this period was the ex-railwayman Llew Heycock of Port Talbot, the dominating patriarch of Glamorgan County Council over many decades, famous for his malapropisms. He was much attacked as a tyrannical boss, but also admired for his genuine commitment to his community, including the causes of the Welsh-speaking minority and the *eisteddfod*. In north Wales, the dominant personality in Welsh Labour ranks was Huw T. Edwards, a fiercely patriotic and administratively gifted transport workers' leader, a pillar of local community life at many levels including local government and, in 1949, the chairman of the first Council for Wales.[23] The older Liberal-chapel ascendancy worked alongside these new conquerors rather than being totally displaced; indeed, it is in many ways the similarity of outlook and ethos between the old national leaders and the new that is striking about Wales after 1945. James Griffiths's brother David, under his poetic name Amanwy, was a famous eisteddfodic bard; Cledwyn Hughes was a disciple of Lloyd George, even while fighting his daughter in elections; in 1951, Abertillery was to be represented by a Congregationalist minister.

Labour rule after 1945 followed the imperatives of the war years and of the party manifesto in the general election. Industries were taken into public ownership; all seemed to thrive in post-war conditions. Coal after nationalisation on 1 January 1947 found renewed strength, and was handicapped not by shortage of demand but by shortage of workers;

the resultant introduction of Italian and (in the north Wales coalfield) Polish workers brought some local controversy. In early 1948, the south-west region of the NCB reported a record weekly production of 592,400 tons. A giant new steelworks at Margam, near Port Talbot, planned from 1947 and eventually employing nearly 20,000 men, spoke of the progress in another long-depressed industry, alongside the new merger of Richard Thomas and Baldwin, and the cold reduction works at Port Talbot, Velindre and Trostre to replace obsolescent tinplate works. The docks of Cardiff, Barry, Newport and Swansea were also galvanised with new life after 1945. Central government used its powers to establish large new works like the nylon plant at Pontypool, the rubber factory at Bryn-mawr and a range of government advance factories, including in long-depressed rural areas like Holyhead and Blaenau Ffestiniog. Trading estates at Bridgend, Hirwaun and Fforestfach, in addition to that at Tre-forest, hugely increased employment opportunities, including particu-larly for women. By the time of Labour's fall from power in October 1951 unemployment in Wales was less than three per cent. The *South Wales Industrial Review* spoke of a second industrial revolution in the valleys.[24] It was due in large measure to the market opportunities temporarily opened up as defeated powers like Germany or Japan strove to rebuild, alongside the assistance of Marshall Aid from America. But Labour claimed the credit for full employment, as well as the welfare state and 'fair shares', and the great majority of Welsh people seemed disposed to agree.

These developments did not differ in kind from those elsewhere in Britain after 1945. Their impact on the Welsh labour movement and on Welsh society and national consciousness was more complicated. Broad loyalty to the Attlee government, local pride in the achievements of ministers like Bevan and Griffiths, were matched by a constant dialogue of query, complaint and protest. In particular, the total failure of Attlee, Morrison and other ministers to show any recognition of the particular needs of Wales and the distinctive outlook of its Labour Party led to much difficulty. The new creation of the Welsh Regional Council of Labour (WRCL), merging the old SWRCL with the constituencies of north and mid Wales in May 1947, was a launchpad to further complaint.

Indeed, the retention of the somewhat insulting word 'regional' was a frequent grievance: Morgan Phillips had flatly refused to accept the title 'Welsh Council of Labour'.[25]

The broader protests of post-war politics did not strike any particular resonance in Wales. Hardly any of the Welsh members joined in the 'Keep Left' protests against Bevin's cold-war policy in 1946. Their supporters were largely English and urban; the Welsh and other union-based old Labour elements remained doggedly loyal. Ernest Bevin blamed 'the Welsh' with their alleged pacifist inclinations when the parliamentary party rebelled against a two-year period of national service in 1947.[26] But even though the leader, somewhat improbably, was the centrist figure of James Callaghan, member for Cardiff South, the large majority of Welsh MPs did not join him. S. O. Davies and W. G. Cove were among those who signed the pre-electoral telegram of support to the left-wing Italian socialist Nenni in April 1948, but again it would be difficult to claim that the Welsh were particularly to the fore in left-wing dissent.

However, they had their own local and national grievances. In 1946, the Welsh Labour MPs *en bloc*, backed by the WRCL and leading union figures like Huw T. Edwards, complained vehemently to Attlee that post-war planning was being carried out with a total neglect of the special needs of Wales. A Cabinet paper, accepted without demur in January 1946, had rejected not merely a Secretary of State on grounds of broad economic planning, but even a permanent advisory council. In language that subsequently seems prophetic, the government urged: 'It is difficult to devise a plan by which such a Council would not become either a dead letter or a dilatory nuisance.' Among the arguments against a Welsh Office was that 'Wales could not carry a cadre of officials of the highest calibre and the services of high English officials would no longer be available'.[27]

But, despite these patronising observations from Whitehall, wartime demands for a Welsh Secretary of State and further governmental de-volution had certainly not gone away. After some frustrating communi-cations, a parliamentary deputation led by Grenfell and Mainwaring met Attlee, Cripps and George Isaacs, Minister of Labour, on 25 July 1946, to complain about the rise of unemployment totals in Wales to nine per cent. It was a somewhat bad-tempered session: the Welsh members complained of bad faith and Attlee criticised them for vagueness of detail.[28] Six days later, Attlee wrote to Grenfell detailing the government's responsiveness to Wales: the annual Welsh debate, the annual white paper, extended regional organisation of government departments. But 'the appointment of a special Minister would not be in the special interests of Wales'.[29] Not surprisingly, the MPs were far from satisfied. On 14 August, Grenfell and Mainwaring on their behalf protested at the inadequacies of the government's response. This time, their complaints had a more obviously nationalist ring: 'The reply of the Government seems to repudiate entirely the claims of Wales as a nation. It will not satisfy the supporters of the Government nor the majority of people in any party in Wales.' They called for a dedicated minister to look after Welsh matters.[30] Attlee's reply, on 5 September, was amiable in tone but offered nothing. He outlined the virtues of formal and regular meetings of the various Welsh regional offices of government departments. But the government believed 'that it would be a mistake to think that Wales could achieve economic well-being altogether apart from considerations of policy for Britain as a whole; nor do I accept the view that the appointment of a Secretary of State would solve the economic problem.'[31]

The matter of Welsh nationality may have been a fringe issue for Attlee and his ministers, but it continued to rumble in a way that anticipates the debates over devolution fifty years later. The Scots had made considerable strides during the wartime years, benefiting from the presence of Tom Johnston as Secretary of State under Churchill. They had gained a Scottish Council of State and a Scottish Council of Industry, along with local developments such as a North of Scotland Hydro-Electric Board. Johnston had been able to terrify Churchill and colleagues with threats of a Scottish Nationalist upsurge if the government did not make these concessions: the return of Dr McIntyre as the first Scottish Nationalist MP in a by-election at Motherwell had given his claims somewhat slender credence. 'We had got Scottish wishes and opinions respected and listened to', wrote Johnston in his memoirs, 'as they had not been respected or listened to since the Act of Union.'[32] By contrast, Wales had got nothing at all. The wartime Welsh Advisory Council had called for a Welsh Planning Authority in 1944 to deal with the post-war special needs of Wales as a region or nation, but that had been ignored.[33]

James Griffiths had been the leading figure on the Welsh Advisory Council. While Aneurin Bevan was sternly centralist and totally hostile to any form of Welsh separatism at this stage, from within the government Griffiths did his best to promote Welsh devolution. In December 1946, he circulated a Cabinet paper (CP 462) which called for the bill to nationalise electricity supplies to constitute the whole of Wales and Monmouthshire as a single Area Board. 'The proposals to divide Wales in the Electricity Bill will be criticised both on grounds of National sentiment and on the grounds that they provide an arbitrary division of areas which, for other administrative purposes, are treated as a single unit.' He pointed out that central and north Wales, including parts of Cardiganshire, would be linked with Merseyside under MANWEB and would cut across the proposals on local authority boundaries made by a recent commission chaired by R. Moelwyn Hughes KC, the erstwhile Welsh Labour MP.[34] But the government dismissed Griffiths's ideas out of hand. In August 1946, Kingsley Martin's *New Statesman and Nation* noted that, in 1945, Welsh Labour had made five main promises: a Secretary of State; a separate Welsh Broadcasting Corporation; an end to the forced transfer of labour to England; a north–south Welsh trunk road; and a central body to plan and develop the Welsh economy. 'All five have now been turned down in Westminster.'[35]

However, the WRCL and a variety of Welsh MPs, from Goronwy Roberts and Robert Richards in the north to George Thomas in Cardiff, continued to press for more attention to Wales in the government's programme. In the autumn of 1948, a government committee, the Home Services Committee, which included both Bevan and Griffiths, debated the possibilities of a Secretary of State, or at least an advisory council of some kind. Bevan opposed even the latter but, in consultation with the Machinery of Government Committee, the Cabinet came up with the idea of an advisory council for Wales. Griffiths wanted this chaired by a minister of Cabinet rank, but Morrison vetoed this as likely to create a 'buffer minister' who would impede efficient government.[36] In a Cabinet paper of his own (CP 228) in October 1948, Morrison spoke of 'the difficulties that would arise between the chairman and other Cabinet ministers'. It would 'strengthen the demand for a Secretary of State for Wales', which Morrison evidently regarded as a crushing argument against the idea.[37] The council's chairman in the end was the influential north Wales trade union leader, Huw T. Edwards, and Morrison himself addressed the council's inaugural meeting on 17 May 1949. It considered a range of important economic and later cultural issues, but quite soon disillusion, even boredom, set in. It enjoyed no executive power and was little more than a talking shop. The council's phantom-like existence petered out in 1966.

The demand in Labour ranks for distinct recognition for Wales continued, despite the heavy-handed undemocratic centralism of Morrison and Attlee. In particular, rising figures in north Wales like Goronwy Roberts, the member for Caernarfon, and Cledwyn Hughes, member for Anglesey in 1951, along with others like T. W. Jones, member for Merioneth in 1951 and Elwyn Jones, member for Conway in 1950–1, all called for greater recognition – at least a Secretary of State, even a Welsh elected assembly. In August 1950, Goronwy Roberts received short shrift from Morgan Phillips and Transport House. He cited two recent decisions imposed on a hostile Welsh opinion: the Forestry Commission taking 20,000 acres in west Wales for afforestation in defiance of the local population, and the seizure of land for military use in Trawsfynydd in northern Merioneth. 'There is a growing feeling in Wales that the Movement is hostile to all suggestions of devolution.' Welsh Labour, he claimed, was 'dispirited and frustrated'. He talked of the difficulty in finding suitable candidates in Anglesey (where Cledwyn Hughes was reluctant to stand again), West Denbighshire, Montgomeryshire, West Flint, Merioneth and Cardiganshire. 'The movement for devolution will gather force. Is Labour to be placed in a position of such hostility to such a natural and indeed traditionally socialist idea', or would it continue to be treated 'as a kind of box room where the rubbish of the United Kingdom may be dumped'? He demanded that Wales be treated as a unit for all government purposes, that the advisory council be treated as a working party for specific Welsh problems, and that either a minister or a national council be set up 'which may focus the whole of Welsh thought and take its views into orderly consideration'.[38] Roberts was brushed aside yet again by Transport House.

A further pointer to the potential tension between centralist socialism and forms of nationalism arose that summer when Lady Megan Lloyd George launched an all-party Parliament for Wales campaign at the traditional setting for such events, namely the spa of Llandrindod Wells.[39] The movement had been stimulated by the cultural pressure group Undeb Cymru Fydd; its secretary, the writer and broadcaster T. I. Ellis was the son of Tom Ellis, the visionary nationalist-prophet of Cymru Fydd in the 1890s, while the presence of W. R. P. George, the nephew of David Lloyd George, was another sign of distinguished ancestry and continuity. The movement eventually attracted the support of no less than five Labour MPs – Goronwy Roberts, Cledwyn Hughes, T. W. Jones, the Merthyr Marxist S. O. Davies, and also Tudor Watkins from Radnor and Brecon – while several defeated candidates in north and mid Wales had also favoured the idea of a Welsh parliament. The support for the dissident five was not widespread, but their presence remained an embarrassment for the Labour Party machine, both Morgan Phillips in London and Cliff Prothero of the Welsh Council of Labour. It reminded contemporaries of an old and abiding argument that remained incomplete even in the glory years of the Attlee government.

Some months before the Parliament for Wales campaign was launched, Wales and the United Kingdom had their opportunity to give their verdict on five years of Labour government. It was clear that, after years of rationing and austerity, the Attlee government's popularity had slipped a good deal, especially in middle-class constituencies in southern and eastern England. However, in the general election of 1950, Wales remained quite as solid as before for what it regarded as peculiarly its own administration. Disputes over Welsh national recognition paled by comparison with the boons of full employment, economic growth, welfare and the National Health Service. While Labour nationally saw its majority fall from over 150 to just six, in Wales its popularity was greater than ever. Churchill was heckled at Ninian Park, Cardiff, over his role at Tonypandy in 1910.[40] Morale was high in the party: individual membership had risen sharply. And Labour's energy was far from exhausted. Particular attention had been paid by the WRCL to the Welsh-speaking areas of north and mid Wales. Labour had never struck deep roots here as it had in the industrial south, but there had nevertheless been a Labour MP for Anglesey as early as 1918 and for Caernarfon, with its slate quarrymen, in 1922–3. Conversely, rural Welsh Liberalism had been in decline since the fall of the Lloyd George coalition in 1922, while Plaid Cymru was as yet a minor force. This campaigning in rural areas was to bear fruit in the 1950 election campaign. There was a high poll in Wales: 85 per cent, the highest in Britain. Labour's share of the Welsh votes was 58 per cent, the same as at the high noon of 1945.

The outcome confirmed that Labour's advance in Wales continued, whatever the result in Britain as a whole. Labour now held twenty-seven of the thirty-six Welsh seats, as against five rural Liberal seats and four Conservatives. With the redistribution of Welsh constituencies, it is difficult to be certain about gains and losses. In some, the absence of a Liberal gave the Conservatives a slight advantage but not enough to count. One clear Labour gain in a new area was in Pembrokeshire, where Desmond Donnelly, a young left-wing journalist of Irish extraction, gained a very narrow victory over Gwilym Lloyd George.[41] Carmarthen remained Liberal by a majority of 0.4 per cent. Conversely, Labour lost one of the Cardiff seats, Cardiff North. In north Wales, there was a narrow Labour victory at Conway, and strong votes again in Anglesey and Merioneth as in 1945. At least nineteen of the twenty-seven Labour MPs were of broadly working-class background, twelve having originally been working miners. One novelty in the macho world of Welsh Labour politics was that there were now, for the first time, women Labour MPs: Eirene White in East Flint, daughter of the redoubtable Thomas Jones, Lloyd George's former secretary; and Dorothy Rees in Barry, a school teacher.[42] There were younger women organisers, such as Peggy England Jones in Swansea and Megan Roach, but a labour movement so close to the unions and the world of hard manual labour was unlikely to give women socialists much encouragement; in any case the total number of women elected in Britain generally was only twenty-one, fourteen being Labour, a decline from 1945. Clearly, however, in a sharply polarised political culture, the Labour dominance of Wales was amply confirmed.

Welsh Labour remained loyal, solid and satisfied with Labour's years in power. In the government, Bevan remained at Health (Attlee refusing to promote him, perhaps on doctrinaire grounds) before moving to the Ministry of Labour in January 1951, at the height of the Korean War. Griffiths entered the Cabinet as Colonial Secretary, while Ness Edwards became Postmaster General. But, generally speaking, the performance of the Welsh MPs did not encourage the party leaders to consider them for promotion.

The final eighteen months of Labour government, with an overall majority of just six, was a very difficult time. From June 1950, it was caught up by the war in Korea, the arguments over the rearmament programme, the Cabinet disputes over health service charges that saw Bevan and Wilson resign, an alarming balance of payments crisis and, finally, possible wars in Persia and/or Egypt in its final weeks in office. On balance, the Welsh remained loyal and gave little encouragement to movements of protest. S. O. Davies voiced public opposition to lending support to South Korea; he received widespread backing for his views, but relatively little within Wales.[43] James Griffiths was but one minister worried about the scale of rearmament and the consequent charges on the health service, but there was no likelihood of resignation or overt protest here. By far the most serious challenge was that from Aneurin Bevan in April 1951. His resignation led to the prolonged civil war between the so-called Bevanites (who may or may not have included Bevan himself) and the Gaitskellite right. Wales, however, gave remarkably little support to the Bevanite persuasion. None of the original fifteen who formed the core of the later Bevanite group in May 1951 represented a Welsh seat, although they included two of Welsh ancestry, Harold Davies and Will Griffiths, both of whom represented English seats. The Welsh were in the main centre-right in these disputes but, in any case, trade unionists such as miners and others were hostile to acts of private rebellion, however worthy the cause. Thus, while Bevan found backing from party activists in Ebbw Vale, his support in the main came from middle-class socialists operating in London, many of them journalists such as Foot, Crossman and Driberg. Among the Welsh MPs, Desmond Donnelly and George Thomas made occasional statements of support, but not consistently. Donnelly in due course was to move sharply towards the far right of the party, and indeed out of it altogether. He ended up as an erratic Tory, before committing suicide. Aneurin Bevan may have been a Welshman, proud of his ancestry, but to the Welsh labour movement it was the cause and not the man that counted.

When the Attlee government went to the country again in October 1951, at a particularly unfavourable time, it was widely anticipated that it would be defeated. So it proved, although the eventual margin was a narrow one and Labour, with 48.8 per cent of the vote, polled 230,000 more votes than the Conservatives. Its percentage of the poll was unequalled in British history until John Major's victory in 1992. Wales, despite the Bevanite rebellion and other problems, was even more solid than in 1950. Indeed, its share of the vote at 60 per cent was higher than in 1945. The Welsh turnout at 84 per cent was again the highest in Britain. Despite a flood of Tory money and propaganda in the press for the Tory cause (the Cardiff-based *Western Mail*, resolutely Tory throughout, made scant effort to give Labour a fair hearing), the Welsh voters held to their old faith. The tally of Labour seats remained at twenty-seven out of thirty-six. Two marginal seats were lost, Elwyn Jones in Conway and Dorothy Rees in Barry. To balance this, Cledwyn Hughes finally triumphed in his third battle with Lady Megan Lloyd George in Anglesey, with a 595-vote majority, and began a long and distinguished tenure of the seat. In nearby Merioneth, T. W. Jones, an elderly ex-miner from Rhosllanerchrugog, Wrexham, defeated Emrys Roberts, the Liberal member since 1945. The Liberals retained Carmarthen, Cardigan and Montgomeryshire with some help from an electoral pact with the Tories.[44] But it made them look opportunist, while Clement Davies, their 66-year-old leader, was a failing force moving to the right. Labour had even stronger credentials to speak as the voice of progressive forces in Wales: only one Communist stood, Idris Cox in the Rhondda, and he lost his deposit. Some rising figures in Labour's ranks came from Wales, notably James Callaghan who had made a strong impression as a competent Admiralty minister. Whereas in Britain as a whole, therefore, the fall of Attlee's government marked a clear shift in national debate, from the ethos of 'fair shares' to that of 'setting the people free', in Wales there was little change. In defeat as in victory, the Labour ascendancy confirmed a turning-point at which Welsh politics resolutely refused to turn.

The years 1939–51 cast their shadow over the Labour Party and Welsh politics for much of the rest of the century. They symbolised people's power, solidarity, a collective response, central planning, a welfare democracy and social citizenship, an ethos diffused through local councils, the trade unions and the public services, to renew the nation after the suffering of the interwar years. The main fabric of Labour's economic achievement, and the instruments of corporate government that ran it, largely survived until the 1980s. It was a period of reform, yet also of social and cultural conservatism. Labour's victory was for the old values. It was based on the communal solidarity of the pit and the choir and the co-op and the Workers' Educational Association, transmitted from the industrial valleys throughout significant areas of the Welsh-speaking north and west as well. Its most characteristic figures were working-class ministers like James Griffiths, trade unionists like Huw T. Edwards, local government bosses like Heycock, relatively senior figures whose outlook was shaped by past experience. It gave socialist values and historic images a new infusion of life: no raging now against the dying of the light. Post-war Wales handed on to future generations the potent legend of Labour in power. The anniversary of the birth of Nye Bevan in 1997, attended by Gordon Brown among others, gave an opportunity to replay the nostalgic tunes of Old Labour. What this pivotal period did not do was relate those achievements and that legend to the concept of a living Welsh nation. That was to remain unfinished business, to beguile or torment comrades yet unborn.

Notes

1   Kenneth O. Morgan, *Modern Wales: Politics, Places and People* (Cardiff, 1995), pp. 108–9; Iorwerth C. Peate, *Rhwng Dau Fyd* (Dinbych, 1976), pp. 122–9.
2   June M. Morris, 'Morale under air attack: Swansea 1939–1941', *Welsh History Review*, 11/3 (1983), 358–87.
3   Stephen Brooke, *Labour's War* (Oxford, 1992).
4   See Kevin Jefferys (ed.), *Labour and the Wartime Coalition: From the Diary of James Chuter Ede* (London, 1987), pp. 178–80.

5 South Wales Regional Council of Labour minutes, 14 April 1942 (NLW).

6 South Wales Regional Council of Labour minutes, 4 October 1941 (NLW).

7 Hywel Francis and Dai Smith, *The Fed: A History of the South Wales Miners in the Twentieth Century* (Cardiff, 1980), pp. 403ff.

8 S. Bloomfield, 'The apprentice boys' strikes of the Second World War', *Llafur*, 3/2 (1981),

9 Aneurin Bevan, *Why Not Trust the Tories?* (London, 1944), p. 25.

10 James Griffiths Papers (NLW), C1/2.

11 D. Jay, *Change and Fortune* (London, 1980), pp. 116ff. He adds, 'I was not entirely prepared, however, for the torrent of Welsh oratory awaiting me in the Valleys.' The memory lingered on, sixty years later.

12 E. Pride, 'The economic province of Wales', *Transactions of the Honourable Society of Cymmrodorion* (1969), 111ff.

13 Francis and Smith, *The Fed*, p. 418.

14 Brecon and Radnor constituency Labour Party papers, 1939–45 (NLW).

15 South Wales Regional Council of Labour, 10 May 1943.

16 Kenneth O. Morgan, *Callaghan: A Life* (Oxford, 1997), pp. 53–4.

17 Morgan, *Callaghan*, p. 54.

18 C. Prothero, *Recount* (Ormskirk, 1982), p. 57.

19 South Wales Regional Council of Labour, 17 September 1945.

20 Personal information.

21 B. Vernon, *Ellen Wilkinson* (London, 1982), pp. 219–21.

22 Kenneth O. Morgan, 'Morgan Phillips', in *idem, Labour People: Leaders and Lieutenants, Hardie to Kinnock* (Oxford, 1992), pp. 231–8.

23 See the Edwards papers (NLW).

24 *South Wales Industrial Review*, 2/3 (January 1950), 12–15.

25 Welsh Regional Council of Labour minutes, 5 May 1947; Prothero, *Recount*, pp. 53–4.

26 L. V. Scott, *Conscription and the Attlee Government* (Oxford, 1993), p. 152.

27 'The administration of Wales and Monmouthshire', CP (46), 21, 23 January 1946 (TNA, CAB 129/6).

28 Record of meeting, 25 July 1946 (TNA, PREM 8/272).

29 Attlee to D. R. Grenfell, 31 July 1946 (Labour Party archives, GS 9/2); also TNA, PREM 8/1569.

30 Grenfell and Mainwaring to Attlee, 14 August 1946 (ibid.).

31 Attlee to Grenfell, 5 September 1946 (ibid.).

32 C. Harvie, *Scotland and Nationalism: Scottish Society and Politics, 1707–1977* (London, 1994, 2nd edn), pp. 29–33.

33 Griffiths Papers, C1/6.

34 'Note on Area Boards covering Wales under the Electricity Bill', 17 December 1946, CP (46) 462 (TNA, CAB 129/15).

35 *New Statesman and Nation* (24 August 1946).

36 'The administration of Wales and Monmouthshire', CP (48) 228 (TNA, CAB 129/30); Cabinet minutes, 15 October and 18 November 1948 (CAB 128/13); Morrison to Griffiths, 13 October 1948 (Griffiths Papers, C2/9); meeting of Morrison with Welsh Regional Council of Labour and Welsh Parliamentary Group, 29 October 1948 (ibid., C2/15).

37 Griffiths Papers, C2/31.

38 G. Roberts to G. Williams, 8 August 1950 (Labour Party archives, GS 9/2).

39 See J. G. Jones, 'The Parliament for Wales campaign', *Welsh History Review*, 16/2 (1992), 207ff.

40 *Western Mail*, 9 February 1950.

41 Desmond Donnelly Papers, B1–3 (NLW).

42 See P. Stead, 'The town that had come of age: Barry 1918–1939', in D. Moore (ed.), *Barry: The Centenary Book* (Barry, 1984), pp. 455–6, for a sympathetic portrait of Dorothy Rees.

43 See S. O. Davies Papers, A16 (South Wales Coalfield Archive).

44 *Western Mail*, 2 October 1951.

11

Welsh Devolution: The Past and the Future

This historic day, 18 September 1998, recalls for me not one anniversary but two. Of course, it marks the first anniversary of the very narrow endorsement of Welsh devolution in the referendum on which I was a television commentator, immured, oddly enough, in Cardiff castle. But a few hours later came the publication of my official biography of Lord Callaghan. One launch of it took place in Cardiff City Hall, hailed that day by the leader of the council as the building that would house the new Welsh Assembly. The coincidence of these two events was striking – not only for me, perhaps. In March 1979, the Callaghan government had been brought down, the first to be defeated on a vote of no confidence in the House of Commons since that of Ramsay MacDonald fifty-five years earlier. And it was devolution, not the industrial troubles of the 'winter of discontent', that finally laid it low. While the three Plaid Cymru MPs, in an interesting comment on the ethos of Welsh politics, voted for the Labour government in March 1979, the eleven Scottish National Party (SNP) members voted against, and the government fell by a single vote. One commentator was subsequently to see Callaghan as the last Labour prime minister, whose life was appropriately being written by the University of Wales's last Vice-Chancellor – both forecasts proving to be quite untrue. But the whole affair re-emphasised the political distinctiveness of Scotland and Wales, with the former's much stronger sense of national and territorial identity. The Scots had at least voted in favour of devolution, if narrowly, on 1 March 1979, while the Welsh, even in Gwynedd, rejected it almost contemptuously by an overall majority of almost four to one.

Eighteen years later, the world had moved on. Again it was Scotland that was to trigger political change. Wales, as we know, now endorsed devolution on a low turnout of only 50 per cent but in a major shift of electoral opinion, which commentators have tended to underestimate. The referendum this time brought not catastrophe but Catatonia – 50.3 per cent of the voters woke up that wet morning (assuming they had been to bed at all) and thanked the Lord they were Welsh. But again it was the Scots who would lead the way, not a candle in the wind but a beacon of hope. Their elected body, endorsed by three-quarters of the voters, would be a genuine parliament with legislative and taxation powers. It would open up fundamental issues for the British polity and constitution, and their relationship with Europe and a wider world. In the run-up to the Scottish elections in May 1999, the opinion polls showed a strong surge of support for the SNP. All this is likely to have its impact on Wales too – not in the Welsh Assembly being dominated by Plaid Cymru (which seems unlikely in any future one can foresee), but in pressure in Wales that its own body should have stronger powers and a more credible role. We historians are erratic prophets. But it seems to me highly probable that, as so often in the past, Wales will emulate changes north of the border. This will happen much more rapidly this time than the seventy-nine years it took to follow Scotland in having a Secretary of State. In the past, one of the more famous insults to which the Welsh took offence was that contained in the *Encyclopædia Britannica*, an entry which encapsulated all the patronising indifference shown by the Victorians towards the Welsh identity: 'for Wales – see England'. A hundred years on, in a very different social and cultural context, in which English nationalism seeks a role, and a rebirth of a Welsh nation seems to have genuinely taken place, we might find another watchword: 'for Wales – see Scotland'.

The historic differences between the two nations are as old as the Scots and Welsh themselves. Modern Scotland is the product of an Act of Union, between two sovereign states, passed in 1707, less than three hundred years ago, which is comparatively recent in the historian's eye of eternity. Modern Wales is the product of an act of conquest, imposed on a defeated and fragmented people by Edward I over four hundred years earlier. In the thirteenth century, when Prince Llywelyn's last bid for Welsh statehood was crushed by the English, the kingdom of Scotland under Alexander III was recognised as enjoying sovereignty. Alexander was to observe in 1278: 'No-one has a right to homage for my kingdom save God alone'.[1] There was a territorial Scotland. For all its acknowledged cultural identity, there was not and never had been, a clearly territorial Wales. 'When was Wales?', the late Gwyn A. Williams memorably asked.[3] It might be added, where or what was Wales? A bishop of St Davids in the later nineteenth century was much abused by Liberals and nonconformists when he referred to Wales as a 'geographical expression', as Metternich had so described Italy prior to its unification. But Bishop Basil Jones was not far wrong in so describing at least the outward forms of one of Karl Marx's classic 'unhistoric nations'. In 1282, Edward I mopped up the fractured Welsh kingdoms, exploiting their rivalries and lack of common identity. Wales was assimilated into the English state and legal system thereafter, culminating in the relatively trouble-free passage of the Acts of Union under Henry VIII in 1536 and 1543. One Welsh institution after another was extinguished, culminating in the quiet demise of the once popular Court of Great Sessions (which had allowed the use of the Welsh language in legal proceedings) in 1830.[4] The Edwardian settlement in Wales had done more than construct powerful, if picturesque, castles around the periphery of the principality. It had also created patterns of English or Anglo-Norman infiltration, which indeed were to be confirmed with remarkable exactitude in the polling of the various Welsh counties on 18 September 1997. The one great rebel over the years was Owain Glyndŵr in the early fifteenth century, on whom Rees Davies has recently written a powerful study. But it was his total failure that made him a figure of legend: 'No Welsh poet or story teller commemorated his deeds as John Barbour did those of Robert Bruce', Professor Davies tells us.[5] He never had the subsequent resonance in popular consciousness enjoyed in Scotland by William Wallace or Robert Bruce, let alone Bonnie Prince Charlie. Owain Glyndŵr has never inspired an epic Welsh *Braveheart* – though perhaps that is just as well.

Scotland, for its part, was unified with the English kingdom in 1603 and with the English state in 1707. But there remained no doubt about Scottish separateness. The Scots and the Irish, after all, in their different ways, provoked the crisis in the United Kingdom in the late 1630s that led to the civil wars, the execution of the king and an eleven-year republic. It is inconceivable that the Welsh, largely docile royalists at the time, could have had a similar impact. Even after the Act of Union, as is universally recognised, the Scots retained crucial forms of institutional and social identity. There were the Scottish Kirk and its established Presbyterian religion, a national banking system, the Scottish educational system at all levels, and perhaps most importantly, a totally distinctive Scottish legal system. The Scottish legal profession became latimers of national identity. In the university world, Glasgow and Aberdeen dated from the fifteenth century, almost challenging Oxford and Cambridge in their antiquity. As recently as the 1990s, I was constantly struck as a Vice-Chancellor by how much greater authority Scotland's represen-tatives in the Committee of Vice-Chancellors and Principals seemed to enjoy in speaking for their system of higher education than the Welsh did for theirs. Wales, then, had nothing like the Scottish institutional inheritance. Its education, fiscal and legal systems were part of the English. The four Welsh dioceses were part of the province of Canterbury, and no one dreamt of their disestablishment. In Scotland, enduring and powerful institutions and images created a surviving sense of Scottish citizenship. A similar sense of Welsh citizenship prior to 1800 lay in the realms of imagination or fantasy.

In the nineteenth century, powerful global forces of integration and of pluralism transformed the world. Naturally, they affected Scotland and Wales in their different ways, and of course Ireland, north and south, as well. Industrialisation, urbanisation, a country-wide financial market, the force of growing literacy, could work in different directions. They could make the United Kingdom more of a homogeneous whole – reinforcing the insular, entrepreneurial, Protestant forms of Britishness of which Linda Colley has written powerfully.[6] But they could also, perhaps to an extent which she underestimated, lend a distinctly national focus to the component parts of a formally united kingdom. Glasgow, Cardiff, Belfast were great imperial cities and ports which exported to the world. They were also, or became, important *loci* of the self-assertive identity of Scotland, Wales and Ulster. The consequences for Scotland and Wales, at least, proved however to be predictably different. Scottish distinctiveness acquired new robustness in an increasingly wealthy and literate age. The Scottish aristocracy, fading flowers of the forest as they had been, became themselves bearers of a new sense of national identity. Their role in fact and legend was popularised by the wizardry of Sir Walter Scott. The Welsh have produced many remarkable men of letters from Dafydd ap Gwilym to R. S. Thomas (and latterly a few women, too) but it is a matter of profound historical significance that there has never been a Welsh Walter Scott. It is not surprising, given the character of nineteenth-century Scotland, that it was members of the Scottish aristocracy, the young Lord Rosebery, the Duke of Argyll, the Earl of Fife, who led the agitation which persuaded Gladstone to set up a revised secretary of state for Scotland in 1885. As Arthur Balfour sagely remarked, 'The best salmon river in Scotland will go a long way'.[7]

Welsh national consciousness and its revival took a very different form. Interestingly enough, Gladstone played a significant part here, too. The Welsh aristocracy, however lengthy their antiquity, had long been symbols of Anglicanism and Englishness in speech, outlook and aspirations. The campaign for Welsh identity, therefore, was, unlike Scottish, much more of a case of historical pressure from below. In the 1840s, it took the form of a campaign to protect the proudest and most distinctive feature of the Welsh as a people – their native language, spoken at the time by perhaps 90 per cent of the population. The dismissive contempt shown it by the Blue Books on Education in 1847, known in popular legend thereafter in treasonous terms as *Brad y Llyfrau Gleision*, documents which correctly showed the stark limitations of Welsh educational provision at that time, stung Welsh nationalism awake. The newly emergent Welsh-language press, editors like 'S.R.', Samuel Roberts of Llanbrynmair, and William Rees and their middle-class readers, symbols of the power of the word, became instruments of protest that took an increasingly national or nationalist form.

After the passage of the Reform Acts of 1867 and 1884/5, Welsh identity became much more overtly political.[8] Welsh national consciousness in its modern form is a function of mass democracy – of course, for men only at this period. A new Liberal ascendancy totally dominated Welsh parliamentary politics and captured virtually all the new county councils as well after 1889. A variety of well-organised national campaigns resulted; indeed, the fifty years from the 1860s to the end of the First World War were a decisive crucible of change in Wales – peaceful, constitutional change – which may be why some of the more colourful commentators on the Welsh scene, seeing the Welsh as eternally rioting and demonstrating, knocking down toll-gates or flattening enclosure walls, tend to pass it by. There was a long propaganda campaign for disestablishment of the Church in Wales, for a reform of the system of landed tenure along the lines of that achieved in Ireland, and for a new educational structure which led to the 'county' schools of 1889 and the national federal University of Wales achieved in 1893. There arose a new generation of young nationally-minded radical politicians. Of these, the most beguiling was the philosopher-patriot Tom Ellis, who became Liberal chief whip and died at forty, but the most spectacular talent of all was 'the little Welsh attorney', David Lloyd George, elected to parliament in 1890 on a strongly Welsh national programme at the tender age of twenty-seven.

They challenged comparison with Parnell's Irish Nationalist Party at the time, and perhaps won quite as many victories. Certainly, they won over key English supporters, Gladstone above all. The champion of struggling nationalities abroad – Greeks, Italians and Bulgarians – himself part Scots, he had married a Welsh woman, lived at Hawarden in north-east Wales, and patronised the National Eisteddfod. The Welsh Sunday Closing Act was passed with Gladstone's vocal support in 1881.[9] It was the first legislative enactment to apply to Wales (though not yet Monmouthshire) a wholly different set of principles from those obtaining in England. It may seem odd now to regard closing the pubs to the thirsty Welshmen and others on the Sabbath as a badge of nationhood, but so it was. Again, the Intermediate Education Act in 1889 created a free, undenominational secondary schools system in Wales, different from and superior to that operating in England. The University of Wales in 1893 was to be a model for the federal National University of Ireland, based on the colleges of Dublin, Cork and Galway, a few years later. Above all, the disestablishment of the Church in Wales (including Monmouthshire this time) in 1920 (something the Scots, with their very different religious complexion never came close to achieving) was in its modest way a remarkable political victory. It was, significantly, passed through parliament while David Lloyd George was in Downing Street – or rather while he was in Versailles signing the peace treaty in 1919, busying himself with extending the principle of nationality among the fallen empires of continental Europe, but keeping his own nation on his agenda as well.

But – and it is a crucial 'but' – all these political achievements for the Welsh were far removed from devolution. In Wales, and indeed in Scotland too at this time, there was no demand for any form of separatism on the lines of the Irish. Wales and Scotland sought national equality within the United Kingdom, not exclusion from it. In a worldwide Victorian empire, they wanted, in Bismarck's famous phrase, their own place in the sun. There was no Welsh or Scottish Parnell or de Valera. During the Anglo-Boer war of 1899–1902, as I had to remind an audience in Pretoria in August 1998, despite Lloyd George's courageous protests, the majority of the Welsh were staunchly imperialist.[10] They cheered the defence of Mafeking and the capture of Pretoria by such alleged Welshmen as Lord Roberts and Baden-Powell. The Welsh members took a very different line from the Irish who actually cheered in the House when news of the British defeat at Spion Kop came through. While the Irish kept on resolutely pressing for Home Rule down to the Great War, and for republican status thereafter as Sinn Féin supplanted the old Nationalist Party, the Welsh rejected the concept of separatism out of hand. The only attempt at a movement for some form of devolution was the Cymru Fydd campaign of 1894–6. It was a political catastrophe which almost tore Welsh Liberalism apart; perhaps it had more to do with the personal ambitions of David Lloyd George than with a grass-roots demand for home rule. Even the scenario of the historian-publicist F. S. Oliver in the imperialist periodical *Round Table* for 'home rule all round' as part of a federal imperial system, got no support. In the 1890s, as later on, the Welsh language was claimed to be a divisive force politically. It ranged the southern coastal cities and ports – the famous 'Newport Englishmen' who shouted down Lloyd George at the South Wales Liberal Federation in January 1896[11] – against the Welsh hinterland, rural and industrial. In 1979 the referendum showed that that division was still there.

The disestablishment of the Church in Wales, unlike Ireland, was not a precursor of separatism but an alternative to it, sufficient in itself. Movements led by worthy politicians like E. T. John for a Welsh secretary of state led absolutely nowhere. Lloyd George in 1920, when prime minister, advised his fellow Welsh Liberals to 'go for the big thing', that is a secretary of state. But he himself did absolutely nothing to further that objective, then or later; even the greatest Welshman of the age had turned unionist, too. It should be added that the Scottish people, in the late Victorian and Edwardian period, were more unionist still. After all, the Scots, as ship-builders, soldiers, doctors and, especially in Southern Africa, as missionaries, felt themselves to be at the heart of empire, the very model of a virile imperial race. In the 'khaki' general election of October 1900, held at the height of the Anglo-Boer war, the Scots results actually showed a small swing to the Conservative and Unionist Party, the one part of the kingdom so to do.

The twentieth century, from the First World War down to the late 1960s, has been for Scotland and even more for Wales an age of central-ism and of unionism. The Conservatives called themselves the Unionist Party from the crisis over Irish Home Rule in 1886 down to the Irish Free State Treaty in 1922. They continued so to designate themselves in Scot-land until well after the Second World War. The emergent Labour Party, which represented a very different class interest and supplanted the Liberals, and came to be dominant in the Celtic nations by 1945, proved in time to be no less unionist. After all, it was essentially a product of the integrative forces of the First World War, in which the trade unions emerged nationally as vital components of a new, if short-lived, corporate order. Until 1918, there had been many symptoms of Labour favouring devolutionist ideas. The Independent Labour Party favoured localism and the politics of community. The Fabian Society endorsed municipal socialism and experiments in local government. There were forces for industrial as well as political devolution – witness the quasi-syndicalists in the Rhondda who produced the tract *The Miners' Next Step*, published by the Unofficial Reform Committee at Tonypandy in 1912, and who wanted workers' control at the point of production, not state national-isation. Keir Hardie, member of parliament for Merthyr and Aberdare, championed Welsh and Scottish home rule, as did Ramsay MacDonald in his youth, seeking to unite the Red Dragon and the Red Flag. Hardie's aim was to create a more pluralist, locally based, genuinely democratic Labour movement in Britain in contrast to the inert bureaucratic Prussian centralism of the German Social Democrats.[12]

But, after 1918, social and economic pressures during the depression years, notably the role of the nationally organised trade unions, made a working-class Labour Party as unionist as the wealthy Tories. Solidarity meant the unity of workers in all nations. Arthur Henderson, as Labour's general secretary, proved to be stoutly resistant to the quasi-separatist pressures of the comrades in Scotland and Wales. Socialism and national-ism were clean different. Not until as late as 1947 did the party create a unified organisation in Wales, called with due modesty the Regional Council of Labour.

Attempts once favoured by Labour and some Liberals at some kind of United Kingdom federalism in 1918 to 1919 – an idea backed by some apostles of imperial federation such as Philip Kerr, now lodged in Lloyd George's 'garden suburb' of private advisers – attracted no interest. Not that this seemed anything less than wholly appropriate during the grim depressed atmosphere of the interwar years. The Scottish National Party was minute: its one MP, Dr Robert McIntyre, elected in the last few months of the Second World War, proved to be a fleeting phantom. Plaid Cymru, founded in 1925, significantly during the National Eisteddfod at Pwllheli, was in the main a pressure group of intellectuals and *littérat-eurs* campaigning on behalf of the Welsh language.[13] Its early politics were complicated and compromised by the politics of its charismatic first president, the poet and dramatist Saunders Lewis. Plaid Cymru was given an emotional boost by the imprisonment of Saunders Lewis and two other nationalists after an admitted arson on a Royal Air Force base in Llŷn in 1936; but it was fundamentally a pressure group. Down to the 1950s it could hardly be designated as an organised political party at all.

Even in this era of unionism, however, the differences between Scotland and Wales were apparent and persisted right down to 1997 and beyond. The contrast comes out with great clarity during the latter part of the Second World War. In Scotland, that famous socialist Tom Johnston made the Scottish Office a powerful laboratory of change.[14] He did so partly by persuading Churchill that if he did not get his way, an upsurge in the SNP would follow. As a result, Johnston was able to create a Scottish Council of State and a Council of Industry, to get planning powers transferred to the Scottish Office in St Andrew's House and to create in Edinburgh the basis for a powerful impulse towards greater self-government. He gained the support of powerful Scottish establishment figures such as John, Lord Reith and John Boyd-Orr. In Wales, by contrast, there was nothing. The Welsh Council of Reconstruction, established in 1942, in which James Griffiths was a prominent figure, failed to achieve any devolution in central economic planning or decision-making. The Attlee government (1945–51) offered nothing to Welsh sentiment in the running of the nationalised industries.[15] There was to be no Welsh secretary of state. Instead of any kind of elected assembly, Herbert Morrison produced a purely nominated and ineffective Council for Wales which limped along until the 1960s. All he and Attlee could offer otherwise as a *douceur* to national sentiment was a Welsh coat of arms (where the location of the leek created problems). Cardiff did not even become a capital city.

The ethos was relentlessly centralist. The Welsh accepted the wisdom of Whitehall.[16] The Parliament for Wales campaign in the early 1950s, which attracted the support of Welsh-speaking MPs such as Cledwyn Hughes and Goronwy Roberts, was allowed to peter out.[17] A Welsh Day debate was held in the Commons for the first time in October 1944, but it was not a success. That doughty socialist, Aneurin Bevan, poured scorn on the whole occasion: it was totally unnecessary: Wales and England were inseparable. How did Welsh sheep differ from English sheep? They grazed on the same grass and were subject to the same environmental circumstances (the fall-out from Chernobyl could not be predicted in 1944). Bevan at that time (he modified his stance somewhat in the later 1950s) was no more a nationalist than his Scottish wife, Jennie Lee, was either a nationalist or a feminist. The different political cultures of Scotland and Wales were thus publicly exposed.

The story of devolution or separatism in Scotland and even more in Wales is thus the history of a non-event until well after the Second World War. But, since the 1960s, that era of change in modern Britain in matters political and sexual, a major transformation has occurred. Celtic nationalism proved to be an offshoot of the 'permissive society': Welsh nationalist students, clambering up television masts, defacing road signs or blockading post offices, were part of the new rebellious youth culture. The creation of the Welsh Office in 1964, with the veteran James Griffiths as first secretary of state, left a legacy of frustrated expectations. The change since then has been considerable, the era of Margaret Thatcher notwithstanding. Scotland and Wales have responded sharply to wider movements in the British and worldwide experience – the end of empire and the emergence of a united Europe, the rise of a global economy, the erosion of a London-centred, Fabian civic culture, all of which questioned the role or authority of Westminster and Whitehall. As before, it was Scotland that led the way. The Scottish National Party proved to be more widely rooted than Plaid Cymru. In October 1974, no fewer than eleven SNP members were elected to parliament; the party could claim local government strength all over Scotland, from the remote Western Isles to Cumbernauld new town in the south. With a few articulate exceptions like Tam Dalyell and the young Robin Cook, the Scottish Labour Party became strongly committed to the notion of a Scottish Parliament. Welsh nationalism, by contrast, as the five Plaid Cymru seats gained variously between 1966 and 1997 suggested, was securely based only in Welsh-speaking rural areas in the north and west; in these areas it managed to establish a permanent presence in place of either Liberals or Labour.

The Crowther-Kilbrandon royal commission, reporting in 1973, noted the differences.[18] In particular, it cited the distinctive Scottish legal system as a major reason for discriminating between the two nations (though the election returns must have been an even stronger factor). It advocated a Scottish Parliament, which indeed the Scots were to endorse very narrowly in the referendum on 1 March 1979. But a proposed weak Welsh elected assembly was, as noted, thrown out by four to one. It was an emphatic action replay of the Cymru Fydd debacle of 1896, with Welsh politics again riven by divisions over regionalism and the language. In Caernarfon, people feared domination by an entrenched south Wales Labour 'taffia'; in anglicised Cardiff, by contrast, there were fears of the potential influence of the Welsh speakers of the distant north. Maverick Welsh Labour MPs, like Leo Abse in Pontypool, fanned the flames with hints that Taffy was a thief, probably resident in the wilds of Gwynedd. So matters seemed to continue throughout the Thatcher years. That period brought several recognitions of Welshness, notably the Welsh fourth television channel S4C, and funding for Welsh-medium primary and secondary schools. These appeared to be enough. The Scots launched an all-party Constitutional Convention in 1989, chaired by Canon Kenyon Wright, to draw up a scheme for devolution. In 1992, the Scottish Labour Party declared itself strongly in favour of a Scottish Parliament with tax-raising powers: this inevitably figured in the party manifesto. In Wales, however, devolution seemed to attract scant support other than from small groups of intellectuals and journalists: the man on the Cardiff omnibus was apathetic if not actually hostile. The Labour Party leader, Neil Kinnock, was himself a Welshman traditionally against devolution, as indeed was Glenys, his Welsh-speaking wife from Anglesey.

On the other hand, the very fact that in 1979 the Welsh had even considered the issue of devolution, for the first time in history, left its legacy on the terms of reference of public debate. In addition, the Welsh Office in the eighteen years of Conservative rule, even if run by a sequence of Englishmen – Peter Walker, David Hunt (on the party left), John Redwood (from the Thatcherite right) and William Hague – quietly changed the terms in which Welsh issues were considered. Almost by stealth, the Welsh Office's extended role after 1979 reinforced the sense of the territorial identity of Wales.[19]

Since 1992, a major historic transformation of opinion has occurred in Scotland and to a lesser degree in Wales. There are a number of reasons for this, many of them external to the principality. First, the pressure for devolution in Scotland became overwhelming. There was the consensual meeting point of the Scottish Constitutional Convention. Labour figures like John Smith and Robin Cook, previously hostile because of concern for maintaining Scottish Labour representation at Westminster in full, were compelled to change; Gordon Brown, on the other hand, author in 1986 of an excellent biography on Jimmy Maxton of the ILP, seems always to have been a robust devolutionist. The very strength of feeling in Scotland had its impact on Wales too. Second, the advent of Tony Blair and New Labour, with its aversion to centralist state planning and the corporatism of old Labour, has meant a distinct change in Labour ideology towards greater local accountability and a reform of the constitution as a means of both economic modernisation and adjustment to a committed role in a united Europe. Devolution was part of that vision, linked by Tony Blair with the legacy of Jeffersonian democracy in his John Smith memorial lecture.[20]

Third, in Wales itself, while the active role of the Welsh Office encouraged an emphasis on local identity, other features of Tory rule appeared to be in stark contrast with it. It is difficult to be sure how much popular resentment was really felt about 'the democratic deficit' inherent in quangos appointed by Tory governments for which only a small minority of Welsh electors had voted. But, certainly, they gave grist to the devolutionists' mill, especially when such fringe figures as the wives of heavily defeated Tory candidates were propelled to the forefront (for example, on NHS trusts) as symbols of Margaret Thatcher's brave new Wales. It may well have added to the air of governmental nepotism, decadence and sleaze that marked the John Major years. A combination of satisfaction with an active Welsh Office and of revulsion at politically unacceptable quangos added to a firmer sense of Welsh identity and, perhaps, of citizenship.

And finally, and of growing importance, there was the overshadowing presence of membership of the European Union. This could encourage the attractive notion of a Europe of nations, nourished not only by the SNP but also in such places as the colloquia held at Freudenstadt in Baden-Württemburg, which several Welsh academics and intellectuals

attended. In an evolving world, in which ideas of centralised governmental planning, the notion of sovereignty, the relation to Europe, and
the contours of the global economy were all in the melting pot, Wales,
like Scotland, would inevitably respond.

The outcome, of course, was the events of 1997. For the historian of
modern Britain, the contrast between 1979 and 1997 is remarkable. In
1979, devolution was reluctantly pushed onto a divided party and an
apathetic public by a declining minority government, manifestly at the
end of its tether. In 1997, by contrast, devolution was enthusiastically
promoted as a legislative priority by a fresh government with an overall
majority of 179 seats and the further backing of the Liberal Democrats
and Plaid Cymru. The opposition of the demoralised and derided Tories
was in itself a bonus – most of all when Lady Thatcher, of all people,
was flown into Glasgow to lecture the Scots on the merits of an un-
changing union. Most attention focused on the massive Scottish majority
of over two-thirds both for the principle of self-government and for
tax-varying powers. But the Welsh result, albeit achieved on a low turn-
out, is also not to be derided. That 50.3 per cent of Welsh voters should
vote for devolution in itself marked a large swing of public opinion
compared with 1979; not only much of the Welsh-speaking heartland
but all the valley constituencies in the south voted 'yes', as also did the
important city of Swansea (strongly resistant to Cymru Fydd a century
earlier). It is not credible to see the Welsh result as the product of a
north–south divide (an east–west divide may be a different matter).

The implications were immense. For the first time in their history,
the Welsh voted, by however narrow a margin, for some element of
power being transferred directly to themselves instead of mediated from
afar at Westminster. Quite apart from the fact that Wales, like Scotland,
rejected every single Tory candidate at the polls in May 1997, the 'no'
campaign was distinctly shadowy. Its major figures included distinctly
elderly survivors like Sir Julian Hodge (resident in the Channel Islands
as a tax exile) and the aged Lord Tonypandy (who died shortly afterwards). The Conservative Party machine prudently kept its distance.

Since the referendum vote in 1997, despite parochial arguments
over the Welsh assembly building (which paralleled those over the

Millennium opera house and rugby stadium), devolution appears increasingly as an idea whose time has come. Opinion polls show an upsurge of national self-confidence, with demands for a local perspective in social and economic planning – not to mention a buoyant Welsh design industry, a thriving Welsh-language cinema and the youthful appeal of such harbingers of Welsh culture as the Super Furry Animals, Catatonia, Stereophonics and the Manic Street Preachers at the turn of the millennium. The old divisiveness created by conflicting views on the Welsh language – the kind of thing that has led to bombings and violence among the Quebecois, the Flemings and the Afrikaaners – has largely disappeared, as *ysgolion Cymraeg* (Welsh-medium schools) and S4C have taken root. Indeed, it could be suggested that the difficulty Plaid Cymru faced in making inroads beyond the mountainous reaches of north-west Wales in itself helped the devolutionist cause. It could not plausibly be argued in 1997, as Leo Abse and others tried to do in 1979, that a devolutionist Wales would inevitably be a separatist Wales, and bring an end to what Hugh Gaitskell called in another connection 'a thousand years of history'.

Will devolution actually make a difference, or merely impose another ineffective, costly layer of intermediate semi-government upon the backs of the already much over-administered people of Wales? In itself, the elected assembly for Wales has limited conferred powers, and this may well lead to frustration with London control. The potential conflict was foreshadowed in the attempts by Labour's high command at Millbank to sideline Rhodri Morgan as potential first minister in favour of the Blairite Alun Michael, following Ron Davies's cumulatively bizarre departure as Welsh secretary. The distinction between the greater, reserved powers of the Scottish Parliament and its counterpart in Wales may well heighten the tension. Another new element since the referendums, of course, is the elected assembly in Northern Ireland, which introduced yet another local variation, along with the shadowy role provided for the Council of the Isles, on which the Welsh and Scottish bodies will be represented. It is not difficult to see prospects of years of wholesale constitutional and legal confusion to bemuse or distract the British people. Edinburgh lawyers could enjoy a bonanza unknown since the Act of Union. The role of the Scottish Parliament may lead to prolonged disputes over such matters as the extent of Scottish legislative autonomy, local taxing powers, the legal system, the future of the Lords and even the monarchy. In social policy, local initiatives may be hard to reconcile with the maintenance of nationwide standards in such matters as health and education, adhered to by governments of all political persuasions earlier in the century. Of more immediate importance, the future of any British Labour government with reduced Scottish representation must be in serious doubt, although the long-term potential weapon of electoral reform and regime-founding in this millennium on the kind of broader coalition basis familiar in continental politics will no doubt play its part.

But devolution is actually happening. I believe it is more appropriate here – and more useful in the longer term – to take a positive view, to regard devolution in Wales as an opportunity, not a threat. In my judgement, there are a number of specific advantages which a reformed system of government in Wales and elsewhere is likely to bring. In the first place, it is probable that Wales will actually be better governed – indeed, it is hard to claim, surely, that the end-of-millennium governmental system could attract mass enthusiasm, especially an emasculated system of local government for which only a diminishing minority of electors can be bothered to vote. It will mean the application of an all-Wales viewpoint at the point of decision-making for the first time in modern history. In this sense, events will move on from, say, the work of the Attlee government after 1945 – courageous pioneers of change in social and economic policy, but remarkably quiescent in areas of constitutional or governmental change. It is instructive to recall that Ernest Bevin and his colleagues were anxious to minimise the role of central government in the newly divided Germany, to underwrite democracy in the *Länder* and avoid the revival of any form of totalitarianism, but that they took an almost exactly opposite approach in the government of the United Kingdom. Not only will the emergence of an all-Wales viewpoint be beneficial in itself in meeting the challenges of the millennium. The power of scrutiny of the administration of Wales in matters great and small by an Assembly seen to be representative of the people as whole could be hugely beneficial, and have a democratically educative effect which the role of a largely invisible Welsh ombudsman to inquire into administrative abuses or errors could never achieve.

Let us illustrate the point with one historic, and dreadful, instance from the past. An elected Welsh Assembly would not have prevented the catastrophe at Aberfan in which one hundred and sixteen children died in 1966, smothered to death by tons of coal slurry from nearby tips. But it might well have prevented, or at least vigorously challenged, the disgraceful abuses that followed, and which my Oxford colleague Iain McLean clearly exposed.[21] One was the power of the National Coal Board to bully the government to avoid a proper investigation of the causes of Aberfan or apportion responsibility among, or take legal action against, Lord Robens (Chairman of the Coal Board) and other officials. Nobody was ever prosecuted. Another was the Board's wilful reluctance to pay proper compensation to bereaved relatives. Yet another was the fact of £150,000 donated by decent, sympathetic people to the Aberfan Disaster Fund being diverted to bail out the money-conscious National Coal Board in meeting the cost of levelling out its own coal tips. (Ron Davies, then Secretary of State for Wales in the Blair government, to his great credit reversed this, thirty years on.) Another has been the carelessness in preserving records of the whole affair, which determined scholars, fortunately, have been able to remedy. The aftermath of Aberfan is an appalling instance of local mismanagement which a probing, investigative Welsh assembly would have confronted and perhaps exposed.

Apart from the avoidance of governmental errors, an inclusive National Assembly, could draw in individuals and groups from far beyond the somewhat enclosed world of Welsh political culture – women, of course (only four of them served as Welsh MPs between 1918 and 1997); younger people, to revive a society that too often looks like a gerontocracy; ethnic minorities, who have played almost no part in our politics hitherto. Within the political world, minority groups would be given a far more positive role, especially Plaid Cymru, among whom able leaders would relish the prospect of responsibility. An assembly could also revitalise the Welsh Conservatives, born losers for well over one hundred years under incumbent voting systems, but offered new hope under the electoral system adopted for the Assembly. All this would be for the good.

As a supplement to this, one can be too defeatist about the limited powers that the Welsh Assembly had at the outset. Of course, it is far less powerful, as matters stand, than the Scottish Parliament: its initial remit did not include powers of primary legislation at all. However, powers over secondary legislation could be far-reaching, not least in the powers over six hundred statutory instruments. Influence over financial powers is also crucial. Jonathan Evans, a former Conservative minister apparently converted to devolution, urged that the Welsh assembly should have more than a mere permissive 'concordat' with central government: he suggested an input over such key matters as rates of interest and the level of sterling, both of central importance to the performance of the Welsh economy and the growth of jobs – which indicates a way for the agenda to move forward.[22] No doubt there will also be a Welsh view offered in the debates over joining European Monetary Union; I take it as probable that, at some stage, the Assembly will acquire financial powers, perhaps substantial ones, of its own – otherwise, as a body exercising executive power without financial responsibility, the Assembly will be on a par with the appointed or nominated quangos of the Tory past. Beyond these matters, any new body will surely acquire a life and personality of its own. Before coming into effect, the prospect of an Assembly might seem less than enticing, perhaps a talking shop for the Welsh chattering classes: but it will want to act, to challenge and question; it will attract publicity and a wider attention in the media; it will have the stimulus of a proactive and probably highly independent Scottish Parliament to encourage it.

Above all, it will have the essential legitimacy that arises from being elected. The Council for Wales, after 1949, raised major issues and had an inspirational first chairman in Huw T. Edwards, but it never got over its origins as Herbert Morrison's Celtic kindergarten. It could advise, encourage or warn, like Walter Bagehot's monarchy, another dignified part of the constitution. But it could never act and, therefore, it could never inspire. Edwards resigned in 1958, sadly complaining of the inability of 'Whitehallism' to understand Welsh aspirations.[23] The Welsh Assembly, by contrast, had from the start the power of a popular mandate. Its first minister would not be simply a prime ministerial nominee.

The people would to an increasing degree be governed by and from Wales, not from Whitehall or Westminster, let alone Wokingham, John Redwood's leafy stronghold in the Thames Valley. Like the constitutional reforms of the Blair government in general, the assembly would have a dynamic all its own.

A quite different, and potentially important, point relates to regionalism. Just as the Scottish Parliament would likely encourage an elected Welsh assembly to be proactive, so the latter might stimulate ideas of local autonomy among the people of England. In 1998, there was already the precedent pushed through by the Blair government of an elected mayor of London, with the status of his counterparts in, say, Paris or New York to aim for. Attempts to eliminate Ken Livingstone as Labour's candidate did not remove the historic potential of what was a new departure. Beyond that, perhaps some at least of the regions of England with a sense of historic identity – the north-east, and Merseyside and the north-west, perhaps East Anglia or the West Country – might want to follow the Welsh example. If this were to happen then, among other things, Tam Dalyell's famous West Lothian question – unanswerable as things stand, insoluble even for the mighty intellect of Gladstone at the time of Irish Home Rule over a century ago, when perhaps it appeared as the Mid-Lothian question – would be made redundant. Instead of glowering at the advantages, alleged or real, acquired by the assemblies of Scotland and Wales, the English regions, one after another, would surely be moved not to beat them but to join them. An English nationalist backlash would not occur. The outcome could be more fundamental changes. For instance it could shape the reform of the House of Lords, not on the basis of prime ministerial personal patronage to create a new and greater quango, but on a regional basis of devolved authority and democratic audit. At any rate, devolution in Wales and Scotland would not merely be a structure but a process – part of an ongoing range of redefinitions as our constitution adapts belatedly to modern circumstances. It was once said that there were no bounds to the march of a nation. Perhaps we might substitute or add the term 'region' as well. Or perhaps, in a post-modernist society, the difference between the two would simply wither away.

A third giant benefit, in my view, is that devolution could lead to a new relationship with the European Union, not only for Wales and Scotland, but for the United Kingdom as a whole. The EU is often condemned for a democratic deficit of its own, with the bureaucratic centralism of Brussels poised against the comparative ineffectiveness of the European parliament other than as a forum of debate; it was surely right that the British government should seek to reform its structures and methods of business. The EU reflects the statist constitutional and legal traditions of the central continental powers, rather than the (alleged) parliamentary basis of the British constitution. It is not surprising that this should be so. Time after time, from the failure to enter the Schuman coal and steel community in 1950 onwards, British governments missed a series of historic opportunities to join, and thereby influence, the new Common Market (later the European Economic Community). Historic or sentimental attachment to the myths of empire or the sea-faring exploits of an island race, a narrow definition of national sovereignty based on an ancient vision of the Crown in parliament, the symbolism of Big Ben chiming out for liberty, a kind of *Dad's Army* sentimentality dating from Dunkirk and the Battle of Britain, recalling how this happy breed fought alone while defeatist or treacherous continentals surrendered to the dictators – all these have played their part. They have particular resonance for the Home Counties: the bluebirds and nightingales which Dame Vera Lynn told us hovered over the white cliffs of Dover or Berkeley Square seldom made it as far as the Rhondda Valley.

But under New Labour it became clear that membership of Europe was central to all aspects of our external policy, with even the likely prospect that the future might see us enter the monetary union as well. But what matters is not only that British foreign policy is shaped accordingly, but also that domestic structures are made appropriate as well. With the process of incorporation into European law under way, the United Kingdom – or its component nations if Scotland were to break away – now requires political incorporation too.

This is where devolution, Welsh and otherwise, comes in. There are some excellent pointers in this direction offered by Sir John Gray and John Osmond, a distinguished ambassador and a crusading journalist respectively, which indicate the kind of opportunities open to a Welsh assembly even within existing structures.[24] In fact, for all its central-isation at the executive level, the European Union operates in some measure within the localities. It is increasingly a regional/national Europe, not a controlled monolith. The Committee of the Regions is a particular reflection of this. In the various regions of Spain, Italy, Belgium or the Netherlands, and emphatically so in the *Länder* of Germany where, for instance, Baden-Württemburg has been a powerful engine of economic growth (even in the difficulties following reunion with the east), decision-making is local, even parochial, rather than central-ised. In the shifting world of an inter-meshed global economy, where change, constructive or destructive, can be so rapid and cataclysmic it is no longer feasible to think simply in terms of the protective shield of central government over the nation-state. The EU operates in practice because its regional or national entities make many of their own de-cisions over trade, investment and employment, and interact with one another.

In a very modest way, I have been a witness to this myself in seeing the way the so-called Motor Scheme, consisting of Catalonia, Rhônes-Alpes, Lombardy, Baden-Württemburg and (thanks to the initiative of the Welsh Office) Wales, operated on an inter-regional basis. It cer-tainly brought benefit for the University of Wales when I was Vice-Chancellor, since our institutions of learning have enormous economic and social clout as well. The research money accruing to the six university institutions in my last year, 1994 to 1995, amounted to over £20 million.[25] Indeed, recourse to the EU could be a more straightforward and agree-able matter than trying to prise funding out of funding councils nearer to home. Further, I was frequently told in Brussels how beneficial it was that Wales's university was a nationwide, federal institution, since it represented a known territory, with its own culture and historic identity, which made it easy for other Europeans to grasp. It is not the least important argument for a national university.

In this and other ways, devolution will help Wales to progress within the European context that surely is our future. It will offer new choices for us at the Council of Ministers (where the German and Belgian regions are represented), on the Commission and in relations with other member-states. A Europeanised devolved Wales may also find other role models. Instead of being obsessed by England as we have been ever since the time of the Tudors, we may look, for example, across the Irish Sea. Ireland proved a remarkable success story within the EU, another largely rural and apparently peripheral nation like Wales, whose rate of growth once made it the tiger economy of Europe, leaving the Germans gasping in admiration and lagging behind. Naturally, the Irish used the system with much subtlety as befits a people with rare political talent. But they also seized on the emphasis on supply-side skills and training, the use of information and other technology, the revamping of education and applied research, as subsequently advocated by New Labour in Britain. So, if global pressures do not derail it, the millennium might bring another novel idea, 'for Wales – see Ireland'.

Devolution in Wales is an important part of a new concept of politics. It reflects a form of political post-modernism in which a more subtle, flexible and contemporary range of relationships will arise between communities: national, regional and local. Even without devolution, the United Kingdom would have had to change. It has been for centuries, at least since Henry VIII, perhaps since William the Conqueror, among the most centralised countries on earth. It has retained, with remarkably little overt change since 1688, a constitution designed for control and conquest. It has not reflected the pluralism of our society. Britain has in the course of the present century transformed itself in fundamental ways, many of them beneficial. It has peacefully shed an empire, it has launched a welfare democracy, it has survived mass depression and world war. Its constitutional structure has remained impervious, but now there is real change here also. The *status quo* is not an option. It may be a rough ride, but to me it is a potentially exciting prospect. For Wales, after its colourful and in many ways unfulfilled history – a story of frequent defeat – the prospects of an imaginatively-designed assembly on the Cardiff waterfront are historically fascinating. Some of us have spent our working lives showing that Wales has a continuous past, the past not of a state but of a living society. But you can have too much obsession with history, too, even if I am hardly the person to say so. Arthur Griffith, in 1922, protested against a hopeless view which saw Ireland eternally poised between the dead past and the prophetic future. Was there not to be, he asked the *Dail*, a living Irish nation in the here and now?

Now is the time to say the same for Wales, to ditch the patrician certainties of the 'gentleman from Whitehall' (or the message-maker from Millbank) in favour of what Bevan called the wisdom of ordinary people. Bevan was an anti-devolutionist who, late on, began to change his mind. He was above all a passionate democrat, who saw in the popular will the agency of historic necessity. He might just be with us now, seeing devolution as the democratic mobilisation of power, saying as he did in his last great speech in 1959, just before cancer destroyed him, that it – and we – represent the future, that the tides of history are flowing in our direction.[26] 'And if we say it and mean it, then we shall lead our people to where they deserve to be led.'

Notes

1 A. Grant and K. J. Stringer (eds), *Uniting the Kingdom? The Making of British History* (London, 1995), p. 91.
2 Gwyn A. Williams, *When was Wales?* (London, 1985).
3 Kenneth O. Morgan, *Wales in British Politics, 1868–1922* (Cardiff, 1980), p. 60.
4 M. Ellis Jones, 'An Individious Attempt to Accelerate the Extinction of our Language: Abolition of the Court of Great Sessions and the Welsh Language', *Welsh History Review*, 19, 226–64.
5 R. R. Davies, *The Revolt of Owain Glyndŵr* (Oxford, 1995), p. 340.
6 L. Colley, *Britons: Forging the Nation, 1707–1837* (New Haven, 1992).
7 C. Harvie, *Scotland and Nationalism: Scottish Society and Politics, 1707–1999* (London, 1999), p. 16.
8 Morgan, *Wales in British Politics*.
9 Morgan, *Wales in British Politics*, p. 42.
10 Kenneth O. Morgan, *Modern Wales: Politics, Places and People* (Cardiff, 1995), p. 46.
11 Kenneth O. Morgan (ed.) *Lloyd George: Family Letters c.1885–1936* (Oxford and Cardiff, 1973), p. 94.
12 Kenneth O. Morgan, *Keir Hardie: Radical and Socialist* (London, 1975), p. 209.
13 A. Butt-Philip, *The Welsh Question* (Cardiff, 1975), p. 13.
14 Harvie, *Scotland and Nationalism*, p. 32.

15 Kenneth O. Morgan, *Rebirth of a Nation: Wales 1880–1980* (Oxford and Cardiff, 1981), p. 377.
16 D. Jay, *The Socialist Case* (London, 1937). Repeated in his post-war edition in 1947, p. 258.
17 J. G. Jones, 'The Parliament for Wales Campaign, 1950–56', *Welsh History Review*, 16 (1992), 207–36.
18 V. Bogdanor, *Devolution* (Oxford, 1979).
19 D. Griffiths, *Thatcherism and Territorial Politics* (Aldershot, 1996).
20 T. Blair, 'John Smith Memorial Lecture', London, 7 February 1996.
21 I. McLean, 'On Moles and the Habits of Birds: The Unpolitics of Aberfan', *Twentieth-Century British History*, 8 (1997), 285–309.
22 J. Evans, 'The Assembly's Economic Hurdles', *Agenda* (Summer 1998), 21–2.
23 Morgan, *Rebirth of a Nation*, p. 333.
24 Sir J. Gray and J. Osmond, *Wales in Europe: The Opportunity Presented by a Welsh Assembly* (Cardiff, 1997).
25 Welsh Select Committee, *Wales in Europe* (London, 1995). Evidence from the University of Wales.
26 Michael Foot, *Aneurin Bevan, 2: 1945–60* (St Albans, 1973), p. 646.

12

Wales and Europe: From Revolutionary Convention to Welsh Assembly, 1789–2014

Twenty years ago, when I served as Vice-Chancellor of the still-important federal University of Wales, I was very aware of the European dimension to higher education in Wales. Three things in particular struck me. First, Wales appeared to be overwhelmingly pro-European. The Euro-scepticism prevalent in southern England seemed to be almost unknown. In Aberystwyth, where I was based, town and gown greatly benefited from the European connection, and knew it. The university there was much helped by student exchange via Erasmus, research collaboration with European institutions, and, to a limited degree, funding direct from the European Union itself – a Monnet chair in Politics and a Celtic lectureship from the committee of Minority Languages. Brussels was seemingly quite as accessible to British universities as were UK funding bodies in London or even Cardiff. The citizens of Aberystwyth enjoyed substantial support from the European Social Fund for rebuilding the Victorian promenade, and upgrading the sports facilities and arts provision at the university which were rightly deemed to be of wider benefit for the town, the county and mid-Wales as a whole. Secondly, there were practical opportunities for giving effect to the European relationship in teaching and research, especially through the Motor Scheme which linked Wales with the thriving European regions of Baden-Württemberg, Catalonia, Rhônes-Alpes and Lombardy, a connection which we owed to the vision of Peter Walker at the Welsh Office. I twice went to Brussels in the period 1993–5, the second time heading a deputation from all the Welsh university colleges: I heard from our European colleagues that the very title 'University of Wales' was pleasing to them since it linked the university with a significant territorial region or nation, not a mere town.

My third impression was less positive, namely that the policy of the Welsh Office (effectively in London) was very erratic, the strongly pro-European Peter Walker and David Hunt being followed by the deeply Eurosceptic John Redwood. When I went to Brussels, I was told by the late Bruce Millan, then an EU Commissioner, that he had in effect to act as Secretary of State for Wales himself since he could not get the Welsh Office to distribute Objective One structural funding to the south Wales valleys. I also had a peculiar experience in my last term as University of Wales Vice-Chancellor in June 1995, when we met the Welsh Affairs Select Committee in Westminster to discuss the University of Wales's links with Europe.[1] The Committee had been told by the Welsh Office that our funding from the EU was around £2–3 million; I told them that I had checked carefully with the vice-chancellors and finance officers of all six of our institutions, and that the actual total was significantly over £20 million. Aberystwyth alone had received more than the Welsh Office suggested had been received by the entire University of Wales. Thus far could Euro-scepticism take you along the path of misinformation.

This, then, is the traditional, received view: an England inclined more and more to Euro-scepticism, ardent for an 'In/Out' referendum, increasingly congenial territory for UKIP, the Celtic nations very much the opposite and eager to be at the heart of Europe. In 2012, a newspaper survey found support for UKIP in Wales to stand at six per cent (in Scotland, even less) but in England at 23 per cent. Things are never static, however, and the situation seemed in 2014 to be far less simple. As throughout England, Euro-scepticism in Wales gathered pace. Statistics garnered by Richard Wyn Jones of Cardiff University early in 2013 seemed to confirm the view that I had long held of Wales, like Scotland, being far more in sympathy with the links, financial and educational, with Europe. 'Surveys show overall a clear preference in Wales for staying in the EU', wrote Wyn Jones.[2] This judgement, which I shared, has become the conventional wisdom, endorsed at the highest level. The Welsh First Minister, Carwyn Jones, has declared that leaving the EU would be a disaster, with 150,000 jobs depending on the single market, and the whole community benefiting from EU Structural Funds (£2 billion over the next seven years).[3] After 2020, indeed, Wales will be the only part of the United Kingdom still receiving resources from these funds. In Wales, Labour, Plaid Cymru and the Liberal Democrats have always been generally strongly pro-European, and even the Welsh Conservatives are sympathetic. There has been something close to a Welsh consensus on Europe, among politicians and commentators alike.

But some recent polls of Welsh opinion appear to show the reverse. In July 2013, the Cardiff-based Beaufort Research showed that 37 per cent of Welsh people would vote to leave the EU in a referendum, and only 29 per cent to stay in. Every part of Wales would vote to come out, with especial hostility shown (43 to 23 per cent) to EU membership in the valleys. Yet the valleys had been by far the greatest recipient of European largesse, with £3 billion of aid since 2000, along with a further £3 billion of matching funds from within Wales. Almost every age group endorsed a 'no' vote. The three groups, all significant ones, which showed a majority for staying in the EU were the youngest age group, the most affluent social classes ABC1 (38 to 34 per cent), and speakers of Welsh (36 to 31 per cent).[4] This startling result had already been anticipated in a BBC Wales poll back in February 2013, which showed that 49 per cent felt that, on balance, Wales would be better off outside the EU, while 45 per cent felt that it was advantageous to stay in.[5] These figures, showing a markedly greater degree of hostility to Europe than shown in Scotland, were hardly a surprise. After all, back in 2009, UKIP had polled the respectable total of 87,585 votes in the Welsh Euro elections, 12.8 per cent of the total. More importantly, Wales now had a UKIP parliamentary representative. The fourth and final MEP to be elected in 2009, relegating the struggling Liberal Democrats to fifth place on the list, was a UKIP candidate, John Bufton from Llanidloes in Powys. In an earlier venture into politics, standing as UKIP candidate in Ceredigion in a by-election, he had come fifth with a paltry 1.9 per cent of the vote. Now he sat in the European Parliament in Brussels/Strasbourg to speak for Wales, so far as that restricted body would allow. Gains in the next Assembly elections were not unlikely through UKIP's regional list vote. At the 2014 European elections, UKIP showed even more strength in Wales, gaining 27.55 per cent of the Welsh vote (just below Labour's 28.15 per cent) and having Nathan Gill elected as one of the four Welsh MEPs. The tides of Welsh Euro-scepticism might be lapping around Cardiff Bay. Meanwhile, alarming lurches within the Eurozone – Ireland, Portugal, Spain, Italy and Cyprus all sunk into massive indebtedness and recession and having to be bailed out, the hapless Greeks virtually going into receivership, even mighty France in deep trouble and turning more Euro-sceptic with the advance of Marine Le Pen's Front National – hardly added to the attractiveness of the European panacea in economically struggling Wales. The hazardous entry of little Latvia in January 2014, against the wishes of most of its people at the time, was no great reassurance.

If the present day presents a rapidly changing, multi-faceted picture of Welsh attitudes towards Europe, so does the evidence from our history. It shows that the very idea of 'Europe' in Wales has had a rich variety of meanings and implications. It shows too that, in our view of Europe as in so many other respects, the Welsh are very different from the English. It is this aspect that I wish to focus on here, the varied visions of the European idea held by significant Welshmen down the years. On four of them in particular, I want to place a particular emphasis – the Europes of David Williams, Tom Ellis, Saunders Lewis and Rhodri Morgan – since their Europeanism was central to their outlooks and, by extension, to the international outlook of Wales itself.

David Williams (1738–1816) was a Presbyterian minister from Caerphilly who found his way to a chapel in Highgate in London, and another in Frith Street, Soho.[6] Here he evolved a distinct and original Deist religious philosophy, accompanied by experimental proposals for a rationalised Church liturgy. Williams's Europe was a revolutionary, republican Europe, a Europe of reason, of nature and enlightened thought. He established a wide range of intellectual contacts with French *philosophes*: he was the friend of Condorcet, and corresponded with Voltaire, Rousseau and even Frederick the Great of Prussia. Another correspondent was Benjamin Franklin. Williams's *Letters on Political Liberty* (1782) were a robust defence of the American Revolution, and a call to arms on behalf of democracy and popular sovereignty. He responded equally strongly to the events in Paris in 1789 and, like his fellow-countryman Richard Price, vigorously condemned Burke's assault on the French Revolution. It was in 1790–1 that Williams's Europeanism reached its most dramatic phase. He became close to the Girondins, especially to Jacques-Pierre Brissot, the excitable editor of the democratic newspaper, *Le Patriote Français*, on whom Williams's *Letters* had a particular impact. He was invited to attend the debates in Paris on the constitution of 1791, and was actually granted honorary French citizenship. Events thereafter greatly disillusioned him: he disapproved of aspects of the 1791 constitution as it eventually emerged; he opposed Brissot's pugnacious calls for a national- ist war to strike out at France's counter-revolutionary enemies; he de- plored the fate of the moderate Girondins, and the execution of their leaders, including finally Brissot himself; above all, he condemned the execution of Louis XVI, which soured his enthusiasm for revolutionary constitution-making. Williams would have echoed the Girondin Madame Roland's despairing cry, 'Liberty, what crimes are committed in thy name!'

The later David Williams was a far more cautious and conservative figure, and indeed a less interesting one. He became politically suspect on both sides of the Channel as a go-between, operating secretly with both the French and British governments. His most visible surviving creation today is the distinctly philanthropic Literary Fund for the assistance of indigent authors. Still, he retained his reputation as an important philosopher of democratic revolution: Madame Roland's praise of him as 'a deep thinker and a real friend to mankind' refurbished his radical credentials.[7] Williams is remarkable, almost unique, for the directness of his engagement with European revolutionary doctrines, and his legacy for Wales, along with contemporaries such as Richard Price, was of much importance. They left a tradition of internationalist, rationalist, republican 'Jacobinism' (not a strictly accurate term for the pro-Girondin David Williams) that underlay the radical ideology to which many dissenters subscribed throughout the Napoleonic wars and their aftermath. There were strong echoes of it during the riots in Merthyr

275

in 1831, Wales's Peterloo. Williams and his colleagues left a legacy of dynamic social and political democracy which Gwyn A. Williams has brilliantly chronicled. It has its still-living embodiment in Gorsedd y Beirdd at the National Eisteddfod, Iolo Morganwg's eccentric reinvention that still testifies to visions of natural man, republicanism and organic transformation. The picturesque ceremony to initiate its Bards (of which I have the honour of being one) embodies timeless, cosmic values that speak to us all.

Tom Ellis (1859–99) was a very different character, the Methodist son of a Merioneth tenant farmer, Liberal MP for Merioneth 1886 until his death, who became his party's Chief Whip under Rosebery in 1894. But he was a politician without precedent, a cultural nationalist and a visionary prophet.[8] His Europe was emphatically a Europe of libertarian nations. Like his near contemporary, the preacher-poet William Rees, his idea of Wales was strongly influenced by continental apostles of nationhood, the vision of Count Szechenyi in Hungary and especially Guiseppe Mazzini in Italy. Mazzini's ideal was nationality, not nationalism: it was always subordinated to the wider claims of humanity in general, and it was this gentler creed that captured Tom Ellis's imagination. He was drawn to Mazzini's secular, civic religion of nationality based on free citizenship. The old Italian cherished individual civil liberties and was in no sense the forerunner of a fascist Italy; he wrote to an English friend, James Stansfeld, that 'the principle of nationality is sacred to me. I believe it to be the principle of the future.'[9]

This was, Ellis believed, especially applicable to Wales, where deep-rooted concepts implied collectivity and organic cohesion. 'It has been the land of *cyfraith, cyfar, cyfnawdd, cymorthau, cymanfaoedd*, the land of social co-operation, of associative effort.'[10] The very name of the nation, Cymru, meaning friends or companions, itself conveyed this idea. There was always a socialist side to Ellis. He particularly venerated that pioneer utopian socialist, Robert Owen of Newtown, who 'preached the ancient doctrine of human brotherhood – the hope, the faith, the living fact of human brotherhood'. He was 'the bearer of *Neges Cymru* (the message of Wales) to the modern world.'[11] Ellis thus cherished Mazzini's idea of 'association' and the romantic cult of youth he identified with it. Hence

'Young Wales' on the model of Young Italy: Cymru Fydd, the Wales that is to be. Ellis underlined passages in his private copy of Mazzini's writings to this effect. 'Place the young at the head of the new insurgent masses . . . You will find in them the host of apostles for the new religion . . . Consecrate them with a lofty mission.'[12] Mazzini's vision he regarded as particularly applicable to small, mountainous communities. In 1888 he went with an English friend, Arthur Acland, on an important visit to the Austrian Tyrol, whose *Landtag* might serve as the model for a future Welsh parliament. Then it was south to the Italian lakes where, close to Pliny's villa beside Lake Como, 'we blessed again and again the work of Joseph Mazzini'.[13] For all the disillusion that a united Italy generated afterwards, notably in the era of Mussolini, Welsh Liberals of a particular school continued to venerate Mazzini long after Ellis's tragically early death. An excellent lengthy biography of him, *Mazzini, Prophet of Modern Europe*, was published in 1932 by Gwilym O. Griffith, a Welsh-speaking disciple of Ellis, and a campaigner for Welsh home rule alongside E. T. John before the First World War. Griffith kept the faith in extreme old age. Remarkably, his book was reprinted, thirty-eight years later, in 1970, two years before Griffith's death at the age of ninety. He also published, in 1954, a short pamphlet for an Italian publishing house, *Mazzini Yesterday and Tomorrow*. For men like him, Mazzini's importance was an inspiration not only for Wales itself but for humanity at large. He transcended the ages. Mazzini's outward-looking message encompassed not just a united Italy but vision of a European union of free and autonomous nations. In our own time, his prophecy has come close to being fulfilled.

Ellis's passionate nationalism reached its climax with an emotional, almost mystical, speech in his home town of Bala on 18 September 1890.[14] The emphasis here was on the unity of the national spirit – unity was a more powerful element even than freedom. This was above all a cultural unity. Ellis's European vision thus emphasised arts and crafts, historical records and antiquities, as essential components of an enduring Welsh nation that would live on to fulfil its destiny. He wanted monuments in traditionally Celtic (or Keltic) style to be built to celebrate the Cymric dead, the great patriots of the past from Hywel Dda to Robert Owen, to inspire the feeling of nationality. His published speeches focused on schools for arts and crafts and native traditions of vernacular architecture, perhaps reflecting the influence of Ruskin while he was an undergraduate.[15] He regretted that contemporary Irish nationalism had become so narrowly political and sectarian under the leadership of men like Daniel O'Connell and Charles Stewart Parnell. Its future should rather lie, he believed, in cultural renewal. He cherished, as did his contemporary Llywelyn Williams, the subtler cultural message of the Protestant Irish nationalist, Thomas Davis, editor of *The Nation*, back in the 1840s. This was a fundamental barrier between Ellis and his far more pugnacious, essentially political, colleague David Lloyd George. Ellis's Mazzinian nationalism merged with other ideas in his complex outlook. He was a young man of remarkably wide culture with a curiosity for ideas. At Oxford, he absorbed something of early Fabianism and neo-Hegelian Idealism; he met delegates to the Co-operative Congress; he listened to the radical lectures of Arnold Toynbee on the early industrial revolution, and read the works of T. H. Green which anticipated the future New Liberalism. He also heard John Ruskin lecture in Oxford on 'The Art of England', and actually met the great man. More surprisingly, perhaps, Ellis was attracted by the imperialism of Cecil Rhodes, and the vision of a perhaps confederal imperial dominion which encouraged Rhodes, surprisingly, to give financial support to Parnell's Irish Nationalists. He met Rhodes in South Africa in 1891 and was hugely impressed, in a way that is somewhat reminiscent of Lloyd George's admiration for Hitler in 1936. Ellis wrote of Rhodes to his close friend D. R. Daniel of Rhodes: 'He is truly a strong man with powerful personality and clear brain and large views. I wish he were in British politics. He would soon be the leader of the Liberal party.'[16] This imperialist outlook led Ellis later on to take a distinctly equivocal view of the notorious Jameson Raid in South Africa in 1896, in which Rhodes was deeply implicated. It suggests that during the South African War, Ellis, unlike David Lloyd George, would not have been a 'pro-Boer'. Ellis's early death, after a long period of ill-health, makes it difficult to speculate where his version of nationalism would have led. He was a practical politician, not a mystic, a Liberal Chief Whip, even if perhaps not a very good one. He was also a man who saw the problems and pitfalls of separatism: something very close to modern devolution would have been his desired objective. But he imposed himself on Wales and its international consciousness as no-one else of that inspired generation of *fin de siècle* radicals managed to do. He symbolised a nationality that unites rather than a nationalism that divides. His reputation survived the erosion of late-Victorian Welsh Liberalism. It has left the vivid image of the lost leader, the youthful visionary, who detected a turning-point at which Welsh history refused to turn, a prophet with nobility of spirit frustrated in the last by the pragmatic calculators, the Kossuths, the Cavours – and the Lloyd Georges.

Saunders Lewis (1893–1985), a Liverpool Welshman of the diaspora, was a nationalist of a very different stamp from Tom Ellis.[17] But they shared a common commitment to aspects of European nationalism. Lewis's philosophy was intensely European from the start. It was during his time on the Western Front in the First World War that he began to develop his passionate interest in the Welsh language, of which hitherto he had only scanty knowledge, and it was there also that he fell under the spell of the far right-wing French author Maurice Barrès, whose novels *Le Culte de Moi* Lewis read avidly in the trenches. Barrès convinced him of the need to pursue his own intensely personal cultural roots: '[I]t was Barrès that turned me into a convinced Welsh nationalist.'[18] But where Ellis's nationalism was that of a democrat, committed to the national achievements of pre-war Liberalism, Saunders Lewis had only contempt for that tradition, which he regarded as empty and hypocritical. Central to his ideas was European Catholic civilisation in the middle ages; his conversion to Roman Catholicism was fundamental to his nationalism. Most of what had happened to Wales since the Reformation he deplored, the loss of its old religion, the encroachment of industry and urbanisation, the absorption of Wales by the English state, including the English party system, the constant threats to the language and the priceless literary inheritance of his nation. He founded Plaid Cymru in 1925, assisted by another strong Francophile, W. Ambrose Bebb. From the outset, therefore, the party was strongly internationalist and European in its outlook. Nationalists, wrote Lewis, should be 'Europe's interpreters in Britain'.[19]

But it was always to a very specific form of Europeanism that Lewis turned, one deeply abhorrent to many Welsh democrats – the Catholic anti-republican creed of men like Barrès and of Charles Maurras, editor of *Action Française*, both of them adopting a strongly anti-semitic tone during the Dreyfus affair, and subsequently warm champions of the anti-democratic ethos of Marshal Pétain. He also admired the passionate Catholic message of the poetic dramatist, Paul-Louis Claudel. An acerbic critic like R. T. Jenkins, an equally Francophile devotee of the *philosophes* of the Enlightenment, found the identification of Plaid Cymru's pioneers with France to be obsessive and bizarre. Not surprisingly, Lewis moved sharply to the right in the 1930s, while his colleague Bebb wrote in the party's newspaper in strong and consistent support of Mussolini and his brand of corporatist fascism. This was somewhat to the dismay of others in the party such as D. J. Davies, whose Europeanism focused on agrarian co-operative experiments in Scandinavia, following a visit to the People's College at Elsinore. His colleague, Bebb, wrote in the party's newspaper in strong support of Mussolini's totalitarian regime. Thus, while Lewis and Bebb found inspiration in the Catholic south and west of Europe, D. J. Davies and his Irish wife found it in the Protestant Scandinavian north, especially in the cooperative movement and folk high schools of Denmark. Lewis was the central figure in the famous arson attack directed against the establishment of a Royal Air Force base at Penyberth on the Llŷn peninsula, which led to Lewis and two colleagues to be tried for arson. The judge decided to move the trial from Caernarfon assizes, where the jury failed to agree on a verdict, to the Old Bailey in London, since Welsh jurors might be too biased (that is, too Welsh). Lewis and his two colleagues, D. J. Williams and Lewis Valentine, were sentenced to nine months in prison. By the coming of the Second World War, Lewis's European vision led him to see a moral equivalence between the British Empire and the Axis powers. One was no better than the other. He was thus attacked as a sympathiser with Fascist totalitarianism and, by implication, an anti-semite by Lloyd George's former aide, Thomas Jones. Jones accused Plaid Cymru of envisaging a 'new Promised Land of Fascism' which would plunge the Welsh nation into civil war.[20] Lewis's sympathies in France were strongly with the Vichy regime; his fierce anti-Communism made him deeply hostile towards the French left. His influence waned after 1945, other than in the youthful ranks of the Welsh-language movement. His brand of nationalism found more echoes overseas in ETA in the Basque country, among more extreme Corsican nationalists or fringe neo-fascist movements in Greece. Gwynfor Evans, a cultured humane patriot, and a later generation of nationalists had to steer their party into more mainstream, more democratic waters. Lewis's cultural/linguistic nationalism helped to make him the many-sided man of letters of genius which he was. But his far-right ideology was also a brilliant, brutal aberration linking its values with a form of Europeanism which the democratic instincts even of the more nationalist Welsh felt compelled to reject.

Rhodri Morgan (b. 1939) was a much younger Labour politician, the son of a university professor of Welsh, a graduate of Oxford and Harvard, but a man for whom a strongly European outlook was always fundamental. He grew up in a context where the Welsh had declared their strong sympathy for membership of the European union, with a 64.8 per cent 'yes' vote in the EEC referendum in 1975. Morgan's Europe was above all a Social Democratic Europe, all the more attractive as Britain plunged into neo-liberal Thatcherism, dragging left-wing anti-Thatcherite Wales along with it. An important phase of his life was when he headed the European Community office in Wales from 1980 to 1987. It was part of an important movement within the Welsh Labour Party to link its new commitment to devolution with a strong attachment to Europe, as it re-emerged from anti-European negativism under the strong leadership of Neil Kinnock. This outlook was particularly fostered by three Welsh musketeers who flourished in Brussels, all of them Aberystwyth graduates: Hywel Ceri Jones of the European Policy Centre; Gwyn Morgan, who moved from Transport House to play a major international role for the European Commission from 1973; and Aneurin Rhys Hughes, a prominent figure in the EEC general secretariat in Brussels. Of this talented trio, the most important was Hywel Ceri Jones, who joined the European Commission in 1973 as the head of DG XII, which was concerned with education and youth policies.[21] Thereafter, his impact on a wide variety of policy areas was quite astonishing. He developed the higher education exchange schemes, Erasmus and Socrates; he devised the da Vinci programme for vocational training; he played a significant role in creative new regional policies; he moved on to become acting director-general for social and economic policy. He served in effect as the *chef du cabinet* for Jacques Delors in the 1980s and was effectively the author of the Social Chapter of socio-economic rights for which the Blair government of 1997 signed up after years of delay by the Major government backed by the business community. The stamp of these pioneers was powerful in the pro-European momentum within Wales in the 1990s. Hywel Ceri Jones, for instance, headed the European Strategy Group set up by Ron Davies in 1998 to promote the role of Cardiff within the EU: it issued an influential report in 1998 for the National Assembly, *Wales and the European Union*, urging a far more positive attitude towards the Union.

All this also chimed with an important intellectual initiative, launched by the distinguished Scottish historian, later SNP representative at Holyrood, Christopher Harvie. An academic at Tübingen university, he used the Friedrich Ebert Stiftung and the small town of Freudenstadt in Baden-Württemburg as a forum for discussing the notion of a regional Europe, lively at that time. I attended some of these, and I recall that most national groups in western Europe took part – except the English. There were many other initiatives now flowing in much the same direction. Plaid Cymru, in its revived guise from the 1970s, was strongly committed to the European ideal, in a far wider context than the European vision of Saunders Lewis, seeing the then economic advance of the Celtic Tiger across the Irish sea as a future model for a free Wales. Now it would be 'For Wales – see Ireland'. A Welsh European centre was set up in Brussels in the year 2000 under Des Clifford, flamboyantly hailed by BBC Wales as the first Welsh representative in the European continent for six centuries.[22] An influential publication in 1997 was Sir John Gray's and John Osmond's *Wales in Europe* (1997), the joint work of a former ambassador in the Middle East and a prominent nationalist commentator on Welsh affairs. It urged the future Welsh National Assembly to be pro-active in Europe and to seize the opportunities for collaboration within the EU that were now opening up.

Rhodri Morgan became a pivotal figure in this intimacy between Wales and Europe when he became Wales's first minister in 2001, opening up a new chapter in a wider vision of the work of the devolved government. His predecessor, Alun Michael, also pro-European, had been thought to be too New Labour, too much the creature of Tony Blair. It was now emphasised that Wales was not simply a recipient in the EU, passively accepting Objective One funding to clear up environmental dereliction, but also an active participant in pan-European initiatives, for instance in environmental and communications policy. This was the message of a document published by the Assembly government in 2000, *Wales, a Better Country*. It called for Wales to enhance its European status and led to the Assembly government's European Affairs Committee being set up in 2003. The Maastricht Treaty of 1993 and the Lisbon Treaty ratified in 2009, far from being criticised for strengthening the integrative aspects of the EU as occurred in England, were hailed in Wales for the thrust towards promoting policies for the regions and nations of Europe. It was noted that Maastricht associated the European building process not only with national governments, but also with substate or regional institutions, including devolved bodies like the Welsh Assembly. It was a process encouraged by Romano Prodi as president of the European Commission 1999–2004. Maastricht thus became a beacon for the doctrine of subsidiarity. Henceforth, as Elizabeth Gibson-Morgan has shrewdly noted, it was hardly possible to speak of devolution without speaking of Europe, notably in the field of human rights where the European Court at Strasbourg was particularly active.[23] On the other hand, disappointment was expressed that the Committee of the Regions set up at Maastricht proved to be inactive and ineffective in practice, while the British government's Council of the Isles virtually never met. But there was a clear momentum towards more integration to be observed. Throughout the Labour-led coalitions of Rhodri Morgan and Carwyn Jones from 2001, followed from 2011 by Jones's solely Labour government, the emphasis seemed to be on devolution and Europeanism marching side by side. Morgan himself presided at a cheerful gathering in the National Library of Wales at Aberystwyth in 2006 to mark the six-hundredth anniversary of the pact that the famous national leader

Owain Glyndŵr had made with the French (supposedly) at the tiny village of Pennal in southern Merioneth, nestling in the Dyfi valley of my childhood. He crowned the occasion with a rousing trilingual speech to hail a kind of Franco-Welsh Entente Cordiale. In May 2009, he was to launch a new European Strategy on behalf of the Assembly government, urging anew the case for an even closer involvement with Europe, including, controversially perhaps, the European Court of Human Rights. Europeanism was throughout an important factor in pushing on moves towards further devolution. This emerged now in arguments that a distinctive Welsh law and jurisprudence were needed to mirror the other different national jurisdictions, to foster internationally the rule of law, and the notion of justice based on human rights, as propounded by the European Court at Strasbourg. Over the years, it had become increasingly clear that the two unions – the union-state of the four nations of the United Kingdom of Great Britain and Northern Ireland, and the Union of the sovereign nation-states of Europe – were evolving side by side, and reinforcing each other. All this would make the twin debates in 2014–17 about the future of the two unions a pivotal phase in the history not only of Wales and Scotland, but also of Britain and its future destiny.

Notes

1. HC 393, 1994–5.
2. Richard Wyn Jones, in *Wales, the United Kingdom and Europe* (London, October 2013), p. 12.
3. Speech by Wales's first minister, Carwyn Jones, 8 November 2012, *Western Mail*, 9 November 2012.
4. BBC Wales online report by Martin Shipton.
5. BBC Wales online report, 28 February 2013.
6. There is a good biography of Williams by Damian Walford Davies in the *Oxford Dictionary of National Biography*. There are two biographies available: Whitney R. D. Jones, *The Anvil and the Hammer* (Cardiff, 196); and J. Dybikowsky, *On Burning Ground* (Oxford, 1993). Neither is entirely satisfactory. Dybikowsky, for instance, says remarkably little on David Williams's activities in France in 1792. Sadly, my old mentor, Professor David Williams of Aberystwyth, an authority both on Wales and the French

Revolution and who intended to write a study on his namesake in his retirement, was prevented from doing so by serious illness.

7 Madame Roland, *Appel à l'impartiale postérité* (1795); cited in Walford Davies, entry on David Williams in the *Oxford Dictionary of National Biography*.
8 There is a fascinating analysis of Ellis's ideas in Neville Masterman, *The Forerunner* (Llandybïe, 1972). Mr Masterman, the son of Lloyd George's old colleague, C. F. G. Masterman, celebrated his hundredth birthday in 2012, and I had the joy of celebrating it with him.
9 Denis Mack Smith, *Mazzini* (New Haven, 1996), p. 154.
10 Tom Ellis, *Addresses and Speeches* (Wrexham, 1912), p. 22.
11 Ellis, *Addresses and Speeches*, p. 24.
12 Masterman, *The Forerunner*, pp. 80–1.
13 Ellis to his wife, 26 November 1889, in *T. E. Ellis, Cofiant*, Cyfrol II (Lerpwl, 1948), p. 91.
14 *Baner ac Amserau Cymru*, 24 September 1890.
15 Ellis, *Addresses and Speeches*, pp. 29ff. For the influence of Ruskin on him as a student, see T. I. Ellis, *Thomas Edward Ellis: Cofiant*, Cyfrol I (Lerpwl, 1944), pp. 116–17.
16 Ellis to D. R. Daniel, 11 March 1891 (NLW, Daniel Papers).
17 A thoughtful contribution on Lewis, from a strongly nationalist standpoint, is Richard Wyn Jones, *Y Blaid Ffasgaidd yng Nghymru: Plaid Cymru a'r Cyhuddiad o Ffasgaeth* (Cardiff, 2013), published in English translation in 2014 as *The Fascist Party in Wales? Plaid Cymru, Welsh Nationalism and the Accusation of Fascism*, which argues passionately (and, to my view, correctly) against Lewis being himself seen as a fascist.
18 Bruce Griffiths, *Saunders Lewis* (Cardiff 1979), p. 5, citing Lewis's article on 'Maurice Barrès', *Baner ac Amserau Cymru*, January 1924.
19 *Y Ddraig Goch*, November 1927.
20 See E. L. Ellis, *T.J.: A Life of Dr Thomas Jones CH* (Cardiff, 1992), pp. 460–1. Jones's attack, originally published in the *Western Mail*, 28 February 1942, was later turned into a pamphlet, *The Native Never Returns* (1946).
21 Jones's views appear in *Wales, the United Kingdom and Europe*, p. 21. He richly deserves a biography (or an autobiography?).
22 Jones, *Wales, the United Kingdom and Europe.*, p. 22.
23 Elizabeth Gibson-Morgan, 'Devolution and the European Union in the British Constitution: Concord or Conflict?' (forthcoming).

Postscript: A Tale of Two Unions

All the strains of Europeanism associated with the four men discussed in the previous chapter have left their historical imprint – the rationalist republicanism of David Williams, the gospel of nationhood of Tom Ellis, the militant organic nationalism of Saunders Lewis, the social democracy of Rhodri Morgan. But they have led to different destinations and made the achievement of a national agenda more difficult and divisive. After all, a potpourri composed of Condorcet, Mazzini, Barrès and Jacques Delors would contain highly miscellaneous ingredients. It would be difficult to see the Europhile dream of 'a Europe of the mind', of which David Marquand, Roger Liddle and other Europhiles of the centre-left have written, emerging coherently from these varied components. These historic elements of our cultural heritage have therefore played their subterranean part in making the response of the Welsh towards the idea of European integration increasingly problematic. They have left diverse legacies influential in the momentous national and constitutional debates of the present time.[1]

In 2014, the relationship between the United Kingdom and the European Union was at a critical stage. Nigel Farage's UKIP made large gains in the May 2014 European elections, alongside other right-wing parties such as the heavily racist *Front National* in France and similar extremist nationalist movements in Poland, Belgium, Denmark, Italy and Greece.

Beyond that, the ongoing crisis in the Eurozone could be damaging to the flow of EU funding to Wales compared to the recent past, notably in the process of transferring resources from the wealthier parts of Europe to the poorer ones. Indeed, the definition of which are the poorer parts of the EU might well change with the adhesion of new countries from south-eastern Europe, making Wales appear comparatively richer. In any case, international financial investment in Wales, the poorest part of Britain and a branch economy in Europe at best, may be more at risk in the new global climate. Politically, the European Union could be entering a more pluralist phase, with not only the new eastern European countries coming in, but also smaller 'unhistoric' nations like the Catalans, the Flemish and, of course, the Scots, clamouring for admission. The Scots have been showing impatience with the regional institutions of the EU and have felt confident enough to embark on a path that may lead to independence. Whether the Welsh will ever have anything like the same degree of self-confidence is very debatable, even if nations as tiny as Latvia, Malta and Cyprus are able to sustain their independence within the EU. A larger, more pluralist EU may help the Welsh government to become more assertive, but it also may mean a danger of its being crowded out of decision-making. In the lead-up to the second Silk report in February 2014, Labour's shadow Secretary of State, Owen Smith MP, raised another danger – too glib a comparison being made between Wales and Scotland in relation to tax powers. His point was that Wales was smaller and poorer than Scotland, with half its population living within a few miles of an all-too accessible border with England. The Welsh Assembly government's being granted powers to raise its own taxes and determine the rates at which they are levied might both impoverish Wales and damage its links with the union of the United Kingdom (and the EU for that matter), 'the solidarity and common threads that bind us'. The Labour Party (at Westminster at least, though less clearly so in Wales itself), while still warmly devolutionist and Europhile, appeared resistant to the beguiling slogan, 'For Wales – see Scotland'.[2]

Meanwhile the idea, fashionable fifteen years ago, of a Europe of the regions appears to have stalled.[3] In some countries, the pressure has rather been for stronger forms of autonomy or 'devo-max' within existing national states as in Catalonia and the Basque lands, or alternatively for full-blown independence as in Scotland (which might end up with 'devo-max', just the same). Neither would hold much attraction for Wales, where 'devo-max' would lead to serious cuts in government funding with alarming consequences for public services and social welfare. In the federal German republic, of course, the Länder have for over seventy years enjoyed a high degree of autonomy, including in key areas of economic and fiscal policy. By contrast, Italy, an unstable concept ever since the Kingdom of Italy came erratically into being in 1861, could implode completely into a range of regional territories. Belgium, on the other hand, had ceased to be a unitary country and declared itself to be a federal state back in September 1992. Its Accord de la St Michel set up separate legislative councils for both the Flemish and Walloon regions, and divided up the province of Brabant into two distinct linguistically-based areas. By 2014, Belgium seemed close to a terminal fracture between nationalistic Flemings and Francophone Walloons, with little but the monarchy to keep it together. There were to be heard French right-wing politicians speaking of the possible absorption of the Walloons into a greater France, emulating the conquests of Louis XIV over three centuries earlier. The Welsh relationship with Europe, therefore, faces multiple choices and uncertainties of a basic kind which makes it imperative that a clear, united Welsh response and policy approach should emerge.

The most immediate factor likely to influence the Welsh relationship with Europe lies within these islands, namely the referendum on independence in Scotland in September 2014, to be held emotively on the eight hundredth anniversary of Bannockburn. It could be a very close run thing. The possible reconfiguration of the United Kingdom would have a profound impact on Wales. It is reasonable to say that Wales will be much affected by the outcome of the Scottish referendum whatever the result, since the Union of the United Kingdom and its union with Europe are so profoundly linked up with each other. Obviously, Scotland will be the most directly affected. The Scottish referendum poses dilemmas for voters on both sides. Those supporting the Union and also wishing to remain within the EU know that the 2017 referendum could result in Britain leaving the EU anyhow because of the weight of the

English vote. On the other hand, pro-EU Scots intending to vote for separation are aware that it is far from certain that an independent Scotland would automatically be entitled to rejoin the EU without debate. There has been opposition not just from Barroso and Van Rompuy, the unelected presidents of the European Commission and the EU respectively, but also from the elected government of Spain, fearful of Catalan and Basque separatism within its borders.[4] The prospect of an independent Scotland having to adopt its own currency, debt-sharing and banking arrangements, with large Scottish banks like RBS perhaps migrating across Hadrian's Wall, is another unsettling factor for the EU link for both sides in the Scottish independence debate to consider.

But there could be a moral crisis in Wales too, if the English vote heavily to leave the EU in 2017 against the will of the majority in Wales. In 2014, pressure for an 'In/Out' referendum on Europe, fanned by irrational hostility towards immigrants from Bulgarian and Rumania, continued to grow in strength in England. True, a European Referendum Bill in 2013–14, sponsored as an allegedly private members' measure by two Tory backbenchers, James Wharton in the House of Commons and Lord Dobbs in the House of Lords, collapsed. It was crushed by their lordships' house on 24 and 31 January 2014 by a large majority of Labour, Liberal Democrat and cross-bench peers (including the present writer), and even some Europhile Conservatives such as Lord Tugendhat. However, the prime minister, David Cameron, claimed that the Bill could return to parliament before the May 2015 general election, even if the constitutional implications and historical grasp of his views were unclear. The prospect of a radical divergence between a Eurosceptic England and a Europhile Wales in 2017 remained by no means unlikely, despite recent Welsh opinion polls. This might have the profound consequence of helping to push the United Kingdom more strongly in a federal, or perhaps confederal, direction. Some defenders of the Union, indeed, have argued that a federal Britain, including effective regional governments being created in England, a modern version of the Anglo-Saxon Heptarchy, might be the best way of repelling the separatist appeal of the Scottish Nationalists anyhow. But the English people have shown little enthusiasm for experiment hitherto. A regional government was heavily rejected by the voters of the North-East in 2004, while elected mayors were voted down by every city or town save Bristol in 2010 (joined by Leicester in 2011). For most of the regional English, it seems, the paternalist gentleman from Whitehall who always knows best retains his traditional appeal. The English Question, the governance of Britain's largest nation, thus remains an unresolved dilemma.

So the British governmental revolution, launched by Lord Irvine and the Blair government in 1999, has thus triggered a complex debate over relocating power which has yet to complete its course. It has significant implications for the future of Wales. The relationship of Wales with the European continent, complex and many-faceted since the French Revolution of 1789, may be about to enter an exciting and unpredictable, but also more dangerous, phase. At the start of the twenty-first century, the long march of the Welsh democracy is very far from over.

Notes

[1] These matters are dealt with authoritatively in the forthcoming publication by my wife, Elizabeth Gibson-Morgan, 'Devolution and the European Union in the British Constitution: Concord or Conflict?'.

[2] Owen Smith, 'Wales is not Scotland', Institute of Welsh Affairs website, 7 February 2014.

[3] A stimulating discussion of this idea is Christopher Harvie, *The Rise of Regional Europe* (London, 1994). Michael Keating most interestingly discusses the evolution of minority nationalisms within the EU, in the British Academy's 2013 publication, *Wales, Europe and the United Kingdom* (London, October 2013).

[4] Barroso, astonishingly, said on 16 February 2014 that it would be 'extremely difficult if not impossible' for an independent Scotland to join the EU. The views of his appointed successor, the Luxembourg federalist Jean-Claude Juncker, on this question are not presently known: 'we should keep our silence', he wisely observed in a televised presidential debate, a view echoed by the socialist candidate Martin Schultz. Barroso had, bizarrely, cited Spain's refusal to accept an independent Kosovo as some kind of parallel. Conversely, after his election, Juncker declared (15 July 2014) that he did not expect new members to join the EU for the next five years.

Index